SACRED AS SECULAR

ADVANCING STUDIES IN RELIGION
Series editor: Sarah Wilkins-Laflamme

Advancing Studies in Religion catalyzes and provokes original research in the study of religion with a critical edge. The series advances the study of religion in method and theory, textual interpretation, theological studies, and the understanding of lived religious experience. Rooted in the long and diverse traditions of the study of religion in Canada, the series demonstrates awareness of the complex genealogy of religion as a category and as a discipline. ASR welcomes submissions from authors researching religion in varied contexts and with diverse methodologies.

The series is sponsored by the Canadian Corporation for Studies in Religion whose constituent societies include the Canadian Society of Biblical Studies, Canadian Society for the Study of Religion, Canadian Society of Patristic Studies, Canadian Theological Society, Société canadienne de théologie, and Société québécoise pour l'étude de la religion.

1 The al-Baqara Crescendo
Understanding the Qur'an's Style, Narrative Structure, and Running Themes
Nevin Reda

2 Leaving Christianity
Changing Allegiances in Canada since 1945
Brian Clarke and Stuart Macdonald

3 Everyday Sacred
Religion in Contemporary Quebec
Edited by *Hillary Kaell*

4 Convergent Knowing
Christianity and Science in Conversation with a Suffering Creation
Simon Appolloni

5 Seeding Buddhism with Multiculturalism
The Transmission of Sri Lankan Buddhism in Toronto
D. Mitra Barua

6 The Subversive Evangelical
The Ironic Charisma of an Irreligious Megachurch
Peter J. Schuurman

7 The Public Work of Christmas
Difference and Belonging in Multicultural Societies
Edited by *Pamela E. Klassen and Monique Scheer*

8 Identities Under Construction
Religion, Gender, and Sexuality among Youth in Canada
Pamela Dickey Young and Heather Shipley

9 Prayer as Transgression?
The Social Relations of Prayer in Healthcare Settings
Sheryl Reimer-Kirkham, Sonya Sharma, Rachel Brown, and Melania Calestani

10 Relation and Resistance
Racialized Women, Religion, and Diaspora
Edited by *Sailaja V. Krishnamurti and Becky R. Lee*

11 Sacred as Secular
Secularization under Theocracy in Iran
Abdolmohammad Kazemipur

Sacred as Secular

Secularization under Theocracy in Iran

ABDOLMOHAMMAD KAZEMIPUR

McGill-Queen's University Press
Montreal & Kingston • London • Chicago

ISBN 978-0-2280-0846-0 (cloth)
ISBN 978-0-2280-0847-7 (paper)
ISBN 978-0-2280-0969-6 (ePDF)

Legal deposit first quarter 2022
Bibliothèque nationale du Québec

Printed in Canada on acid-free paper that is 100% ancient forest free (100% post-consumer recycled), processed chlorine free

This book has been published with the help of a grant from the Canadian Federation for the Humanities and Social Sciences, through the Awards to Scholarly Publications Program, using funds provided by the Social Sciences and Humanities Research Council of Canada.

Funded by the Government of Canada | Financé par le gouvernement du Canada | Canada | Canada Council for the Arts | Conseil des arts du Canada

We acknowledge the support of the Canada Council for the Arts.

Nous remercions le Conseil des arts du Canada de son soutien.

Library and Archives Canada Cataloguing in Publication

Title: Sacred as secular: secularization under theocracy in Iran / Abdolmohammad Kazemipur.

Names: Kazemipur, Abdolmohammad, author.

Series: Advancing studies in religion; 11.

Description: Series statement: Advancing studies in religion; 11 | Includes bibliographical references and index.

Identifiers: Canadiana (print) 20210318627 | Canadiana (ebook) 20210320680 | ISBN 9780228008460 (hardcover) | ISBN 9780228008477 (softcover) | ISBN 9780228009696 (PDF)

Subjects: LCSH: Islam and secularism—Iran. | LCSH: Secularism—Iran. | LCSH: Islam and state—Iran. | LCSH: Iran—Religion. | LCSH: Islam—Iran. | LCSH: Iran—Social life and customs.

Classification: LCC BP190.5.S35 K39 2022 | DDC 306.6/970955—dc23

This book was typeset by Marquis Interscript in 10.5/13 Sabon.

Dedicated to those simultaneously engaged
in both *interpreting* the world and *changing* it,
through both *intellectual* and *spiritual* work

Contents

Figures and Tables xi

Preface xv

PART ONE TECTONIC SHIFT

1 Deconstructing Muslim Exceptionalism: Going beyond Philosophy and Theology 3

2 Rethinking Secularity and Causation 22

3 History of Islam in Iran: Critical Junctures 46

PART TWO *L'ÉTAT C'EST NOUS*: FROM DEMOCRACY TO THEOCRACY TO AUTOCRACY

4 Crossing the Trench: Secularism through the Merger of Clergy and State 71

5 Secularizing the State: *Maslahat*, Memoirs, and Minutes 95

PART THREE BACKLASH: STREETS, YOUNG PEOPLE, WOMEN, AND DEMOGRAPHY

6 Secularization on the Streets 115

7 Religiosity among Young People: International Comparisons 129

8 Women: Gender and Demography as Secularizing Forces 144

PART FOUR EARLY WARNINGS AND AFTERSHOCKS IN PHILOSOPHY AND RELIGION

9 A Century of Philosophical Battles 171

10 Everyday Theology: Revealing Episodes since 1979 193

Conclusion: Putting It Together a New Way? 203

Appendix A: Report on *Sunni* Militant Organizations' Conversion to *Shi'ism* 207

Appendix B: Aspects of Religiosity and the 1974/2000 Survey Questions Used to Measure Them 210

Notes 215

References 219

Index 243

Figures and Tables

FIGURES

2.1 Perceptual mapping of the existing conceptualization of the notion of secularity. 24
2.2 A proposed perceptual mapping for the conceptualization of the notion of secularity. 33
3.1 The initial emblem of the MKO. 58
3.2 The emblem of the MKO after the ideological shift of 1975. 60
4.1 State budget allocations (in millions of rials) to seminaries and other religious organizations, 2008–16. 74
5.1 Distribution of the Guardian Council's reasons for rejecting parliament's bills, 1981–2009. 108
6.1 Euclidean distance model of dimensions of religiosity. 119
7.1 Population pyramid for Iran, 2019. 130
7.2 Belief in God (percentage of youths 15–24). 136
7.3 Belief in life after death (percentage of youths 15–24). 136
7.4 Belief in heaven (percentage of youths 15–24). 137
7.5 Belief in hell (percentage of youths 15–24). 137
7.6 How much do you agree with the statement that "those who do not believe in God are unfit for public office"? (Percentage who agree.) 138
7.7 Have you had spiritual moments (prayers, meditation, etc.)? (Percentage who said "yes.") 138
7.8 Do you do daily prayers? (Percentage.) 140
7.9 To what extent do you consider yourself a religious person? (Percentage.) 140

7.10 How often do you go to mosque (for congregational prayers)? 141
7.11 How often do you do Ramazan fasting? (Percentage.) 141
8.1 Average age at first marriage, by sex, 1956–2016. 156
8.2 Marriage-age population in mid–2000 (estimate), by sex and urban/rural area. 156
8.3 Literacy rate of population (six years and older), by sex, 1956–96. 161
8.4 Proportion who agree with the statement "when jobs are scarce, the priority should be given to men." 162
8.5 The gender difference (men minus women) in the proportions of those who agree with the statement "when jobs are scarce, the priority should be given to men." 162
8.6 Everything equal, would you choose men or women for a specific job? 163
8.7 In your opinion, which group – men or women – enjoys more opportunities for self-advancement? 164
8.8 In your opinion, which group – men or women – enjoys more opportunities for self-advancement? Women's responses. 164
8.9 In your opinion, which group – men or women – enjoys more opportunities for self-advancement? Men's responses. 165
10.1 Potential net migration index (in- minus out-migration), 2013–16. 201

TABLES

4.1 Contextual and institutional sources of Institutional Change. 78
6.1 The mean of four indices (dimensions) of religiosity, 2000. 121
6.2 Correlation coefficients for four (indices) dimensions of religiosity, 2000. 121
6.3 Frequency of practising daily prayers (percentage), 1974, 2000. 123
6.4 Frequency of Participating in Collective Prayers (percentage), 1974, 2000. 123
6.5 The influence of religion, or strength of people's religious sentiments, in the future (percentage), 1974, 2000. 124

6.6 The influence of religion or strength of people's religious sentiments in the future (percentage), 1974, 2000. 125
7.1 World Values Survey (wave 4, 2000–04), sample size. 134
7.2 Iranian surveys, sample size. 134
7.3 "To what extent do you agree with the following tatements?" (Percentage who agree.) 139

Preface

Any discussion about Iran – whether it is about international relations or local governance, economics or culture, ethnicity or language, local population or migrants – would run into the issue of religion one way or another; and it has been so for the past four decades. It is difficult to make an accurate observation or have a meaningful conversation about Iran or Iranians without considering religion or having a clear position about it. In a question about religion asked in an Iranian survey conducted in the mid-1970s, more than half of the respondents did not have any particular opinion; twenty-five years later, this number had dropped to zero. In other words, one cannot find an Iranian these days who does not have an opinion on the subject.

This intense awareness, however, has not always come with high levels of accuracy and precision in people's opinions and judgments about religious matters or the roles religion has played in Iran's history. Quite often, people think about it in political terms. Many read its place in the history of the country in reverse order – that is, they start with what they like or dislike about religion today and project that back into the depths of history. This has resulted in many sensationalized, exaggerated, unsubstantiated accounts of this history, in which many important details are accidentally overlooked or deliberately put aside.

This tendency among many Iranians, both scholars and laypeople, has been confounded by another, similarly problematic way of thinking about the Muslim world in the post–9/11 West. Overwhelmed by the magnitude and the spread of Islamist terrorism, and in their rush to understand and explain it, many Western observers adopted a neo-Orientalist perspective, based on a notion of "Muslim exceptionalism."

They assumed that Muslims, due to the nature of their religion and the contents of its teachings, have a unique connection to their faith that makes them behave in a way that is distinct from all other faith communities. Together, these two layers of misconceptions have severely impaired the understanding of religious developments in Iran, resulting in over-simplified, imprecise, and factually inaccurate accounts and descriptions.

This book is a modest effort to address these problems, by examining religious developments in Iran through a sociological perspective and empirical data. While the volume's discussion revolves around the issue of sacred and secular, and its empirical details are related to the case of post-revolution Iran, I hope that its broader theoretical arguments will have useful implications for other debates involving Muslims and Muslim societies and beyond.

As someone who experienced political socialization during the time of Iran's Islamic Revolution[1] of 1979, I had some existential questions of my own to address as well. My goal was to add, through this study, a macro-level context around my own micro-level personal observations and experiences. In that sense, it would be fair to say that, while the writing of this volume has taken me several years, I have been thinking about its contents for several decades. That puts me in intellectual debt to many friends and colleagues with whom I have had, during some four decades, conversations about the various topics discussed below. Too many people, indeed, to name them all here; but I have benefitted from my conversations particularly with Mohsen Goodarzi and Ali Rezaei. I am also indebted to my students and research assistants for their excellent work throughout the years; many of them are now themselves scholars: Sayed Hamid Akbary, Taha Azizi, Ata Heshmati, Fateme Ejaredar, and Ebrahim Mazaheri.

Staff members at McGill-Queen's University Press have been a pleasure to work with, as we brought the initial manuscript to this print version: Jacqueline Michelle Davis, Filomena Falocco, Kathleen Fraser, Robert Andrew Mackie, Kyla Madden, and Elli Stylianou. I am particularly thankful to John Parry, for his excellent copy editing of the manuscript, which improved it significantly. I acknowledge as well three anonymous reviewers of the manuscript, who provided enormously helpful critical feedback as well as encouragement for this book project.

As is the case with all my previous works, the huge amount of time and attention I paid to this book has been denied to my immediate and extended families, as well as my friends. I hope that after reading this book, they find the choice that I had made somewhat justified. The real test, however, would be the satisfaction of my readers; may this volume prove helpful, either answering some of their questions or raising new ones.

PART ONE

Tectonic Shift

1

Deconstructing Muslim Exceptionalism

Going beyond Philosophy and Theology

A HISTORICAL-PHILOSOPHICAL MOMENT

Some historical events stand out not because of their huge influence or the many people they touch, but because they present a philosophical dilemma or challenge fundamental beliefs and assumptions. The Lisbon earthquake of 1 November 1755 was one prime example. To be sure, it disrupted many lives, demolished a thousand houses, and killed and injured thirty thousand people; but it also, according to Durant and Durant (1965, 720), sent "its tremors throughout European philosophy." As a result of this philosophical aftershock, an old theological question resurfaced – i.e., what was God's purpose in all this suffering? – which none of the existing authorities and standard modes of reasoning could answer satisfactorily. Unlike in the past, Protestants could not present it as God's punishment of Catholics, as on 18 November a similar quake shook the largely Protestant Boston; Catholics could not claim it to be a scourging of sinners, as Lisbon's casualties included many very pious Catholics as well as several hundred priests and nuns who had gathered that morning to celebrate All Saints' Day; Muslims could not portray it as divine retribution against Christians, as the same quake had also destroyed the great Al-Mansur mosque in Rabat, Morocco (Durant and Durant 1965). All pre-constructed answers proved unsatisfactory.

The COVID-19 pandemic of 2020 appears to be acting like another such philosophical moment. The fast, worldwide spread of this coronavirus to virtually every country in the world, and the struggling of many developed countries to bring it under control, undermined the confidence of many industrialized nations in their economic power and democratic governance. Its unstoppable nature initially challenged religion and raised people's confidence in science; but the questions around the quickly developed vaccines, followed by their problematic rollout, eroded some of that confidence and paved the way for some to view the pandemic as nature's or God's punishment for humanity's arrogant attitudes, neglectful behaviour, and careless way of life. A few other historical developments – such as the fall of the Roman Empire in the fifth century, the rapid geographical expansion of early Islam in the seventh century, the quick fall of vast swaths of eastern and central Europe before the Ottoman onslaught during the late Middle Ages, and the rapid collapse of Communist rule in eastern and central Europe in 1989 – were other such historical-philosophical moments.

Iran's Islamic Revolution of 1979 was perhaps another – at least, it was so for the French philosopher Michel Foucault. During the latter half of 1978, when Iran was at the peak of its revolutionary movement, Foucault visited it twice to observe not just a political event but what he felt was an intellectual and philosophical turning point. At the time, there were several other political revolutions under way in the world – including Nicaragua's socialist revolution against dictator Somoza and Zimbabwe's anti-colonial revolution against Britain – but none of those attracted Foucault's attention as much as Iran's. He saw the massive participation of people, the absence of political leadership, and the absence of internal conflicts over issues such as class, gender, ideology, and ethnicity as signs of an entirely different species of revolution (for a detailed account of his observations, see his interview with two journalists from the daily newspaper *Libération*, in Foucault 1988). He had previously argued that, after the end of colonialism in the 1960s, Western thought and modern philosophy had reached a dead end and that, if there was any hope of a future for philosophy, it had to emerge either outside Europe or in the encounter between Europe and non-Europe (Afary and Anderson 2005, 2–3). He saw, in the Islamic Revolution of Iran, a potential birth of that future.

Foucault was not alone in his sentiments. More than a year earlier, the same sentiments had been expressed by Ali Shariati, a Sorbonne-educated Iranian sociologist who was posthumously given the title "Teacher of the Revolution" (*mo'allem-e enghelab*) by the revolutionary masses. In an emotional letter to his father, a few hours before his journey to self-exile in London and death three weeks later in Southampton, Shariati wrote:

> It is clear that Islam is being reborn … I think the most effective cause of this rebirth is the dead-end currently faced by today's intellectuals, the defeat of science, and the incapability of ideologies, especially the shortcomings and problems of the Marxist socialism and Western social democracy, which had raised so much hope among all the humanitarians and social-justice warriors and those seeking people's salvation, yet ended in Stalinism and Maoism or governments such as those of Schmidt, Guy Mollet and Callaghan. Also, science, instead of substituting religion as it claimed, produced nuclear bombs and became a servant of capitalism and dictatorship … All of these sad experiences have paved the way for a new dawn of faith. (A. Shariati 1977)

Even more remarkably, more than half a decade before Foucault and Shariati, another Frenchman, Henry Corbin, had a similar observation about a return of Iranians to religion: "Twenty years ago one could rarely come across a young Iranian intellectual with whom one could have a conversation about the philosophy of *Molla Sadra Shirazi*. But, this is no longer the case today. While we may never be able to show this with statistics, something new is being born here" (Corbin 1971, 36). It was this rebirth, this surfacing of the future, that Foucault went to Iran to witness. He wanted to see these occurrences "not in books expressing them, but in events manifesting [them] … in struggles carried on around ideas" (quoted in Afary and Anderson 2005, 2–3). He called this newborn phenomenon "political spirituality."

"MUSLIM EXCEPTIONALISM"

For Foucault, "political spirituality" was notable because it had surfaced outside the existing Western paradigms of liberal modernity and Marxism and had the potential to restructure the whole world order. This was a potential that he believed could not be found in other religions, because "Islam … [was] not simply a religion, but an entire way of life, an adherence to a history and a civilization" (Afary and Anderson 2005, 4). There were two elements in Foucault's way of thinking that found enormous appeal in the following years: understanding "ideas" as the driving force of history, and a belief in the "uniqueness of Islam." These two ideas found their reflections in academic accounts of the Iranian Revolution of 1979. First, a new line of research focused on "Iranian intellectual history" (Matin-Asgari 2018).

Second, it reinvigorated an old interest in studying *shia* Islam; but, this time it emerged with a new twist – rather than explaining the faith's historical growth in Iran (for a classic example, see Petroshevsky 1971), it explored *shi'ism* as a revolutionary religious tradition with a powerful anti-establishment tendency (see, among others, Cole and Keddie 1986; Dabashi 2011).

In the following years, both of these elements – the primacy of "ideas" and the "uniqueness of Islam" – spread beyond Iran and began informing debates and discussions about the whole Muslim world. After the events of 11 September 2001 ("9/11"), Muslims were increasingly viewed as "distinctive" in their presumed higher attachment to their religion and in its unique contents. So the sources of Muslim attitudes and behaviour were sought in the teachings of Islam, whether the subject at hand was democracy, human rights, tolerance, women's rights, blasphemy, violence, terrorism, secularism, or whatever. The various parties in such debates seemed to share an assumption – explicit or implicit, positive or negative – that there exists a "*Homo Islamicus*"[1] that stands outside history and geography, as a different species with its own distinct operating system (for an empirical evaluation of the validity of this assumption, see Fish 2011).

These conceptual biases – about Islam's and Muslims' distinctiveness – have appeared in full swing in the discussions about secularism in the Muslim world. Ernest Gellner succinctly captured Muslims' perceived "exceptionalism" vis-à-vis secularism (1993, 36): "In the social sciences, one of the commonest theses is the secularisation thesis, which runs as follows. Under conditions prevailing in industrial-scientific society, the hold of religion over society and its people diminishes. By and large this is true, but it is not completely true, for there is one major exception, Islam … the one striking counter-example to the secularisation thesis." This notion is shared by many scholars, both Muslim and non-Muslim, religious and non-religious, with pro-Muslim views or without (see, for instance, Lewis 1987; Nasr 2010; Nikfar 2016; Shoja'i-Zand 2002a, 2002b; S.J. Tabatabayee 2017).

This book challenges these biases about Islam and Muslims, exploring the place of religion in Iran since its 1979 revolution. At the broadest and most general level, my central argument can be summarized as a twofold statement. First, "ideas" are not the prime movers of history; hence, religion is *not* driving socio-political developments in Iran, and is itself affected by powerful economic, social, and political forces, as part one below reveals. Second, religious changes in post-1979

Iran, rather than evading the rule, resemble some of the most extreme cases of secularization in the modern West. I make this argument by examining empirically in parts two and three the evolving role, function, and place of religion in the lives of Iranians during the forty-some years since 1979.

My approach has two defining features. First, it is empirical, in that I try to make my case with data (whatever types of data are appropriate and available), as opposed to simply offering theoretical possibilities. Second, I take what can be called a Durkheimian sociological viewpoint, which explains social developments in terms of social forces (as opposed to philosophical, psychological, or theological factors). The main conclusion of the book is that Iranian society, contrary to the intended goals of the state's Islamization project, has become deeply secular. Such an outcome is probably a perfect example of the contrast between what Robert Merton (1968) called "manifest" and "latent" functions – to distinguish "between conscious motivations for social behavior and its objective consequences" and "between categories of subjective disposition (needs, interests, purposes) and categories of generally unrecognized but objective functional consequences" (115–16).

THE NEW DEBATES ON SECULARITY, THE MUSLIM WORLD, AND IRAN

Over the past four decades, religion has made a comeback in the social sciences and established a central place in many debates on societal development. This new tide has challenged two century-old, axiomatic concepts: secularization and secularism. Secularization is defined broadly as the withdrawal of religion from human consciousness, while secularism is the withdrawal of religion from social institutions, captured most vividly in the phrase "separation of church and state." "Secularization" referred generally to a sociological phenomenon, and "secularism" was a political ideology recommending a particular type of institutional arrangement. In that sense, secularization was mostly a description, and secularism a prescription. In the late 1960s, both were taken for granted, perceived as universal concepts that were part and parcel of the global process of modernization; and the future was viewed as secular in both senses of the word (for various takes on this trend, see Ausmus 1982; P.L. Berger 1967; Fenn 1978; Glasner 1977; Martin 1978). Underlying these theoretical positions lay, according to Ahmet Kuru (2009, 2), a normative argument that "religion should not play a substantial public role in a modern democratic polity." As a consequence, many social-science disciplines had found the topic of religion uninteresting, and a feature of the past; hence, they had turned away from it and towards what they considered more exciting and urgent matters.

The first challenge to this consensus was the place of religion in the United States, a modern industrial nation, but one with a high degree of religiosity. How could this combination exist? The secularization theorists invoked "the American experience" (Hadden 1987; Joppke 2015; Warner 1993), variously by calling it an "American exceptionalism"; by ruling out the evidence that it deviated from the general trend; or by labelling it a variation of the general trend, whereby religion secularized from within – "internal secularization" (Casanova, 1994). The second challenge to the consensus came from the post-1945 experiences of central and eastern Europe, where, driven by a communist ideology, the states launched "secularization from above," in clear contrast to what had happened in western and northern Europe, which had secularized largely from the bottom up. Relating these two challenges to Max Weber's views on secularization, Robinson (1999, 232–3) proposes: "Weber's theory [of secularization] is regarded as offering only one possible perspective over secularization in the West. It does not explain … the American case of immigration, religious revival and the secularization of theological content; nor does it account for the East European path of secularization from above." There seemed to be a western European rule, with two exceptions, American and eastern European. The secularization theory remained Euro-centric.

In the last quarter of the twentieth century, another, perhaps more serious challenge to secularization theory questioned its main premise and weakened its European focus. Since the mid-1970s, an unexpected wave of religious revivalism has swept many countries around the world, most notably the rise of religious sentiments in the Middle East, the emergence of Catholic "liberation theology" in Latin America, the towering role of the Catholic church in Poland's Solidarity movement, the rise of Evangelical Protestantism in the United States, and the issues surrounding Muslims in Europe, particularly in France (Norris and Inglehart 2004). Similar events followed elsewhere, such as the rise of religious movements among Orthodox Jews in Israel, Hindus in India, and Buddhists in east Asia. At the dawn of the twenty-first century, religion seemed to have made a loud comeback everywhere in the world – except in western Europe – hence the phrase "European exceptionalism" (P. Berger, Davie, and Fokas 2008; Davie 2002, 2006). The collapse of the Communist Soviet Union and the disintegration of the eastern bloc in the early 1990s fostered even more religiously informed movements in Europe and central Asia. Signalling a conspicuous return of religion to public life, and viewed as instances of "de-secularization" or "sacralization," these tectonic shifts challenged the idea that secularization was both inevitable and universal in the modern world.

The return of religion to public life in the last quarter of the twentieth century startled many social scientists. Peter Berger, for instance, who had helped formulate secularization theory in the 1960s, declared in the late 1990s that the "whole body of literature by historians and social scientists loosely labeled 'secularization theory' is essentially mistaken" (P.L. Berger 1999, 2). Stark and Fonke suggested that secularization theory belonged in the graveyard of failed theories (Stark 1999; Stark and Finke 2000). Others, such as Norris and Inglehart (2004, 4), considered complete abandonment premature but suggested that scholars move "beyond studies of Catholic and Protestant church attendance in Europe ... and the United States, if we are to understand broader trends in religious diversity in churches, mosques, shrines, synagogues, temples around the globe." Berger et al. (2008, 140) similarly argued that "an approach which compares *only* the United States and Europe becomes increasingly inadequate."

Even Europe, as the bastion of secularism for more than two centuries, faced a dilemma that unsettled its understanding of secularism. As a political ideology, secularism had its genesis in the European response to the devastating wars of religion that began with the Protestant Reformation in the early 16th century and went on till about the early eighteenth century (Asad 2003; Taylor 1998). Calling for a political ethic entirely independent from all religions (Taylor 1998), secularism found its first institutional manifestation in post-revolution France in the separation of church and state and remained, for the next two hundred years, the dominant and widely accepted model in western Europe for relations between state and religion. In the 1980s and 1990s, however, growing international migration to Western nations increased both religiosity and religious diversity in those societies, where managing religious differences became much more complex and challenging (Joppke 2015). Serious doubts were raised, and a wave of controversies, discussions, and debates about the suitability of secularism for this new reality ensued (see, among others, P. Berger, Davie, and Fokas 2008; P.L. Berger 1999; Cliteur 2010; Freedman 2004; Taylor 1998, 2007; Warner, Vanantwerpen, and Calhoun 2010).

While the focus of the new wave of research and theorization about secularism remained largely Western and Christian, it increasingly incorporated the experiences of the non-Christian religions, particularly Islam. Some scholars, such as Turner, had previously called for that, but more as a contrast to the Western world and to better explain the concept of secularization, because "the secularization of Islam is likely to be very different from the secularization of Christianity" (B.S. Turner 1974, 159–60). Others saw that as a way to illuminate the European experience, as the presence of Muslims forced Europeans "to rethink the place of religion within Europe as well as outside" (P. Berger, Davie, and Fokas 2008, 3).

More recently, in *The Secular State under Siege*, Joppke (2015, 4) mentions Muslims in the West and the Christian right in the United States as the two main challenges to the notion of the secular state in the West. He admits the absence of non-Western societies from his own work: "The regional focus on the West ... excludes, now regrettably, the rest of the world, such as the Middle East or South-East Asia, where religious conflicts may be far more dramatic and central to the political life than in the temperate zones – this part of the world is simply beyond my competence (also linguistically)." This appreciation of the resulting gap in global debates has led to a gradual incorporation of more voices (see, for instance, Bhargava 1998; Kunkler, Madeley, and Shankar 2018). None the less the Muslim world is still largely left out of the debates on secularity.

THE MUSLIM WORLD IN THE GLOBAL DEBATES ON SECULARITY

The Muslim world poses a particularly complex dilemma to the theory of secularization and the ideology of secularism. Three recent changes have contributed to this complexity: first, the reinvigoration of an old assumption in the West that Islam and Muslims are inherently different from other religions and faith communities because Islam merges the "Kingdom of Heaven" and the "Kingdom of Earth"[2]; second, the recent emergence of Islamist political and social movements in the Muslim world, with a clear claim on state power and a blueprint for running societies, which reinforced those pre-existing assumptions; and third, a growing identity politics in the West vis-à-vis Muslims, as a result of growing migration from Muslim countries to western Europe, North America, and Australia. A new set of debates has surfaced on the state of religion among Muslims, whether as nations or as minorities in non-Muslim countries. Some participants supported long-held assumptions about Muslims, others noted their mismatch with realities on the ground (for an excellent discussion of the validity of those assumptions when they are examined against the empirical data, see Fish 2011).

At the heart of these assumptions about Muslims lie two concepts that affect theorizations about secularity. The first is the idea that Muslims have a particularly strong attachment to their religion. As Christopher Hitchens writes, "They are more religious ... their religion dominates their lives ... It [their religion] cannot be fenced out or fenced in" (quoted in Norton 2013, 8). The second is the perceived impossibility of secularism – as the separation of religion and state – in Muslim societies because of Islam's contents. Bernard Lewis (1991, 2–3) summarizes this point: "The distinction between church and state, so deeply rooted in Christendom, did not exist in Islam." Along the same lines, Huntington (1996, 36) argues that, contrary to the Catholic and Protestant belief in Jesus' injunction (Matthew 22:21 and Mark 12:17) to "render unto Caesar the things that are Caesar's, and unto God the things that are God's," "In Islam, God is Caesar; in China and Japan, Caesar is God; in Orthodoxy, God is Caesar's junior partner."

The assumptions about the distinctiveness of Islam and Muslims were not limited to Western scholars; many scholars of Muslim backgrounds, with or without religious inclinations, also felt the same way – that Islam basically prevents secularization in the Muslim world. Two prime exponents are Seyyed Hossein Nasr and Javad Tabatabayee, both of Iranian background, but the former a practising Muslim and the latter not. For the latter, "secularization, in the way that it happened in Christianity, will not happen in Islam" (S.J. Tabatabayee 2017, 36:42). I discuss at length below Tabatabayee's emphasis on "the secularization of religion" – as opposed to the secularization of the followers of a religion – or what some observers had called "secularization from within" (mostly in reference to American exceptionalism). Tabatabayee links this to what he sees as another *im*possibility in Islam: that of experiencing a Reformation similar to what Luther introduced in Christianity in 1517. His argument is that Luther called for a return to the holy scriptures – the Bible – as a way to bypass the church's system of authority; but, due to the different nature and content of the Quran, in Islam a return to the Holy Book would be a return to what created the problem in the first place (S.J. Tabatabayee 2017).

Nasr's (2010) more elaborate view on the impossibility of secularism among Muslims revolves around a notion of "European/Christian exceptionalism." According to him, the secularization and secularism that transformed Christian western Europe was a historical anomaly, simply because only Christianity and Buddhism divide the world into the mundane and sacred, leaving the first to the state and the latter to religion, and this bifurcation paved the way for European secularization. The other great religions, including Islam, merge these two realms, leaving "church" and state virtually inseparable. Shoja'i-Zand (2002b, 2002a) expresses a similar view but bases it on Islam's capability to embrace this-worldly realities within a religious framework, which, he believes, Christianity lacks.

Despite his stance, Nasr acknowledges that even Europe, during the Middle Ages, merged these two sources of authority:

> One of the reasons that Western Christianity became weakened as no other religion in history, except for the late Greco-Roman religions, ... is that the laws used by Christian people in Europe were not drawn directly from the source of Christian revelation and the fountainhead of their religion, except for spiritual laws and personal moral codes such as the Ten Commandments. What do I mean by that? I mean that Judaism, like Islam, has a religious law that embraces all of life, and traditional Judaism holds exactly the same position as Islam in this matter. There is no such thing as secular law as we understand today in these religions. (Nasr 2010, 307)

So, in Nasr's view, the Muslim world is unlikely to experience secularism in the way that the Christian world did, not because Islam is an anomalous religion, but because Christianity is.

Another nuanced view, almost diametrically opposed to Tabatabayee's and Nasr's, has been presented by Abdulkarim Soroush. Noting the clergy's different roles in Islam and in Christianity, he argues that a life faithful to Islamic teachings does not, in any way, require the clergy's involvement. In other words, a pious Muslim can connect directly to God and the holy scripture(s) without the need for a mediating clergy.

Thus Islam, as a personal faith that regulates the individual's relations with God and does not officially sanction a religious establishment, has always been secular:

> Islamic jurisprudence has a very good affinity with or inclination towards secularism ... One of the meanings of secularism is the rejection of the clerics' authority; and that has always been the case in Islamic culture ... For your prayers, for your worship, for your marriage, for your divorce, and so on and so forth, you won't need any clergy ... you can do all of these yourself ... There is actually nothing ... no religious practice in which you need the presence of a cleric ... And this is part of the meaning of secularization or secularism; which has already been there, embedded in the teachings of Islam. There is only one single issue or area, which has been disputed, and that is the role of the political leadership ... Otherwise, the rest is supposed to be secular ... In Islamic teachings, in Islam, most of what you do is already secular. You do not need to secularize it again; it is only politics which may need secularization. (Quoted in Kamyab 2008)

So we have at least three conflicting views here: that Islam can never become secular like Christianity; that it should never try to do so; and that it does not need to do so because it already is. How can we square the circle here? I believe that one major source of confusion is the focus on the secularization of Islam as opposed to the secularization of Muslims. As a result, these views have remained heavily philosophical and focused largely on Islam's teachings, with little reference to the realities and the lived experiences of Muslims and the way they understand and relate to their faith. As well, they remain preoccupied with secularism – which refers to the relationship between political and religious establishments – and not with secularization, as something pertinent to the relations between individuals and religion. The first preoccupation has moved these debates towards theology, the second, towards political philosophy, and in both cases away from empirical examination of the realities of lives lived.

An example of an alternative approach, which looks more at views and behaviour than at scriptures and doctrines, comes from Norris and Inglehart (2004). Using data from their World Values Survey, they find the Muslim world to pose one of three widespread challenges to the universality of secularization trends, along with the persistence of exceptionally high religious sentiments in the United States and the religious revival in central/eastern Europe after 1989. So, although their conclusions resemble those of Nasr, Tabatabayee, and Shoja'i-Zand about the distinctiveness of Muslim experiences, they reach them by using empirical behavioural and attitudinal data, not merely theological arguments. This different mode of inquiry points to a fundamental problem in understanding Muslim realities in today's world, which the current study is trying to ameliorate, however modestly.

Against the broader background of the virtual exclusion of Muslims from the debates on secularization, the few existing works on this subject tend to ignore the "eastern" part of the Muslim world. According to Shoja'i-Zand (2002a, 196), even people such as Brian Turner, a scholar deeply interested in the Muslim world – or Max Weber before him, whose views on Islam Turner considered inadequate – have focused on the "western" parts of the Muslim Middle East – countries such as Egypt, Morocco, and Turkey – and ignored the predominantly shia Muslims in Iran and in neighbouring countries once ruled by Persia/Iran. That historical lacuna, plus the notable religious changes in Iran since 1979, call for more attention to Iran in the debates on religion and secularity. José Casanova (1994, 10), in his seminal *Public Religions in the Modern World*, compares secularization trends in the United States, Poland, Spain, and Brazil but adds: "It would have been highly desirable to include the Iranian revolution as an additional case study."

IRAN AND THE ISLAMIC REVOLUTION: THE EXCEPTION OR THE RULE?

As we saw above, Iran's Islamic Revolution of 1979 was one of the main triggers of the recent rise of interest in religion among scholars of various backgrounds. It came as a surprise to many international observers of recent Iranian history, mainly because it happened after more than half a century of rapid modernization and secularization in the country. It announced, loudly and undeniably, the return of religion to the public sphere, and it triggered a massive wave of radical Islamism in the Middle East and beyond, with enduring implications for international politics. Inside the country, it resulted in the launch of a massive Islamization project by the post-revolution state, which reshaped government institutions and the way of life of its populace. The combination of these two developments – pre-1979 secularization and post-1979 Islamization – resonated in debates on secularization in the world.

The pre-1979 efforts by Iran's ruling Pahlavi dynasty reconfigured the nation's institutions to fit a secularist ideology. According to Kazemipur and Rezaei (2003, 348), they

> severely curtailed the influence of religion in its major institutional territories: the control of religious institutions over land was severely limited; the family law that was along the lines with the traditional Islamic law was modified to reflect more secular views such as granting women the right to work outside the home, to vote, and to divorce, and at the same time, limiting men's right to divorce [at will]; the publication of religious books became monopolized in the hands of government, as opposed to the clerical institutions; the justice and education systems were freed from the influences of clergy and the seminaries; and most conspicuously, the constitutional power of the religious authorities to veto and stop un-Islamic laws was systematically ignored (see also Abrahamian 1982; Azmuzegar 1991; Faghfoory 1993; Hashemi Rafsanjani 1998).

All these secularizing efforts, however, came to an end with the triumphant return of religion to the public scene on the eve of the Islamic Revolution. Afterwards, drastic changes undid most of the pre-revolution secularization in most institutions – political, legal, cultural, and, less dramatically, economic – to make them more in accord with Islamic principles. Islamization touched even on subtle matters, such as segregating seats in public space by gender (public transit, university classrooms, government offices, and so on), restricting (mostly women's) dress, and banning a wide range of musical styles as corrupt and "westoxicated."

The revolution and the resultant "Islamic Republic" immediately entered discussions about secularity. For some observers, they reconfirmed Muslim exceptionalism – Muslims' particular attachment to their religion (hence no secularization) and Islamic teachings' closely intertwining religion and state (so no secularism). Some others tried to disregard them as reflecting an "Iranian exceptionalism" rather than the Muslim world writ large.

The notion of Iranian exceptionalism feeds on a historical development related to Iran's being the largest of the few shia-majority nations in the Muslim world (like Azerbaijan, Bahrain, and Iraq). A popular storyline among some scholars of Iran was that shia Muslims' almost-permanent minority status throughout Islam's history had turned them into a permanent opposition force to almost all political regimes that ruled their country. This status had led to a political theology in shia Islam whereby, until the return of the shias' twelfth Imam (the "occulted" Mahdi, born in 870), all states were considered illegitimate. Accordingly, the argument goes, the shia clergy remained politically and financially independent from the state. These dual features then provided Iran's shia Muslims in the 1970s with the elements for a successful revolution: an oppositional ideology, financial independence, and an effective mobilization network (see, among others, Cole and Keddie 1986; Dabashi 2011). So, in that sense, the Islamic Revolution was viewed as a shia-related anomaly in the *sunni*-majority Muslim world (shias make up about 10–15 per cent of Muslims worldwide).

The establishment of an Islamic Republic in Iran soon triggered a debate inside the country – involving mostly religious circles, the clergy, and religious intellectuals – about whether Islamic teachings allowed for the kind of merging of state and religion that happened after the revolution. Various interpretations emerged, ranging from support for the clergy's political rule to seeing Islamic teachings as a source of only spiritual inspiration and not a basis for regulating social and political life. Even supporters of some kind of public role for the religious establishment disagreed among themselves: people like Ayatollah Ruhollah Khomeini believed in the full merging of state and religion, while some other grand ayatollahs felt that the clergy should govern only activities normally outside the state's jurisdiction (for a full discussion of these views, see M. Kadivar 2001). As the Islamic Republic became more settled, those debates became less fiery, and many previously opposing participants came to accept the merging of state and religion. In recent years, however, the debate has flared up again (for a discussion of this, see N. Hashemi 2018).

Most current discussions of these questions, however, lack an empirical basis and suffer from great conceptual confusion. An example appears in the arguments of the prominent Iranian religious scholar Seyyed Hossein Nasr. While admitting that "the direct rule of the 'ulama' [Muslim clergymen] as we have in Iran today is a recent phenomenon, and we never had such a thing in the history of Islam before" (Nasr, Jahanbegloo, and Moore 2010, 311), he adds that there was no need for it:

> The Iranian kings were not simply secular figures. They were supposed to be protectors of religion and were even called the shadow of God on earth even through the Pahlavi period. In the Iranian Constitution of 1906, it is said that royalty is a gift bestowed by God. In fact, kingship in any civilization can never be completely secular. Even before the Revolution it was not as if you had the body of 'ulama' as the church and the monarchy as the state, which were separate as church and state are separate in the United States. The situation was not like that at all. (Nasr, Jahanbegloo, and Moore 2010, 310)

So, if Iran's institutions have always connected religion and state, what makes the last four decades different? The logical extension of Nasr's argument is that there is no difference, as the two were not separated before the revolution, or after it.

Basing his judgment on some labels – such as the kings' being the "shadow of God" – as a sign of a merger of state and religion leads Nasr to misunderstand, I believe, relations between sacred and secular not only in Iran but in the rest of the world. About the state of secularism in the West, for instance, he says:

> Even in the West, the so-called separation of church and state does not hold true in the same way for all nations. In England, the queen is the head of the Church of England and in principle there is no separation of the church and state at all in that land. In Sweden, the most secularized of all societies in Europe, the Lutheran Church was the official church of the country until a short time ago. Now, they are planning to change the laws because there are not only Christians, but also Muslims, in Sweden today, and consequently you have different religions which have to be considered in their relation to the state. (Nasr, Jahanbegloo, and Moore 2010, 310)

In addition to their conceptual confusion and lack of empirical data, many of the existing arguments rely, in some cases exclusively, on Islamic textual sources. Whether stating so or not, this approach assumes that Muslim realities are direct consequences of Islam and its teachings. Thus, to understand those realities, one need only consult with their source, the religious texts. Fish (2011) has convincingly documented the serious problems with this approach, by showing the many areas in which Muslim societies do not follow Islamic teachings. Such a problem is highly visible in the debates about religious and secular in Iranian society. In this book, I try to examine this issue relying on empirical data.

Let's recap the discussion so far. Since the mid-1970s, there has been a new surge of religious sentiment all over the world, and increasing study of religion. In this new wave of popular and scholarly debates, the topics of secularism and secularization have been of special interest. However, Muslim experiences with religion and secularity have been largely absent from these debates, treated more like exceptions to general global rules. This chapter discussed some of the conceptual reasons behind such an oversight, as well as the theoretical blind spots with regard to Muslim realities. In the analysis of the experience of secularity in the Muslim world, Iran serves as a special and particularly informative case study.

OUTLINE OF THE BOOK

The book is divided into four parts. In part one, chapter 2 provides the conceptual backdrop and theoretical framework of this study, and chapter 3 sketches in its historical context. In part two, chapters 4 and 5 examine the merger of state and religious establishment in the post-1979 era, and its consequences for both of those institutions. Part three analyses the deep secularization that has been under way in various areas of life in post-revolution Iran, among variously the general population (chapter 6), young people (chapter 7), and women (chapter 8). Part four explores the effects of post-revolution developments on debates in philosophy (chapter 9) and everyday theology (chapter 10). To examine empirically what was happening in such diverse areas, one needs to use various types of data and a range of methods, which I outline in the corresponding chapters. Chapter 11 offers a wrap-up of the conclusions and implications of the study.

The current chapter, up to here, outlines the contours of the study, by introducing its research question – i.e., the implications of the Islamic Revolution for the place of religion in Iranian society – and situating it within the various current debates going on around the globe about the place of religion in the world, in the Muslim world, and in Iran.

Chapter 2 discusses the two conceptual building blocks of the study – secularity and causation. It "unpacks" the concept of secularity and discusses causation in the social sciences as they pertain to religion and religious developments. In the chapter's first section, while assessing current global debates on secularity, I reveal the relative silence on Muslims' experiences. The chapter illustrates how the philosophical and theological assumptions of some Western and Muslim scholars and their notions about Muslim exceptionalism have presented themselves in their scholarly works and have resulted in inaccurate conclusions about the state of religion in the Muslim world. It then makes a case for the study of secularity in the Muslim world in general, and in Iran in particular. The information in this section comes from the existing literature on religion and Islam in English and Farsi (Persian). The central argument is that the conventional conceptualization of sacred and secular as mutually exclusive neither explains the current world nor yields any practical implications for how to change it. Instead, the chapter offers a more nuanced picture, which better captures the diversity of experiences with secularity.

The second section of chapter 2 introduces the theoretical backbone of the study: the concept of "causation." Critiquing an underlying assumption among many scholars of Islam and Muslims societies, who consider "ideas" the driving forces of history, this chapter first reviews the philosophical distinctions between "reason" and "cause" and, second, offers examples of "reason-based" and "cause-based" theoretical approaches in historical research. It then ends, third, with examples of such theoretical approaches to religious developments in Iran. It makes a case for a cause-based approach in studying secularization in Iran. The discussion in this chapter draws on the existing literature in English, but I take examples from the literature in both English and Persian.

Chapter 3 outlines the history of Islam in Iran, using the cause-based approach. For a systematic study of this history, both as a faith and as an institution, I have used, as Hashemi (2018) proposes, the conceptual framework from the sociological perspective known as historical institutionalism. Rather than viewing institutions as fixed and continuous, this perspective analyses them as both continuous and evolving by looking at the roles of "exogenous forces," "critical junctures," and "path-dependency." Major changes in the broader environment act as exogenous forces on institutions and force changes in the path-dependent ways they function. The resulting critical junctures – historical moments of uncertainty and indeterminacy – allow various players to influence the institutions and introduce qualitative changes. Those alterations then create momentum, or inertia, that incrementally changes, even reshapes, how the institution functions, leading to a new path-dependent mode of operation (Capoccia and Kelemen 2007, 341).

Using this perspective, I organize my outline of the history of Islam in Iran in chapter 3 around six critical junctures:

- Early sixteenth century: adoption of *shi'ism* as the official religion by the Safavid dynasty.
- Early twentieth century: Reza Shah's adoption of secularism, in order to remove the influences of the religious establishment from the state, and later the launch of "secularization from above," under Reza Shah Pahlavi.
- Mid-1960s: the emergence of militant Islamism as a political ideology, through the Mojaheddin-e Khalgh Organization (MKO) and Ali Shariati.
- Mid-1970s: the ideological shift in MKO from Islam to Marxism, and the consequent eruption of a reactive conservative Islamism.
- Late 1970s: the Islamic Revolution and the launch of Islamization.
- Late 1980s: the incorporation of the notions of *zarura* (necessity) and *maslahat* (expediency) into the foundations of the Islamic Republic's political philosophy.

Each of these six critical junctures ushered a new element into Iran's religious landscape that helps explain historical developments and the current state of affairs. I have tried to use information available in English, but have also consulted many historiographical sources in Persian.

Each chapter in part two (chapters 4 and 5) and part three (chapters 6–8) focuses on one aspect of religious life in Iran since 1979. Chapter 4 discusses the sea change whereby religion became the state's junior partner. This "special case of secularism," as I call it, resulted from the merger, rather than separation, of religion and state. The database for the chapter consists mostly of Farsi sources. Many of the main players have published memoirs in the tradition of oral history, invaluable portraits of post-revolution Iran.

Chapter 5 examines the changes in the political philosophy of the Islamic Republic over the past four decades, whereby the needs and exigencies of state trump conventional religious principles. This, I argue, is a bold move towards a secular ideology, however autocratic, that reduces the impact of religion on state policies. Like chapter 4, this chapter also draws on Farsi documents.

Chapter 6 takes a close look at the changes in Iranians' religious beliefs and behaviour. Several nationwide, longitudinal surveys (looking at the same variables over time) traced a significant shift away from religion towards secularity. Together, they offer a longitudinal picture of the changes in Iranians' beliefs and attitudes.

Chapter 7 uses the sources for chapter 6 to explore religious beliefs among Iranian young people and supplements them with international data from the World Values Survey to compare young people in Iran with those in Egypt, Turkey, Britain, Canada, and the United States.

Chapter 8 examines the role of Iranian women in the process of secularization. As one of the main targets and subjects of Islamization, they have been at the forefront of pushing back the religious boundaries. I argue that a unique post-1979 baby boom rendered the traditional and religiously informed life cycle and life paths no longer viable for many Iranian women, so they opened new, secular social frontiers. This chapter uses census data and secondary statistics.

In chapter 9, I discuss how the strong secularization of Iranian society has reflected itself in the philosophical debates of the post-revolution era, illustrating this process through the ideas of two prominent Iranian philosophers, Abdulkarim Soroush and Ahmad Fardid. These scholars represent the two main camps within Iran's religious circles, which divide somewhat like Europe's analytical and continental philosophies. Through detailed analysis of their central ideas, I trace the signs of a secularizing trend in Iran's philosophical landscape. Almost all the literature I cite in this chapter is available only in Persian.

Chapter 10 discusses six main events and trends in the post-revolution era that helped form the nature and functions of religion in today's Iran. These are the impact of the Iran–Iraq War of 1980–88, the rise of religious ceremonial, the deepening of the religious–secular divide, the emergence of new spiritualities, increasing migration from the country, and women's rights movements.

In the final chapter, "Conclusions and Implications," I situate the findings of the study in the broader landscape of research on religion in Iran, while discussing how these findings relate to some better-known views and studies on this issue, both in English and in Farsi.

I now turn to current debates on secularism and the place in those debates of the Muslim world and Iran.

2

Rethinking Secularity and Causation

Some years ago … [at] a dinner at Princeton University … I witnessed a revealing exchange between an eminent European philosopher … and a Muslim scholar who was seated next to him. The Muslim colleague was indulging in a glass of wine …

"How come … you are drinking wine? … "

"We are the Muslim wine-drinkers … "

"I don't understand."

"Yes, I know, but I do."

Shahab Ahmed[1]

Either God can prevent evil and he will not; or he wishes to prevent it and he cannot.

Will Durant[2]

The two quotations above embryonically introduce the two main topics of this chapter. Take the imagery of a "Muslim wine-drinker"! The images of Muslim non-drinkers and non-Muslim drinkers are familiar, but the combination of Muslim-ness and wine drinking has been mostly a symbolic concept in *sufi* poetry. In reality, however, there are many examples of Muslims who combine both Islamic and non-Islamic elements, religious and secular elements, in their daily routines. This notion challenges the customary contradistinction between sacred and secular in discussion and writing. The first section of this chapter explores this conversation.

The Durant quotation refers to two other concepts often mixed up in analyses of religion in the Muslim world: "reason" and "cause." "Reason" refers to ideas, "cause" to material forces; and studies of Muslim populations tend to rely on reason much more than on causes.

The second section of this chapter analyses the differences between these two concepts, and between the analytical approaches revolving around each.

UNPACKING THE CONCEPT OF SECULARITY

There are probably few concepts surrounded by as much controversy and disagreement as the concept of secularity. As a result, some scholars, such as Charles Taylor, have argued that the concept is obsolete and should be replaced with something more precise (quoted in Soroush 2017). Towards this goal, we need, first, to unravel the concept and identify its possible constituents; second, to assess the degree of their explanatory power vis-à-vis the real world; and, third, to refine them and relate them to empirical observation.

The easiest way to conceptualize "secular" is to contrast it with "sacred," which idea originated with Durkheim's ([1912] 2008) well-known distinction between "sacred" and "profane." In this mode of understanding, everything – e.g., individuals, institutions, societies, policies, even things – is either religious or secular, blessed by a faith or shaped by this-worldly forces. This dichotomy reflected the sixteenth-century beginning of the modern age as a turning point in history, with a sharp shift away from the "sacred" towards the "secular." This break was understood to happen both in individual consciousness and in institutions, constitute an irreversible transformation, and occur in all societies sooner or later.

Challenges arose in the 1970s and 1980s, as a series of political movements heralded the return of religion to the public scene: the rise of Islamic fundamentalism in the Middle East, the emergence of liberation theology in Latin America, the involvement of the Catholic church in the anti-communist Solidary movement in Poland, and the surfacing of Evangelical Protestantism in the United States. The deep-seated belief in the inevitability of secularization, however, had rendered social scientists ill-prepared to grasp this new phenomenon; hence, new methods to make sense of these changes were slow to emerge. In the first section of this chapter, I offer a perceptual map of research on the notion of secular and introduce the concepts of secularization and secularism in the way that I apply them in the present study.

Figure 2.1 provides a schematic view of how these two concepts have been understood and how they break down into secondary categories.

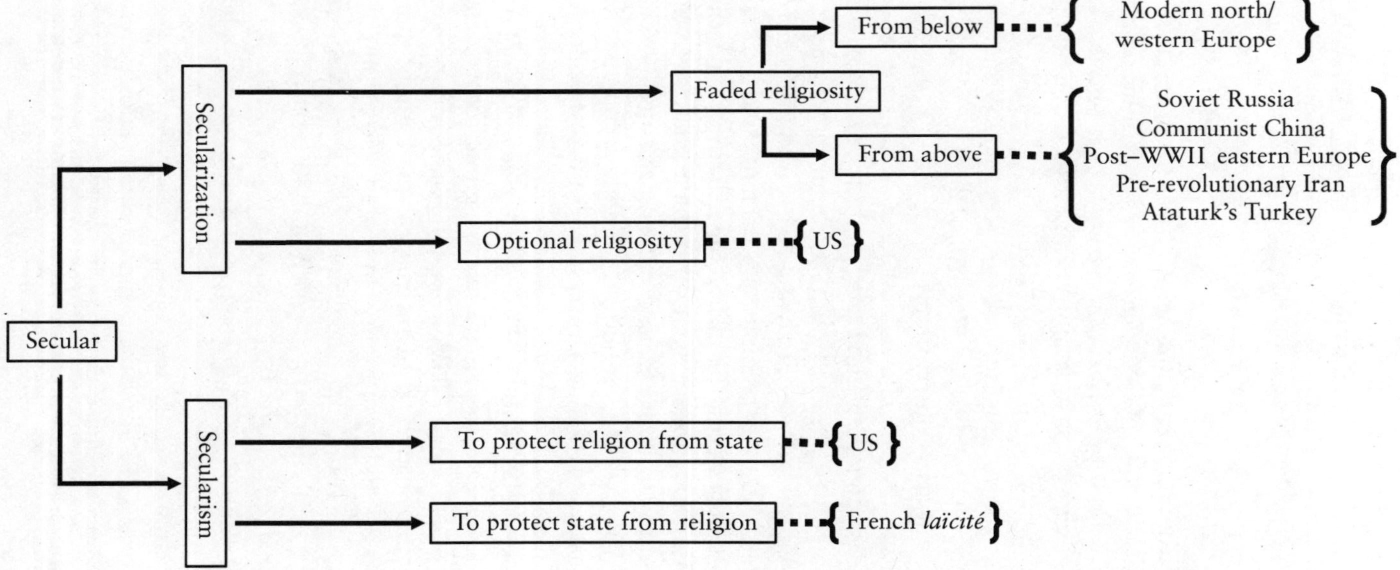

Figure 2.1 Perceptual mapping of the existing conceptualization of the notion of secularity.

The left half of this figure outlines the concepts and the resultant scenarios, and the right, the corresponding countries.

Any discussion of secularity starts usually with the distinction between "secularization" and "secularism" (see Berger et al. 2008; Casanova 2009; Gole 2010). Berger et al. (2008) comment succinctly: "Strictly speaking, 'secularization' is a process subject to empirical examination in accordance with the norms of social science ... 'Secularism' ... like all 'isms' – is an ideology" (33). In other words, secularization refers to what *is*, secularism to what *ought to be*; secularization *describes*, secularism *prescribes*. Secularization refers to a *process*, whereby religion loses its influence on an individual's mind, thinking, and decision-making, but secularism is a *project* that prevents religion from influencing the state (hence "separation of church and state").

Yet secularization and secularism do connect in reality. Societal secularization in western/northern Europe, for instance, created a demand for, and resulted in, a secular state. In other words, the retreat of religion in people's minds and lives resulted in restrictions on the church's ability to meddle in various aspects of state functioning, such as education, justice, taxation, and political appointments. This is what I have called "secularization from below." In such cases, it follows, any increase in the level of people's religiosity might pose a challenge to the state's secularism. Such a dynamic is currently at work in many western European countries, where the growing number of more religious immigrants, mostly from Muslim backgrounds, has triggered serious debates about the nature of secularism in those countries.

In contrast to western/northern Europe, in the Soviet Union, post-1945 central and eastern Europe, and Communist China, the causal influence between secularization and secularism was reversed. There, first a secularist state came into existence, and then it launched a project of social secularization. Influenced by a Marxist view of religion as a superstructural epiphenomenon and an example of a false ideology at the service of a class-based society, such states took it upon themselves to rid society and people of the "yoke of religion." Some non-communist countries in the developing world – such as Turkey under Mustafa Kemal Atatürk and Iran under Reza Shah Pahlavi – followed a similar path, with the secularization of people an adjunct of the western-European model of nation-building and modernization. In this "secularization from above," state secularism preceded, and caused, secularization among people.

Such societies – i.e., those that have experienced "secularization from above" – tend to develop an additional feature. Since their secularization has been imposed by an authoritarian government, any popular revolt against the state is often accompanied by a return to religion. Iran's Islamic Revolution of 1979, the rise of Erdoğan's Justice and Development Party to power in Turkey, and the strengthening of attachment to Catholicism and Orthodox Christianity in central and eastern Europe after 1989 are all pointed examples. A similar dynamic could be found in Egypt, as Saba Mahmood (2015) outlines in her study of its Coptic Orthodox Christian and Bahá'í minorities. Her *Religious Difference in a Secular Age* postulates that "modern secular governance has contributed to the exacerbation of religious tensions in postcolonial Egypt, hardening interfaith boundaries and polarizing religious differences," so secularism has not been "a solution to the problem of religious strife" but "a force in its creation" (1–2). All of these examples highlight the inadequacy of the simple distinctions between sacred and secular, secularism and secularization.

Religion in the United States also poses a major challenge to the simple dichotomy of sacred and secular. Secularization theory tells us that a high level of industrial modernization (such as has occurred in the United States) should bring a reduced level of religiosity; a combination that has not materialized in that country. This anomaly is sometimes referred to as "American exceptionalism" (Robinson 1999, 232–3). Scholars differ on the defining feature of this uniqueness. MacIntyre, for instance, considers it a case of secularization from within: "American religion has survived in industrial society only at the cost of itself becoming secular" (quoted in B.S. Turner 1974, 158).

Charles Taylor (2007, 2–3) looks at American religiosity as "a move from a society where belief in God is unchallenged and indeed, unproblematic, to one in which it is understood to be one option among others." Taylor labels it a type of secularity, where embracing religion exists as a choice, "rather than as a default setting into which people are born." In Taylor's view, what he calls "secularity 3" – to add to the withdrawal of religion from the public sphere and its withdrawal from individuals' minds – is one in which a belief in God or spirituality is present, but adopted through some kind of "reflective" process, as opposed to being "naïvely" attached to it; and it is happening in a social milieu in which the default is unbelief. Studying this "secularity 3" will inevitably involve examining the "conditions of belief" or the "context of understanding in which the moral, spiritual or religious experience and search takes place" (Taylor 2007, 3).

Taylor's suggestion allows us to view the two "opposing" elements sacred and secular as intertwining and part of one larger complex. In figure 2.1, I call Taylor's secularity 3 "optional religiosity," to mark it off from the "faded religiosity" of secularization from below.

Besides "faded" and "optional" religiosity, we can imagine a third type as well, called "scope-reduced religiosity." I base this concept on a hint from Durkheim ((1897) 2013), recently picked up by Casanova (1994), Chavez (1994), and Yamane (1997). Viewed this way, secularization does not totally erase religion in an individual's mind but shrinks its scope. For Durkheim, this differentiates Protestant faith from Catholicism, given that many Protestants were not any less religious than many Catholics; rather, the former applied their religious instruction to much less of their lives, leaving more to their own personal conscience, interpretations, and secular decision-making. Durkheim used this theory to explain Protestants' higher rates of suicide, attributing it to their weaker communal bonds, themselves due to their greater egoism and loneliness, which results from the individualized nature of their faith.

Along the same lines, Chavez (1994) and Yamane (1997) introduced "neosecularization" as an alternative to both "old secularization" and "postsecularization":

> According to its critics, the 'old' secularization paradigm has been tried, convicted, and executed by recent scholarship in the social sciences of religion, and is being replaced by a 'new' (postsecularization) paradigm which highlights the continued vitality of religion in modern societies. This paper argues that claims to have definitively refuted secularization theory are exaggerated. It mounts a defense of a neosecularization paradigm which retains the core insights of the old paradigm while incorporating criticisms leveled against the hubris and laziness of some deployments of the concept of 'secularization.' Following Chaves (1994), [I argue] that the core of neosecularization theory is the proposition that secularization means not the decline of religion but the declining scope of religious authority at the individual, organizational, and societal levels of analysis. (Yamane 1997, 109)

Secularization in this sense happens, according to Yamane (1997, 115), "when religious authority structures decline in their ability to control societal-level institutions, meso-level organizations, and individual-level beliefs and behaviors." He then elaborates on these three levels, quoting Chaves (1994, 757) as saying:

> Secularization at the societal level may be understood as the declining capacity of religious elites to exercise authority over other institutional spheres. Secularization at the organizational level may be understood as religious authority's declining control over organizational resources within the religious sphere. And secularization at the individual level may be understood as the decrease in the extent to which individual actions are subject to religious control. (Yamane 1997, 115)

This proposition allows for more theoretical possibilities and more explanatory power. Other scholars seem to have used the same concept, even if in different terms. An example is the arguments of José Casanova, the prominent scholar of religion and neosecularization. For him, secularization consists of at least three components that do not always act in tandem:

> What usually passes for a single theory of secularization is actually made up of three very different, uneven and unintegrated propositions: secularization as differentiation of the secular spheres from religious institutions and norms, secularization as decline of religious beliefs and practices, and secularization as marginalization of religion to a privatized sphere … The fruitless secularization debate can end only when sociologists of religion begin to examine and test the validity of each of the three components independently of each other. (Casanova 1994, 211)

Such an approach allows for a much more refined picture of secularization. For instance, one can imagine an individual or a society becoming simultaneously more secular and more religious: more secular because of reduced scope, yet more religious because of stronger attachment to that reduced scope. This dual process seems to capture the experiences of many early Protestants, who, as described by Weber ([1920] 2010), were as pious, if not more so, than their Catholic counterparts; but, as described by Durkheim ([1897] 2013), had much less of their lives informed by religious instruction and decided much more on their own.

This possibility tweaks the concept of secularization, which was based largely on the dichotomy of sacred versus secular, and permits us to more accurately capture religious experience in Iran.

REVISITING SECULARISM

In a broad sense, secularism has referred to an institutional arrangement that separates religious and political authorities, that is, a separation of church and state. As Casanova (2009) puts it, it can reflect a mere organizational principle of statecraft, not based on a particular philosophy, or it can manifest an ideology based on a substantive historical-philosophical theory of religion. As a statecraft principle, it could be used either to protect state from religion or vice versa. In the global debates on secularism, this distinction is often used to contrast secular dispensations in western Europe and in the United States. A major explanatory factor, according to Berger et al. (2008), is the presence of a dominant church in many western European countries, as opposed to the many smaller denominations in the United States. The latter situation, combined with a higher degree of religiosity among early settlers in the American colonies, required a political arrangement that allowed no one denomination a monopoly over the state and that prevented the state from interfering in citizens' religious affairs. In Europe, in contrast, the main concern was to ensure that the dominant church would not undermine the state. So, both went for a separation of church and state, one to protect religion, the other to protect the state.[3]

The western European notion of secularism, particularly as articulated in the French notion of *laïcité*, however, was more than just a statecraft measure; it was often accompanied, at least in its formal articulation, by a philosophical perspective on the history of religion. According to Casanova (2009, 1054), this perspective viewed religion as a pre-modern force to relegate to a minor position as societies modernize: "To be secular means to be modern, and therefore by implication to be religious means to be somewhat not yet fully modern." Of course, adopting such a stance did also affect the non-institutional domain, and secularity permeated the whole consciousness of the modern human being. As Casanova points out, this particular philosophy of religion has made the ideology of secularism appear a universal, even inevitable consequence of modernization. This perceived or imposed notion of universality – itself flowing from an overgeneralization of a particular historical evolution in western Christendom (Warner et al. 2010) – has dampened efforts to theorize in this area, reducing conceptual choices to a "modern and secularist" political philosophy committed to separating church and state and a "pre-modern and theocratic" one that merged the two.

The case of post-revolution Iran, however, points to a third theoretical possibility that may seem somewhat paradoxical at first glance. As I propose in the remainder of this book, what has happened in Iran over the past four decades has triggered a unique process that has resulted in a secular state, not through a separation, but through a merger of mosque and state. The merger of the two realms did not give religion the upper hand; rather, through a complex process and a deliberate project, religious institution was relegated to a subservient position. This project, founded on the concept of *maslahat-e nezam* (state exigencies), aimed not to protect religion from the state but to protect the state from religious interference. The outcome transformed the Islamic Republic's political philosophy from one based on religious teachings to one informed by pragmatic considerations of the state apparatus.

The post-1979 Iranian scenario resembles Charles Taylor's (2007) "secularity 3" – where religion is adopted as an option and as a consequence of pragmatic and secular considerations, unlike traditional societies, where religion was the default and did not involve much individualized thinking – but with a twist. While in Taylor's "secularity 3" the sacred is arrived at through a secular process, in post-1979 Iran, the state, I argue, has undergone a similar process but in reverse; here, a theocratic state has moved to a secular political philosophy through the pressure of secular and pragmatic considerations. Both of these imageries – "secularity 3" and "secularity 3 in reverse" – interconnect sacred and secular, and allow for frequent passages from one to the other, and in both directions. This intertwining is what I have meant to convey in the title of this book, *Sacred as Secular*, as a challenge to the understanding of the two concepts as mutually exclusive.

RECONCEPTUALIZING SACRED AND SECULAR

I would summarize the above discussion in the following four points, whereby I reconceptualize the relations between sacred and secular in the present study.

First, sacred and secular as non-essentialist, historically shaped, and socially constructed phenomena: Prevailing theoretical perspectives on secularism can be placed, as Kuru (2009, 15–22) suggests, under three broad headings: *modernist*, which views secularity as an inevitable product of modernization; *civilizational*, which treats it as an essentialized concept for use only in the equally essentialized Christian civilization, but not in, for instance, the Islamic world; and *rational-choice*, which considers it the product of rational decision-making by states to maximize their political stability and economic growth and minimize unrest, instability, and other opportunity costs. Kuru himself suggests a fourth possible view of secularism, as the outcome of *ideological struggles* in a society: "A religion's close relations with political authority create certain negative perceptions against it among the authority's discontents," and, as de Tocqueville argues, "it sacrifices the future for the present" (Kuru 2009, 22–3).

Of Kuru's four perspectives, the first two are too deterministic, and the third is too individualistic, to adequately explain the variety of religious developments in today's world. In this study, I adopt Kuru's fourth perspective – based on ideological struggle – and look at religion and secularism as part of the political landscape, and as phenomena that both shape and are shaped by the other forces in this landscape. Conceptualized this way, the secular (and the sacred) are understood not as a permanent civilizational feature nor as an inevitable outcome of a long historical process or of a personal cost-benefit analysis, but as a product of some short- and medium-term social forces that can move in a variety of directions. In the case of our study, this would allow us to explain the extreme secularization of Iranian society during the mid-twentieth century and its extreme sacralization since 1979.

Second, sacred and secular as linked concepts and forces: In his *A Secular Age*, Charles Taylor (2007) considers the perceived opposition between sacred/spiritual/religion and secular as falsely placed and largely exaggerated; an opposition that, according to Warner et al. (2010, 17), "appears only as a late and retrospective misrecognition." For Taylor, Western secular society is "an *unanticipated* [emphasis added] result of the reformers' efforts to police the properly spiritual" (Warner et al. 2010, 16). This vantage point summons two new concepts that can powerfully explain religious developments in contemporary societies. First, the sacred and secular do not always (or perhaps ever) form distinct territories or act as two elements in a zero-sum game; rather, they are part and parcel of broader, multidimensional processes that can involve mutual weakening of both, mutual strengthening of both, and the transformation of one into the other (see, for instance, Asad 2003; Gole 2010; Turam 2012). Second, the outcomes of social projects – such as sacralization or secularization – do not always align with the architects' intended goals. A project that aims to secularize a society can lead – *unanticipatedly* and *unintendedly* – to further sacralization, and vice versa (see, for example, Mahmood 2015). In our study, this helps us explain the deep secularization that has been under way in Iran alongside, and as a result of, the heavy Islamization of the country since 1979.

Third, the segmented and scoped nature of secularization: According to Yamane (1997, 115), secularization does not always manifest itself as a consistent and multi-fronted fading of religiosity; rather, it can be very segmented, reducing religiosity in certain dimensions and keeping it intact or even strengthening it in others. It is therefore possible to imagine a secularizing process that does not weaken religious sentiments overall, but reduces the scope of religion's influence. For religion in post-revolution Iran, I argue that both processes – overall weakening and scope reduction – have been at work, with the former explaining religious trends among the younger generation, and the latter among the older.

Fourth, the possibility of secularism through the merger of religion and state: Building on Casanova (2009), I make a distinction between secularism as a technical decision of statecraft, to protect either church or state, and as an ideology based on a – mostly negative – philosophical reading of the place of religion in human history. I argue that state-building in post-1979 Iran shows a unique combination of both, through a four-step process. First, it started with a positive reading of religion in human history; second, it established a state based on Islamic teachings and safeguarded by incorporation of the religious establishment into the state apparatus; third, facing conflicts between religious principles and the pragmatic necessities of statesmanship, it introduced an innovation in statecraft, which subordinated religious institutions to the state and its needs; fourth and finally, it became a unique type of secular state that combines a religious appearance with secular content. (For a good summary of the different possible combinations of societal and state processes, see Fish [2011], chap. 2.).

Given these four points, I would like to suggest figure 2.2 (a modified version of figure 2.1), which highlights the potential contributions of the current study to the literature on sacred and secular in four areas. First, it suggests secularism-religiosity as a continuum, as opposed to a binary option. Consistent with the multidimensionality of religion

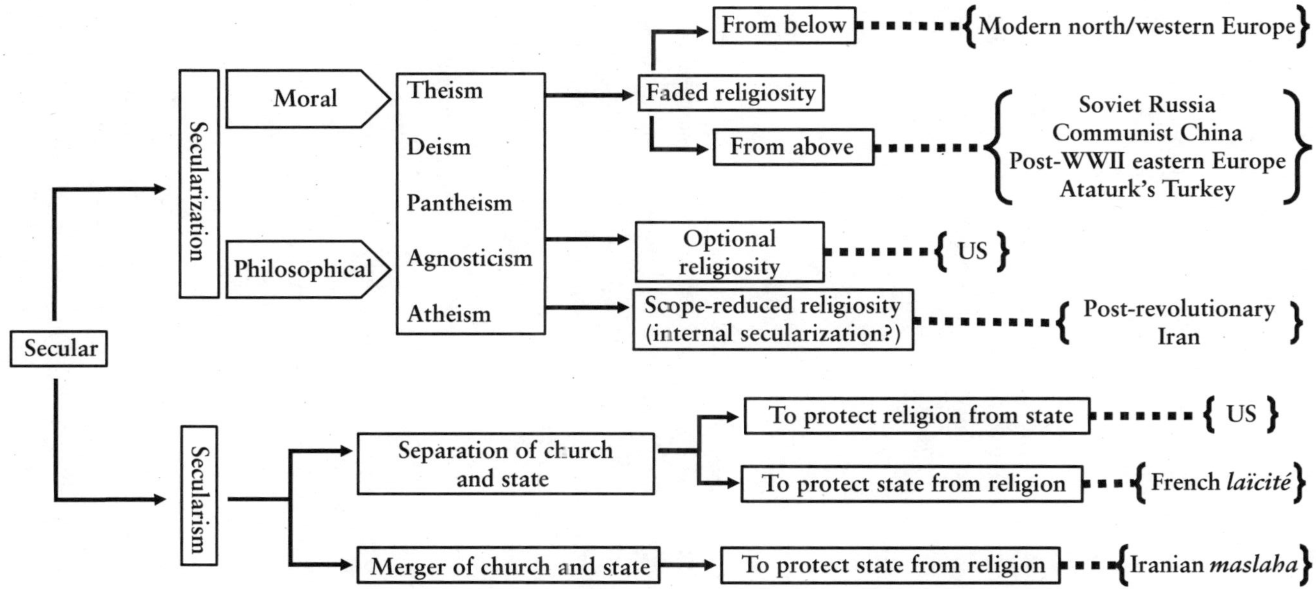

Figure 2.2 A proposed perceptual mapping for the conceptualization of the notion of secularity.

and religiosity, this allows for five possibilities instead of two (as suggested by Dabbagh 2014): theism, deism, pantheism, agnosticism, and atheism. Second, it divides the notion of secularization – i.e., Berger's "subjective secularization" – into philosophical and moral subcomponents (as suggested by Soroush 2014). Third, it suggests a third possible way to conceptualize secularization – besides faded religiosity and optional religiosity (Charles Taylor's "secularity 3") – namely scope-reduced religiosity, in which secular and sacred coexist in the mind, where religion remains influential in certain areas of thought and is absent in others. Fourth, it offers the possibility of a state that appears theocratic but is secular in nature, not because religion and state are separate but because they have merged, and with religion pushed to a subservient position, along the lines of Samuel Huntington's (1996, 70) description of Orthodox Christianity, in which "God is Caesar's junior partner."

REASONS AND CAUSES: HOW TO EXPLAIN SOCIAL TRANSFORMATIONS

The above discussion was about one conceptual pillar of the study – secularity. Here, I introduce the other – causation. I first provide a critique of the perspective that considers that ideas determine and shape history. Then, I offer an alternative stance – derived largely from Durkheim – that makes broad "social and structural" forces central and emphasizes the epiphenomenal nature of "ideas."

As I mentioned on the opening page of chapter 1, on 1 November 1755 a strong earthquake shook Lisbon, demolishing thirty churches and a thousand houses, as well as killing fifteen thousand people and injuring the same number. But, according to Durant and Durant (1965, 720), it also "sent its tremors throughout European philosophy." In this philosophical aftershock, an old theological question resurfaced: what was God's purpose in this? None of the existing and ready-made answers worked. It was in this moment of great confusion that Voltaire wrote a passionate poem, whose essence, according to Durant (1933, 247), was the old anti-God statement that "either God can prevent evil and he will not; or he wishes to prevent it and he cannot."

Voltaire's pronouncement introduces two very distinct modes of explanation, not only for God's behaviour vis-à-vis Lisbon's earthquake, but also for the ways in which we analyse individual behaviour and social transformations in general. This distinction is crucial for the conceptual framework I adopt in the present study. If "God can prevent evil and he will not," God's action is considered to be determined by His intentions, His rationale, His purpose; a mode of operation that we can call *reason*-based. If, however, "he wishes to prevent it and he cannot," His intentions have been undermined and overridden by outside forces that overpowered Him and His ideas; let's call this mode of operation *cause*-based.

The *reason*-based perspective on human conduct has been dominant throughout history, both because it is intuitive and because it gives humans agency. It looks at humans as coming up with an idea and a blueprint for action and then acting on them. The starting point is therefore the idea(s) formed in an individual's mind, and the end point is the actions carried out in the world. This mode of explanation was used for both individual behaviour and social developments; in the latter case, the society was first reduced to individual actions, and then those individual actions were explained with reference to the individual "reasons" behind them. Viewed this way, the solution to all human problems was the refinement of individuals' thoughts and the correction of their thinking process; hence education was the magic bullet to fix all human ills.

The oldest version of a reason-based perspective is probably Socrates and Plato's notion of "the close connection between virtue and knowledge" (Russell [1946] 2005, 97).[4] Initially, this was a proposition in ethics, which began with Greek philosophy and continued in Catholic theology during the Middle Ages. But, during the eighteenth-century Enlightenment, knowledge (as the product of intellect) was used to explain human behaviour (whether individual or social). Knowledge was no longer counterpoised to other human qualities such as courage, humility, fear, and selfishness; instead, it was counterpoised to ignorance and superstition. In other words, knowledge was divided into false and correct, with the former the source of all human evils, and the latter the way to counter them.

This Enlightenment monopoly of *intellect* faced some serious challenges before the eighteenth century was over. Durant (1933) reports the sentiments of this revolt against intellect: "What was this intellect that proposed to destroy with a syllogism the beliefs of thousands of years and millions of men? Was it infallible? Or was it one human organ like any other, with strictest limits to its functions and its powers? The time had come to judge this judge … The time had come for a critique of reason" (278–9).

The first and most enduring revolt against intellect was staged by Jean-Jacques Rousseau and Romanticism. This was a shift away from the Aristotelian notion of human intellect emphasized by the Enlightenment thinkers, towards what Romantics called *la sensibilité*, "which meant a proneness to emotion, and more particularly to the emotion of sympathy" (Russell [1946] 2005, 615), emotions that were at the basis of art, literature, aesthetics, and morality. In the nineteenth century, Romantic ideas inspired several philosophers, each emphasizing a different non-intellectual element – Schopenhauer emphasized *will*, Nietzsche the *will to power*, and Bergson *intuition* – but all denied centrality to the intellect in informing human behaviour. In doing so, they were indeed referring to "causes" – as opposed to "reason" or "intellect."

But all the above propositions were still situating the "causes" within individuals, in the same way that intellect or reason was an individual property. It was the advent of social sciences in the second half of the nineteenth century that not only spurred cause-based explanations, but also located causes outside individuals and within the realm of the social. Even though the "*social cause*"–based explanation found its fullest articulation late in the nineteenth century, it had appeared in a rudimentary form in Edmund Burke's *Reflections on the Revolution in France*, published in 1790, a year after the French Revolution. The French, casting doubt on the main premise of their revolution – i.e., establishing a new society on the basis of rational principles, while ignoring the nation's history and national character – soon proved to be not so philosophical or rational. Burke felt that the revolt's aftermath confirmed that, according to Mitchell (1999, xv), "history was more important than philosophy." In other words, "cause" overrode "reason."

The social cause–based perspective found its most articulate expression in Marx and Durkheim. Karl Marx uncovered the source of human behaviour in the individual's position within the societal class structure. He relegated ideas, philosophies, artistic expression, and religion to epiphenomena that merely reflected "non-ideational" and truly "real" – material – forces; the epiphenomena belonged to a superstructure that was determined by the economic substructure. Along the same lines but expanding on Marx's perspective, Émile Durkheim grasped that individuals' behaviour was driven by "social forces," which could be material, like those that Marx emphasized, but also political, demographic, even psychological.

So, what distinguishes causes from reasons? Buss (1978, 1311) proposes: "Causes are that which bring about a change; reasons are that for which a change is brought about." This distinction is useful, because each concept can explain one of the two types of events – occurrences and actions: "Behaviors that happen *to* a person – that is non-intentional … – is [*sic*] an *occurrence* and is explained with causes; behavior that is done *by* a person – that is intended, that has a goal or purpose – is an action and is explained … with reasons" (1311). This distinction increases the explanatory power both of causes and of reasons and allows for extensive refining and precision.

Later works have added factors such as the explainer's tendency to invoke causes or reasons, the impact of whether the explainer is an actor or an observer, changes over time in the attachment to these two modes of explanation (e.g., the shift from reason- to cause-based explanation with modernization and science), the role of personal desires in promoting particular reason-based explanations, and the differences in using causes and/or reasons in lay and expert languages (for some of these discussions, see A.R. Buss 1978, 1979; Hinkle and Schmidt 1984; Macklin 1972).

USING REASON AND CAUSE TO EXPLAIN MUSLIM REALITIES

Observers have applied both reason- and cause-based modes to explain Muslim realities, and I offer some examples of each. One using both is the European debates about the involvement of Muslim youths in violent and/or terrorist activities in Europe in the aftermath of 9/11. In those debates, some commentators considered the violent teachings of Islam as the *reason* for such involvement, while others invoked Muslims' poor living conditions as its *cause* (for an elaborate discussion of those debates, see Kazemipur 2014). In an article in *Le Monde* after the terrorist attacks that shook France in November 2015, Olivier Roy, a French scholar and a keen observer of Muslim affairs, illustrated the difference between these two perspectives. He suggested that Muslims' participation was the outcome not of the "radicalization of Islam" but of the "Islamization of radicalism" (Roy 2015). While the former characterization finds the reason in Islamic teachings, the latter focuses on the cause, for which Islamic beliefs are only a façade.

Another illustration of the reason/cause distinction comes from the Iranian philosopher Abdulkarim Soroush (Soroush 1988, 2000b, 2016b).

He distinguishes between cause- and reason-based religiosities, with the former being the outcome of living in a particular social and cultural environment and the latter the result of independent and personal reflections and intellectual work. Extending this conceptual distinction, one can imagine two types of secularization as well; one triggered by causal forces, the other by rational thinking. Along these lines, Soroush further uses this distinction to interpret the Quranic verse, "Most people do not believe in God" (i.e., *fa aksarohom la yo'menoon*), to show the futility of the Islamic Republic's Islamization project, as well as the need for religious pluralism. He says that such a goal – making everyone religious – was not achieved even by God, either for a reason or for a cause. If it was due to a reason, God did not really plan or wish to make everyone religious; if it was due to a cause, even if God so desired, practical obstacles might have made this goal unachievable. Soroush concluded that, whichever explanation Islamic Republic authorities accepted, they should not aim for the impossible.

Peters (1958) has observed that ordinary-language explanations of human action invoke reason much more often than cause. They typically involve "stating one's intention or goal and/or justifying the means used in attaining the goal" (quoted in A.R. Buss 1978, 1313). A cursory look at records of discussions and debates on Muslim realities indicates a similar reason-bias, which has confounded understanding of the Muslim world. This bias puts Muslims' beliefs at the root of all their behaviours – Islam drives their conduct. It follows that, since any undesirable behaviour by them is assumed to have been triggered by a perverted interpretation of Islam, any corrective measure should also start from a re-interpretation of the faith. Such a view was dominant in the old Orientalist literature and received a boost from new Orientalism after 9/11.

This pro-reason bias, however, affects not just Western Orientalist observers but also many scholars of Islam or of Muslim backgrounds, whether or not they're religious. A perfect example appears in an account of the Iranian psyche by Seyyed Hossein Nasr (2000):

> Because of this long period during which the Persians have become Islamicized in the deepest sense possible, the worldview of the Persian today is determined more than anything else by the teachings of Islam. Like other Muslims, the vast majority of Persians are born, live and die with the verses of the Noble Quran echoing in their ears. They see the world about them

> in light of the conception of the Divine and His creation as delineated in the Noble Quran. There is, in fact, in spite of the secularist tendencies of the past fifty years, still no conception of a way of life among the vast majority of Persians in which religion would be seen as only one element among many or of a worldview in which the religious factor would be only one dimension. The total worldview is religious, and even the apparent negation of religion by certain people has itself a religious significance … There are some who do not heed the voice of the Divine, but there is practically no one who doubts the presence of 'His voice.' That is why after a life of debauchery a man may become suddenly devout, and even in the midst of the most profane life remains aware of the presence of the transcendent dimension of life … Most Persians feel that they are performing a religious duty when they work to make a living, even if the particular work they perform is not itself of a traditional religious nature. (157–9)

Aramech Dustdar also acknowledges an underlying religious outlook among Iranians but judges it negatively and as the source of an intellectual impasse. In *The Impossibility of Free Thinking in a Religious Culture*, Dustdar (2004) traces this outlook's origins to the country's pre-Islamic era and the teachings of Zoroaster. According to him, it has historically impeded free thinking and thereby blocked socio-political evolution. Like other reason-based explanations, Dustdar considers the abandoning of religious beliefs the starting point of any social reform in the country.

In contrast, cause-based theories tend to start with socio-economic forces and then show how they have affected certain ideas. A great example is Morteza Motahhari's ((1973) 1978) *The Causes of the Adoption of the Materialist Philosophy*, based on a speech the author gave in the early 1970s. Motahhari tries to explain the popularity of dialectical materialism among Iranian youths, without conceding any merit in it. His explanation switches from a reason- to a cause-based argument that suggests the following factors: the violence exerted by the Catholic church in the Middle Ages, the use of a religion-based argument in justifying authoritarian regimes, the idiotic and easily falsifiable nature of some pro-religion arguments, the offering of religious instruction in a way that conflicts with other basic human drives and desires, the presence of mental and/or social environments that are conducive to immoral behaviour, and the active participation of Marxist materialists in the global struggle against colonialism, authoritarianism, and exploitation. A direct quote from Motahhari on this last point conveys the clear contrast between reason- and cause-based explanations:

> Today, in the minds of the youth, it is so that one has to be either religious and indifferent [to social injustice] or materialist and active in fighting against colonialism, exploitation, and authoritarianism … How did this [false dichotomy] come about? … The answer is simple. These are not the logical derivations of two schools of thought; but, the youth do not care about the logical imperatives … They see that the materialists are leading the movements against injustice and the pious are inactive and indifferent. For them, this is sufficient grounds for denouncing religion and supporting materialism. At the moment, the bulk of the heroic fights against authoritarianism and exploitation are led by people who have materialistic inclinations more or less … We have to admit that the religious teachings in our time are depleted from any epic spirits (Motahhari [1973] 1978, 179–80)

Thus a decision about how to relate to religion or to its various dimensions is not always intellectual, settled by philosophical and theological reasons, but may be influenced more heavily by social, political, and economic forces.

Viewing it through the dichotomy of reason- versus cause-based modes of explanation, we can group the existing literature on the history of religion in Iran into two relatively distinct clusters:[5]

Reason-based analyses:

- Presenting the eleventh- and twelfth-century "cultural renaissance" in the broader Muslim world as the product of shia academic institutions (Karimi-Zanjani-Asl 2006).
- Attributing the formation of a sixteenth-century shia Safavid state in Persia to the migration of the *shi'i ulema* from Jabal Amel in Lebanon to Persia and the consequent transfer of the ideas of the Lebanese shia thinker Shahid Aval (Farhani-Monfared 1996).

- Viewing Iran's Constitutionalist Revolution of 1905–11 as a consequence of the maturation of shia culture among Iranians (Ramezan-Nargesi 2010).
- Emphasizing the eclectic ideology of Iran's Mojahedin-e Khalgh Organization as the reason for its ideological conversion from Islam to Marxism in 1975, versus causes such as the global spread of Communism, the presence of Communist China and the Soviet Union, the non-ritualistic nature of Marxism, and so on (see Jafarian 2004, 729).
- Attributing a range of social and political changes in Iran, including 1979, to doctrinal elements of shia Islam in Iran (Arjomand 2016; Cole and Keddie 1986; Dabashi 2011; Eshghi 2000; Mozaffari 2008; Naghibzadeh and Amani-Zawarem 2003).
- Citing the conflict between secular and religiously informed political cultures as the reason for the Iranian revolutions of both 1905–11 and 1979 (Alavian 2003).
- Invoking the notion of jurist-ruler (*velayat-e faqih*) and the essential connection between Islam and recent Iranian politics (Derakhsheh 2005).

Cause-based analyses:

- Attributing the gradual rise of jurists (*faqih*s) and the decline of Sufi orders during the Safavid dynasty, as well as the gradual triumph of the "literalist" (*akhbari*) school of religion and the decline of the "prinicipalist" (*osooli*) school, to the sixteenth-century formation of the Safavid state (Sefatgol 1982).
- Identifying five distinct narrations and modes of understanding for the Ashura events on 10 Murraham commemorating Imam Hossein's martyrdom (tragic/emotional, epic/mythological, mystical, Christianized, predestinational) and attributing the dominance of each narration to the socio-political environment at the time (Ranjbar 2010).
- Attempting (unsuccessfully) to analyse the formation of shia Islam as the outcome of competition over scarce resources such as power, wealth, and social status (Ghaffari-far 2011).
- Detecting a populist mode of thinking among shia clergymen in Iran and attributing that to the financial system that collected religious alms, making the clergy financially dependent on followers' donations (Motahhari [1962] 2003).

- Viewing childhood hardship as a factor in shaping the political behaviour of the clergy, particularly the Sources of Emulation (*maraje'e taghlid*) (Hashemian-far 2011).
- Following the evolution of the political discourses in *shia* Islam through history and explaining it by historical developments (Esmaeeli 2007; J. Kadivar 1999; Mir-moosavi 2005; Zargari-Nejhad 2008).
- Explaining changes in religious mourning ceremonies as responses to new state needs and societal imperatives, both before and after the 1979 revolution (Mazaheri 2011).
- Looking at the transformation of religious discourses as a response to inter- and intra-elite political conflicts in post-1979 Iran (Ayatollahi-Tabaar 2018).

The Issue of Causality

The above discussion introduced the properties of, and the differences between, reason- and cause-based perspectives. A related question concerns the relationship between causes and reasons, with three possible answers: that the former always results in the latter; that the latter generates the former; and that there is some kind of correspondence between the two, without a clear directional causality. Below, I offer the contours of my answer to this question and the possible answers.

The question has a long history in sociology, dating back to the discipline's founding fathers, particularly Max Weber. In *The Protestant Ethic and the Spirit of Capitalism,* Weber ([1920] 2010) suggested the concept of "elective affinity," which he had borrowed from the novel *Elective Affinities* by Goethe ([1809] 2008), who had taken it from chemistry texts, where it referred to the mutual attraction between elements that can result in the breaking up of some old bonds and the formation of new compounds. In his novel, Goethe moved this concept to the relationships between the four main characters. Weber gave it new life by using it in his analysis of social trends and development. In his hands, "elective affinity" became the mutual attraction between different psychological and cultural tendencies, as well as the connection between them and socio-economic and political forces. This latter usage could suggest a link between reasons and causes.

Weber's use of "elective affinity," however, has left many scholars puzzled about his exact definition and theoretical orientation and has generated various interpretations (see, for instance, A. Buss 1999;

R.H. Howe 1978; McKinnon 2010; Reed 2020; Runciman 2005; Thomas 1985; Treiber 1985). Providing a comprehensive overview of those opinions, Thomas discusses two interpretations: a materialist one – represented by scholars such as Gerth and Mills, Giddens, and Parkin – who give primacy to material forces, which seek the ideas with which they have affinity; and a non-materialist one, as in Bendix and Parsons, who suggest the reverse process. McKinnon (2010) seems to offer a third possibility, much more symbiotic and relational, in which both material and non-material elements need and find each other. Werner Stark sums it up:

> [The social world] is no place for disembodied spirits; even ideas must have bodies if they are to last, and so they are on the lookout for appropriate social groupings who can take them in and carry them along. But human groupings, of whatever kind, will, for their part, always be on the lookout for appropriate ideas to give expression to their essence and their strivings, for, material as this life is, it nevertheless has a spiritual side to it. Thus, there will be a gradual convergence between the substructures and superstructures, not convergence *ab initio*. (Quoted in McKinnon 2010, 109)

This relational perspective offers more explanatory power and a more flexible theoretical possibility, so I adopt it in the present study but add another concept – a distinction between path-dependency and critical junctures, as suggested by historical institutionalists.

HISTORICAL INSTITUTIONALISM: PATH-DEPENDENCY AND CRITICAL JUNCTURES

As a theoretical perspective, historical institutionalism emerged during the 1980s, as a counter-perspective to behaviouralist and rational-choice theories' overemphasis on the role of individual reasoning in determining both individual behaviour and social patterns. It also offered a better account of how institutions persist and how they change; how they influence and contain the behaviour not only of individuals but also of institutions. To do so, it introduced two concepts: "critical junctures" and "path-dependency." As Capoccia and Kelemen put it:

> The historical institutionalist literature postulate(s) a dual model of institutional development characterized by relatively long periods

> of path-dependent institutional stability and reproduction that are punctuated occasionally by brief phases of institutional flux – referred to as critical junctures – during which more dramatic change is possible. The causal logic behind such arguments emphasizes the lasting impact of choices made during those critical junctures in history. These choices close off alternative options and lead to the establishment of institutions that generate self-reinforcing path-dependent processes. (Capoccia and Kelemen 2007, 341)

These two concepts, however, have a broader appeal and can address the age-old dilemma of structure versus agency in the social sciences. Path-dependent periods can be taken to approximate the solidity of structures, and critical junctures – also referred to as turning points, crises, unsettled times – as moments of structural fluidity that allow players to have a larger role and affect the course of history.

The critical junctures often emerge when an "exogenous force" shocks the existing structure and interrupts its path-dependent routines. Such a shock would inevitably demand a response from the area or part thereof it most heavily affects. In such circumstances, and depending on the strength of the force, the major players would adjust, rearrange, or even radically transform. The degree and content of the resultant change reflect the strength of the exogenous force and the strength of the institution. The revolutionary moments are examples of critical junctures, or, as Lenin comments: "When those at the top cannot and those at the bottom do not want to continue" – comparing how a society operates before and during a revolutionary moment. The critical junctures therefore are singularities, not regularities.

Linking critical junctures and path-dependency to causes and reasons would engender a framework for explaining the nature and the process of social change. During path-dependent periods, causes are more powerful, always on the lookout for the reasons that best justify the status quo. During critical junctures, causes fail to exert their force and open the space for ideas (reasons) to play a more formative role. This distinction gives us the conceptual flexibility to analyse both regular historical periods and singular moments (for a discussion of the details of the historical institutionalism, and its application in the study of the rise of post-secularism in the West, see Zarei 2018, 2015).

One final corollary: when, in critical junctures, reasons are more influential, the outcome may not always be what the player had initially intended. Quite often, there are many more unintended consequences, which may be much more important than the intended ones. Sometimes, the unintended easily overrides the intended. Making this distinction is vital for a thorough and accurate social analysis; Robert Merton (1968) warned sociologists against "confusion ... between conscious *motivations* for social behavior and its *objective consequences*" (114). As an example, he cites Durkheim's distinction between the social functions of punishment for the criminal (manifest) and for the community (latent); while the former works against the criminal, the latter works for the community, by uniting it against crime and clarifying the society's moral boundaries. So it is quite possible to imagine consequences of an action that run contrary to the intentions of those who did that action. A social analysis that limits itself to actors' intentions misses the important unintended component.

Using this conceptual distinction, this book argues that the state-led Islamization of Iran since 1979 has, inadvertently and contrary to its planners' expectations, intensified secularizing trends in society, state, seminary, and philosophy. The various chapters in parts two and three discuss those developments.

SUMMARY

This chapter introduced the two conceptual pillars of the study, one revolving around the concept of secularity, the other on the distinction between reasons and causes in the explanation of social developments. On secularity, my conceptual framework transcends the limitations of the Western-based perspectives and allows for a more satisfactory analysis of sacred and secular in the Muslim world and particularly in Iran. The discussion of causality rests on three pillars: the distinction between cause and reason as the bases for two different views of social change; the notion of elective affinity, as a way to connect causes and reasons; and the use of path-dependent phases and critical junctures to separate long periods of structural stability/continuity from episodes of structural anomie, respectively; while in the former causes and structural forces have the upper hand, in the latter reasons and agency dominate. Finally, besides the planned outcomes of an action, unintended consequences can override planned outcomes. I use these concepts throughout parts two and three to construct a more refined analysis of religious changes in Iran since 1979, starting with a cursory look at critical junctures in the history of Islam in Iran in chapter 3.

3

History of Islam in Iran

Critical Junctures

[In the 640s, with the advance of the Muslim army into] Syria and Egypt the defeated and dispossessed Byzantine magnates could withdraw to the Byzantine capital [Constantinople] and central provinces, leaving their former subject lands and people to new masters. No such escape was available to the [Sassanid] magnates of the Persian empire, whose imperial capital was in Arab hands and who, with few exceptions, had to stay where they were and find their place as best they could under the new regime.

Bernard Lewis[1]

Until very recently, discussions about Islam's place in Iran and Iran's place in the Muslim world were overwhelmed by a popular narrative that kept resurfacing every time there was a new interest in the topic. This narrative could be schematized as follows. First, in the Muslim world, Iran is the largest nation with a shia-majority population. Second, Iranians adopted *shi'ism* so early after the rise of Islam because its political philosophy, based on hereditary succession of the Twelve Imams (hence the shias' name "Twelvers"), fitted with Iran's long tradition of hereditary monarchy. Third, shia Muslims' belief in the occulted twelfth Imam (Mahdi) as a messianic figure who would return at some point to make peace and justice prevail on the earth has rendered all states *illegitimate* until his return. Fourth, this belief in turn has led shia seminaries and leaders to rely on their followers' voluntary donations. And fifth, the shia clergy's financial independence from the state facilitated its involvement in oppositional politics and its leadership (as happened during Iran's 1979 revolution). The various components of this narrative have been suggested by a range of thinkers, from historians of early Islam to scholars of modern Iran (see, among others, Cole and Keddie 1986; Dabashi 2011; Petrushevsky 1985).

Despite its relative coherence, this narrative does not fit the history of Iran's relationship with Islam, and I see at least two major problems with it.

First, for most of its fourteen-century history during the Islamic era, Iran was not actually a shia-majority country. To be sure, there were large pockets of shia Muslims (mostly in the northern and northeastern provinces of Tabarestan and Khorasan), and notable periods of rule by shia dynasties (such as the Buyyids [934–1062]). The shift to shi'ism followed a massive and violent state-led project of *shi'i*fication early in the Safavid dynasty (1501–1722), which involved mass killings of sunni Muslims and forced conversions. Many people adopted the faith for purely practical reasons and /or out of fear for their lives.

Second, even if one accepts the relative independence of the shia establishment from the state throughout Iran's history, this independence ended with the Islamic Republic in 1979. The new state began ruling in the name of Islam and incorporating the shia clergy in its apparatus; shia Islam shifted from anti- to pro-establishment. This sea change made the older narratives less helpful for understanding the current situation of religion in Iran. Shortcomings and simplifications like these call for a more detailed, precise, and nuanced historical account of the relationship between faith and country, both before and after 1979.

This chapter sketches this long history in terms of six "critical junctures" directly related to the focus of this book. I work in chronological order, starting with the Safavids' official adoption of shi'ism as the state religion, but then dwelling on the twentieth and twenty-first centuries. As we saw in chapter 2, these are periods when existing structures lose their power to shape society, and the agency (of people, activists, politicians, and so on) becomes more influential. The six critical junctures are as follows:

- Early sixteenth century: the Safavids' adoption of shia Islam as the official religion.
- Early twentieth century: the state's adoption of secularism and the launch of secularization from above by the Pahlavis.
- Mid-1960s: the emergence of militant leftist Islamism, through the Mojahedin-e Khalgh Organization (MKO) and Ali Shariati.
- Mid-1970s: the MKO's conversion to Marxism, triggering a reactive conservative Islamist reaction.
- Late 1970s: the Islamic Revolution and subsequent Islamization.

- Late 1980s: *zarurat* and maslahat grounding the state's political philosophy.

In the following pages, I discuss each of these critical junctures at length.

EARLY SIXTEENTH CENTURY: THE SAFAVIDS ADOPT SHIA ISLAM

A turning point in the history of religion in Iran occurred at the early 1500s, when the new Safavid dynasty adopted shia Islam as the official religion of the nation (for details, see Zarrinkoob 1999, chap. 14). This shift was a shock to the society, where sunni Muslims constituted the majority. According to Zarrinkoob (1999), even in Tabriz, the Safavids' first capital, where they announced this policy, fewer than one-third of residents were shia Muslims. Furthermore, the new dynasty's association with shi'ism was not strong or clear. The sufi circles that formed the Safavids' initial basis of power had complex relations with both shia and sunni Islam. To prove their shi'ism, members and supporters had to reinterpret many sayings of their previous leaders to align them with shia beliefs or justify their sunni-leaning actions and sayings as diversionary tactics to survive in a predominantly sunni environment. All in all, the decision to adopt shia Islam officially was difficult, and its implementation bumpy and bloody.

Given the above difficulties, why did the Safavids adopt such a policy? Answers differ, emphasizing variously "reasons" and "causes" (see chapter 3). Reason-based analysts look to religious teachings and contents. Farhani-Monfared (1996) cites the migration of some high-ranking shia clerics to Iran from Jabal Amel in southern Lebanon. Those clerics, he argues, carried to Iran the views of the shia thinker (1334–1385) known as *shahid-e avval* (the First Martyr). He had proposed clerics' right to collect followers' alms on behalf of the occulted Mahdi (shia Muslims' twelfth Imam), and their resulting wealth allowed them to think of forming states, running governments, or joining the state apparatus. In other words, in this perspective, a particular jurisprudential (*fiqhi*) view transformed Iranian history.

The alternative, cause-based perspectives look to the region's geopolitical map. In the early sixteenth century, Persia was threatened by its sunni Uzbek neighbours in the northeast, by sunni Ottomans in the northwest, and, to a lesser extent, by Christian Georgians and Armenians in the north. Shi'ism therefore would distinguish Persia from all these neighbours and might help unify the country by "othering" them. This was a common nation-building strategy at the time, very similar to what Anthony Marx (2003) describes for France, Britain, and Spain, each solidifying a religious identity in contradistinction to an "other" religious group: Protestants became the "other" for Catholic France, Catholics for Protestant England, and Muslims and Jews for Catholic Spain. So, coinciding with European nation-building projects and following models similar to them, the Safavids adopted shi'ism to help construct their unique national identity (Amanat 2017).

The Safavids' new policy required them to transform Iran's religious institutions and its society. They created a shia religious establishment – by importing shia religious scholars from Jabal Amel, Lebanon – to create religious legitimacy for the state. While this establishment was initially diverse, over time its specific function narrowed its institutional place and religious content. Sefatgol (1982) points to two such factors: the gradual rise of jurists (faqihs) and the decline of sufi orders (which had founded the Safavid dynasty), and the gradual triumph of the literalist (*akhbari*) theological school over the principalist (*osooli*) one. Both of these changes reflected the needs of the new state: jurists, to justify it theologically, a task that the sufis' experiential orientation could not; and the literalists succeeded because they lacked the intellectual creativity and independence of the principalists. In other words, state needs forged the new religious establishment.

A similar process occurred in society. Because most Persians were sunni, shi'ification required a heavy hand. Towards that goal, public speakers were mandated to recite shi'ite statements in their speeches; the Muslim call-to-prayer (*azan*) received additional clauses recognizing Ali as the legitimate heir of his father-in-law, the Prophet Muhammad; and state officials were ordered to persecute sunnis and force them to convert. Later, by importing shia scholars like Karaki from Lebanon, a fuller system of "Twelver" shia faith was developed and a shia clergy began to take form (Amanat 2017; Zarrinkoob 2006).

This identification of Persia as a shia nation, which pushed state and shia establishment closer together, continued till about 1900. During these four centuries, shi'ism remained the nation's official religion, despite differing levels of commitment by various dynasties (Safavid, Afsharid, Zand, and Qajar) to shi'ism and the shia clergy – most notably, Nader Shah Afshar's lukewarm attitude towards religion and Karim-khan Zand's promotion of religious diversity. Also, with some reinforcement from shia communities in other countries such as Lebanon and Iraq, including the importing of some high-ranking shia scholars, Iran set up a shia seminary in Qom, which quickly gained economic power and socio-political influence. By the early twentieth century, the shia establishment owned large amounts of donated, or endowed land (*vaghf*), had a visible presence in the judiciary system, and shaped the religious contents of the school curricula. All these bases of power, however, came under attack under the Pahlavis.

EARLY TWENTIETH CENTURY: THE PAHLAVIS LAUNCH SECULARIZATION FROM ABOVE

The Pahlavi dynasty consisted of two kings – Reza Shah (reigned 1925–41) and Mohammad Reza Shah Pahlavi (1941–79) – who ruled Iran for more than half a century. During this period, the nation rapidly modernized its institutions – such as the economy, education, government structure, and military – as well as expanding its infrastructure. The political system, however, remained mostly authoritarian, except for a couple of brief episodes in which war, political succession, and social movements weakened state control. In religion, this period witnessed not only the state's adoption of a secularist ideology but also the secularization of culture and society, both enforced from above. Secularization was much more intense under Reza Shah than under his son (or at least the first two decades of the latter's reign). Following in the footsteps of Turkey's Mustafa Kemal Atatürk, Reza Shah severely curtailed the influence of the religious and clerical establishment in one of the most decisive episodes in religion-state relations in Iran, which has intrigued scholars since 1979.[2]

This sea change began in the early 1920s, after years of soul-searching and experimenting after the Constitutional Revolution of 1905–11, its perceived failure, and its aftermath of chaos and regression. The almost-complete failure of all state and social structures during the 1910s created a true critical juncture and opened the country to new ideas and visions. Matin-Asgari (2018) has brilliantly documented the intellectual ferment of the period, which he considers an understudied yet extremely influential decade. Iranian intellectuals and politicians began exploring, and experimenting with, European nation-building models, searching for one appropriate for their country. And, largely through the publications of a group of Iranian intellectuals in Berlin, the seeds of Reza Shah Pahlavi's social-development model were planted.

Matin-Asgari (2018) discusses three such publications: *Kaveh*, *Iranshahr*, and *Name-ye Farangestan*. The first promoted a liberal-bourgeois democracy, with "universal" values of reason, progress, science, and secularism. The second, influenced more strongly by the German anti-Enlightenment and anti-modern philosophical line – originating from the Romanticism of Rousseau, and exemplified in the ideas of Nietzsche, Spengler, Bergson, and others – promoted a nationalistic "soul," a critique of modernity, and openness to Eastern religion and spirituality (for more details, see Durant 1933). This vision sought a uniquely Iranian model, with a place for shi'ism, as a domestic version of Islam. The third pushed for an authoritarian model led by an "enlightened despot," aiming to modernize not only state and economy, but also culture and society. It was this that Reza Shah adopted: a top–down, dual process of secularism (separating mosque and state) and secularization (weakening popular religious belief). Like the Safavids' top–down adoption of shia Islam, this was also part of a nation-building project.

Rahnema (2000, 3-4) lists six initial sets of measures through which Reza Shah secularized the country. First, he subjected clerical education to the Ministry of Education, which reduced the clergy's control. Second, he took over administration of the vast religious endowments (*vaghf*), which weakened the clergy's economic power and undermined its independence from government. Third, lawyers – many of them clergymen – now had to obtain a law degree. Fourth, the shah secularized the processing of legal documents – another traditional clerical function. Fifth, he required a special government permit to wear clerical attire – frock and turban. And sixth, wives of government employees now had to wear Western-style hats instead of traditional Islamic veils, which excluded most clerics from holding government office. Other, similar changes followed, including: revising family law (allowing women to work outside the home, to vote, and to divorce, and limiting men's right to divorce); giving the state oversight of the publication of religious books; and, perhaps most conspicuously, limiting religious authorities' power to veto un-Islamic laws (for detailed discussion of these developments, see Abrahamian 1982; Amuzegar 1991; Faghfoory 1993; N. Hashemi 2018; Hashemi Rafsanjani 1998; Zarrinkoob 1999).

Reza Shah intended to secularize not merely institutions but also the nation's culture. While the institutions were pretty clearly transformed, information on culture is largely anecdotal and inconclusive. The official histories of the post-1979 state cite pockets of resistance, in the traditional corners of society, as signs of a complete failure. However, Razavi (2018) quotes high-ranking clerics from that period and disagrees. Those witnesses complained about people's lack of support for clergymen confronting government agents; widespread ridiculing and harassing of clerics; falling numbers of seminary students (to about only 300); and declining religious donations. Ayatollah Khomeini himself concurs, in his *Secrets Revealed* (*kashf-ul-asrar*), published in 1945:

> In those days, Mullahs stood up to the government several times ... but their efforts failed, due to people's lack of support ... From the very first days, Mullahs found Reza Shah's rule to be against the interests of the country ... but the propaganda succeeded in belittling them in the eyes of people ... The poor Mullahs were defeated and the way was paved for players of the "golden age" ... [who] created dark pages in your [people's] history ... *This is the punishment of a nation ... who turns their back on religion ...* Reza Shah and the dark years of dictatorship are now gone, and we were expecting that people would wake up ... and learn the lessons of history ... and crush those who were promoting the abandoning of religion ... but *they are still asleep* and have forgotten their own dark days. (Khomeini [1944] 1999, 9–10, italics added)

The joint British–Soviet invasion of Iran in August 1941 forced the abdication of Reza Shah, whose son succeeded him, although parts of the nation were under Allied occupation till war's end. While after 1945 the youthful king may have wanted to follow in his father's footsteps with regard to religion, the political scene had changed too much, both domestically and internationally. At home, leadership of shia institutions (seminaries, mosques, endowments) had moved from Najaf in Iraq to Qom in Iran; after several high-ranking Najaf-based Sources of Emulation (*marja'a*) died in a relatively short time, the next in succession in 1945–46 was Qom-based Ayatollah Hossein Boroujerdi. Internationally, the postwar world was split between the Americans and the Communist Soviet Union, which had a long border with Iran and in August 1941 had occupied the far north of the country in hopes (later dashed) of establishing another Soviet republic in the northwestern corner. During the late 1940s, Tudeh, a pro-Soviet communist party, had become the most powerful political force in Iran.

All these events convinced the young king that the Soviet-backed communists formed the main threat to his power, so the shia establishment could serve as a potentially effective ally. For these reasons, he decided to tolerate the clerics and, unlike his father, chose to ignore, rather than confront them (N. Hashemi 2018).

Nothing shows the contrast more clearly than his seeking the approval of the grand ayatollahs in Qom in the late 1950s when he was planning to marry an Italian Catholic, Princess Maria Gabriella of Savoy, as his third wife. He asked those senior clerics for their *fatwa*s on the religious permissibility of such an action, and then abided by their decision after Ayatollah Boroujerdi ruled against it (Rahnema 2005, 26). He even tried – though perhaps unsuccessfully – to clear his father's image of its anti-religiosity and anti-clericalism. When Reza Shah died in exile in Johannesburg in 1944 and his body was returned to Iran for burial, his son arranged for the body to pass through many cities, but politically active seminary students and instructors in Qom mounted strong and well-organized opposition (Rahnema 2005, chap. 6). The new king's policy of toleration and, from time to time, collaboration with the religious establishment continued for his almost four decades in power, although it became more confrontational towards the end.

His policy seemed to be driven by a twofold belief: that the clerics posed no major threat compared to the communists, and that occasional religiously motived political opposition could be isolated and eventually defeated with the help of mainstream forces and moderate clerics. In the light of the Islamic Revolution of 1979, of course, this perception now seems rather out of touch. But for a young and not-too-confident king it seemed perhaps a useful story, and successive US governments, as his main international ally and supporter, seemed to agree, which fact several key players in Jimmy Carter's administration admitted after Pahlavi's fall. These figures included Stansfield Turner, then director of the Central Intelligence Agency, and Gary Sick, on the staff of the US National Security Council, who indicated that both governments missed the rise of the political Islamists in Iran because of their preoccupation with the communist opposition and Soviet espionage (for discussions of this in the memoires of the authorities at the time, see Riedel 2008; Sick 1985; S. Turner 1985).

The Pahlavis' plans for secularization from above, despite their many initial successes, generated forceful backlash during the 1970s. Strong signals were announcing a return of religion to Iranian public space. A rare general social survey, conducted by two Iranian sociologists about 1974, revealed the country's secularization, but pointed also to a rise in the popularity of religion among the younger generation. When asked "whether, in your opinion, the society is becoming more/less religious in the future," respondents aged fifteen to twenty-four reported the highest percentages for "more." A similar pattern had also surfaced for "how frequently you attend mosque" (with the youngest reporting the highest percentages for more than two to three times a week); "whether people do pay more attention to religion than before"; and "whether people should pay more attention to religion" (for the full report, see Asadi 1977; see also Abdi and Goodarzi 2017). These findings suggested perhaps a religious wave about to erupt – as it did four years later, during the revolution.

Hashemi (2018, 190) argues that the backlash against Reza Shah Pahlavi's secularization project resulted from its association with autocracy: "A set of top–down, forced modernization, secularization, and Westernization policies by the state within a short span of time generated widespread social and psychological alienation and dislocation." Religion returned not only to people's minds or private lives – "subjective" religiosity – but also to the public sphere and politics. As Hashemi (2018, 189) postulates, "An autocratic modernizing state, often with critical external support, suffocated secular civil society, thus forcing oppositional activity into the mosque." A new generation of political activists and oppositional forces turned to militant political Islam. Its prime manifestation was the guerrilla Mojahedin-e Khalgh Organization (MKO) and a Sorbonne-educated scholar of comparative literature, named Ali Shariati.[3]

THE MID-1960S: THE EMERGENCE OF MILITANT LEFTIST ISLAMISM THROUGH MKO AND ALI SHARIATI

In the mid-1960s, Iran witnessed a new wave of political activists, willing to engage in full-time activism, armed struggle, clandestine operations, and organized guerrilla warfare against the shah's regime. This new militancy was triggered by the violent suppression of political unrest in June 1963, when the arrest of Ayatollah Ruhollah Khomeini for a speech denouncing the shah provoked massive demonstrations, as well as the government's rejection of peaceful protest and nonviolent political activism. It was also influenced by violent protest and guerrilla warfare in many other developing countries. It reflected the zeitgeist both inside and outside the country.

Disciples of this new worldview included both secular and religious activists. The secular strand consisted of several Marxist-Leninist groups, which emerged in the mid-1960s, initially as intellectual circles later transformed into the paramilitary Organization of Iranian People's Fadāʾi [Fedāʾi] Guerrillas (Sāzmān-e Cherikhā-ye Fadāʾi-e Khalq-e Irān), which began military activities in 1971 (for an excellent history of this organization, see Rahnema 2021). The religious strand started with several political-intellectual groups that morphed into guerrilla organizations, most notably the MKO, or *sâzmân-e mojâhedīn-e khalq-e īrân*, which formed in September 1965 and armed in 1971.

Shortly after its appearance, the MKO found a ready-made pool of potential recruits among the students and the young audience of Ali Shariati, a Sorbonne-educated professor of comparative literature and history and a public lecturer. He arrived back in Iran from Paris in June 1964 and gave his most influential lectures in Hosseinie-ye Ershad religious institute in Tehran 1969–72. The MKO and Shariati's followers found in each other what each was lacking: a revolutionary ideology, on the one side; and revolutionary cadres and organization, on the other.

The common ideological framework that Shariati developed had emerged in the ideas of the post-1945 Movement of the God-Worshipping Socialists (MGWS) (*jonbesh-e khoda-parastan-e socialist*). In Iran's postwar power vacuum, several new political groups filled a wide political and religious spectrum. At the secular end stood the pro-Soviet Tudeh party and the National Front, both posing serious challenges to the regime; at the religious end, Qom's mainstream clergy followers of the Grand Ayatollah Boroujerdi, who believed in a conservative Islam and also minimal engagement in politics. His main concern was Iran's strength and stability as the largest shia-majority nation in the world. The more politically engaged Ayatollah Abol-Ghasem Kashani had a history of activities against the British in Iraq and wanted to influence government policies and even participate in making them. In 1952–53 he was elected to Iran's *majlis* (Parliament) and became its speaker. An initial ally of his was the radical Fadaian-e Islam, led by the young radical cleric Seyed Mojtaba

Navab-Safavi, whose main goal was to create an Islamic state. Comfortable with violence, this body assassinated four prime ministers (Hazhir, Razmara, Ala, Mansur), one minister (Fatemi), and one intellectual critic of Islam (Kasravi), and tried to kill the shah. Mid-spectrum lay the much smaller and less influential MGWS, which inspired both the MKO and Shariati's Islamist ideology (for a detailed and very thorough discussion of these groups, see Rahnema 2005).

While the members of all these religious groups were practising Muslims and their political activism was influenced by Islamic teachings, the nature of this influence differed radically between the MGWS and the other three. The latter groups despised the state's disregard for Islamic teachings, as exemplified by its appointing Bahá'ís to top positions, which "allowed non-Muslims to rule over Muslims" (and, by extension, tolerating Israel's rule over Muslim Palestinians); discouraging the wearing of *hijab*; legalizing liquor stores and alcohol-serving places; and permitting women to vote and file for divorce. While these groups occasionally made references to the poor, they expressed little concern about economic inequality and injustice.

For the MGWS, however, the main social problems were economic inequality, lack of political freedom, social and cultural alienation, and foreign imperial/colonial influences. It believed that Islam could offer something of a "middle road" – combining socialism with spirituality – to fix economic inequality and counter the alienating forces of modernity. It proposed the equality of all humans in the eyes of God as the philosophical basis for a democratic political system that would respect the equal rights of all citizens. It also suggested a "middle bloc" in international affairs, an entity between the communist and "imperialist" worlds (Rahnema 2000). These views won the MGWS the support of the new, educated middle class, as opposed to the traditional urban merchant class (the *bazari*s), which supported mostly the three more traditional Islamist currents.

The political activities of all the oppositional organizations came to an end with a 1953 military coup orchestrated by the British and US governments, which overthrew Mohammad Mossadegh's elected government, which proposed to nationalize the oil industry.

In 1963, following the advice of US President John F. Kennedy's Democratic administration, the shah introduced a series of political, social, and economic reforms as a way to de-radicalize society and to undermine the appeal of communist platforms. This package reformed landholding, expanded education, improved rural health, and allowed women to vote and stand for Parliament. Triggered mostly by the last element, some politically active clerics, including the high-ranking Ayatollah Khomeini, gave a series of fiery critical public speeches against the shah and his government. Mass demonstrations followed in early June, and clashes with the anti-riot police. This wave of public protest – the 15 Khordad Uprising (Jonbesh-e Panzdah-e Khordad) – was eventually suppressed; the leaders were imprisoned or sent into exile; order was restored; many activists were put on trial; and, again, freedom of expression was severely curtailed.

After a few years of soul-searching, new political forces began to emerge. The closing of the political realm had pushed many activists underground and provided fertile ground for much more radical political activism, even guerrilla warfare. New organizations formed mid-decade and went public in 1970. The religious strand, as we saw above, was represented by the MKO and Ali Shariati, both reflecting the values and ideas of the MGWS. The MKO's emblem (see figure 3.1) captured these ideals, with four elements: a clutch of anvil, sickle, and branch of wheat, representing workers and farmers as the MKO's social base; a rifle, standing for its armed struggle; a Quranic verse praising *mojahedin* over the politically inactive, for its Islamic ideology; and a map of Iran alongside a meridian and two parallels, emphasizing its focus on Iran and its commitment to internationalism.

The arrival of mojahedin and Shariati signalled, for religious political activists, that Islam was no longer a goal in itself but a means to achieve social justice. This in turn justified the borrowing of ideas from other schools of thought, including Marxism, and the engagement in dialogue and collaboration with the Marxist-Leninist guerrillas. A corollary was lack of respect for, or commitment to, clergy and seminaries. While the Marxist tendencies of mojahedin and Shariati did not sit well with the Islamists, the latter supported the former for almost half a decade. The aftermath of 15 Khordad had shattered their leaders and supporters, but they could see in the mojahedin and Shariati a force that could and would silence Marxist rivals and promote Islam.

In other words, beginning in the mid-1960s, the more traditional, conservative, and petit-bourgeois Islamists ceded centre stage to the more modernist, ideological, and socialist Mojahedin and Shariati. But in the mid-1970s an ideological crisis in the MKO transformed the political landscape – with enormous consequences for religion in the country.

Figure 3.1 The initial emblem of the MKO.

THE MID-1970S: THE MKO'S CONVERSION TO MARXISM

The years 1975–77 saw a cumulative political earthquake in Iran in three stages: an ideological crisis in 1974–75 within the MKO that led it to abandon Islam for Marxism-Leninism; a series of heavy blows by Iranian secret police in 1976 against guerrilla organizations – both the (Marxist-Leninist) Organization of Iranian People's Fadā'i Guerrillas and the MKO – that wiped out their military and operational capability; and Ali Shariati's death in self-exile in England in June 1977. The MKO's ideological conversion reconfigured Islamist political activism, planted the seeds of the "Islamic Revolution," and, according to Ebrahim Yazdi, "changed the whole course of Iranian history," as it "drastically weakened the whole progressive movement within Islam, and thus had paved the path for the triumph of the backward-looking clergy" (quoted in Abrahamian 1989, 164).

The essence of this ideological shift was captured in a manifesto published by the MKO's Marxist-Leninist wing: "At first we thought we could synthesize Marxism with Islām and accept historical determinism without dialectical materialism. We now realize that this is impossible ... We have chosen Marxism because it is the true road for the emancipation of the working class" (quoted in Abrahamian 1989, 145). The MKO's new emblem depicted these changes (see figure 3.2). The Quranic verse disappeared from the top. The wheat branch was removed, downplaying farmers in favour of industrial workers, as emphasized by Marx. The original rifle gave way to what looks like a Soviet Kalashnikov. The meridian and parallels became more pronounced, perhaps as a symbol of solidarity with the international communist movement. Finally, the year of founding disappeared, implying the birth of a new organization.

The underground MKO's ideological makeover had little to no resonance in the broader society, thanks to strict censorship; but, a somewhat stronger impact on other guerrilla organizations, which followed it closely; and a particularly powerful effect in the shah's political prisons, where all political factions were represented.

In the broader society, such intra-organizational turmoil went virtually unnoticed, due to the heavily underground and clandestine nature of guerrilla warfare. A little coverage appeared in state-run media, the contents largely dictated by the secret police SAVAK to undermine the guerrilla organizations and fighters; hence its dubious credibility and lack of useful details.

There was more discussion within and among the guerrilla organizations. Specifically, within the next two to three years, there was a series of debates between the Marxist-Leninist branch of MKO and the Organization of Iranian People's Fadā'i Guerrillas, about how the Marxist mojahedin had conducted themselves and treated their comrades (for details, see Mojahedin-e Khalgh Organization 1974, 1975a, 1975b, 1977a, 1977b, 1977c, 1977d, 1977e).

The most intense debates, however, occurred inside the political prisons, which had representatives of all political groups and active connections with the outside world. Unlike their comrades outside, who had constantly to look over their shoulders and dodge the security forces, political prisoners had ample time to discuss all the details.

These prisoners took variously one of five main positions on the MKO's ideological shift and its repercussions, including the assassination of some Muslim members who did not go along with the new Marxist leadership. First, some embraced the ideological shift and switched to Marxism inside the prison. Second, other Muslim members, some of them MKO founders, insisted that it should keep its religious posture, and that the new Marxists should have left after changing their ideologies. This group was particularly upset about the assassination

Figure 3.2 The emblem of the MKO after the ideological shift of 1975.

of some religious members by the new Marxist leaders. Third, other Marxists, mostly belonging to the Organization of Iranian People's Fadāʾi Guerrillas, who initially criticized how the MKO's Marxists had acted, but later softened their position, and their leaders outside the prison began negotiating with the Marxist wing about forming a united communist entity. Fourth, other Muslim prisoners, remnants of the former Fadaian-e Islam – whose political activism was triggered primarily by concern about Islam and had been uncomfortable with the MKO's closeness to Marxism and communist fighters – felt the change in ideology confirmed their initial suspicions. Fifth, a small group, consisting of some former MKO members and sympathizers, was, like the fourth group, asking for a critical review of the organization's initial ideology, but, unlike it, was not prepared to boycott the Marxists or even break away from the MKO entirely. Unable to join any of the other groups, these individuals became heavily isolated inside the prisons – one called it "a prison within the prison" (for a detailed history of MKO, including some of the post-ideological-shift era, see Meisami 2008a, 2008b; Mirzayee 2014; Mohammadi-Gorgani 2017; Moomivand 2014; Rastgar 2014; Shahsavandi 2014).

Confrontation ensnared the second and fourth groups: MUSLIM MKO members and their more conservative, clergy-oriented rivals. Rather than criticizing the MKO's Marxist elements, the latter blamed the Muslim members, arguing that the shift was caused by the MKO's eclectic Islamic-Marxist ideology, its soft positions towards Marxist fighters, and its criticism of Muslim clerics. Soon the two factions stopped collaborating in prison, even refusing to eat at the same table. The imprisoned, conservative clergymen issued a joint religious decree (*fatwa*) declaring Marxists *najis* (unclean/untouchable). The same group also maintained that the Muslim MKO members who had declined to join the conservatives in condemning all Marxists were indeed Marxist themselves and using Islam only as a disguise (for an informative account of the existing divisions among various political organizations inside the prisons, as well as a personal account, see Jafarian 2004, 723–60; Mohammadi-Gorgani 2017).

These conflicts hopped over the prison walls. Discouraged by them, and by the MKO's ideological shift, some conservative Islamists applied for parole and were released – an action heavily frowned on by political activists as lending legitimacy to the government. A few years prior, when the conservative Islamists were cranking up similar criticisms against Ali Shariati – i.e., that he was mixing Islam and Marxism and undermining basic shia beliefs in favour of sunni Islam – some of them suggested that they stop opposing the state and defend Islam against Shariati's influence. In a classified report by SAVAK, an informant quotes the high-ranking Ayatollah Mohammad Hadi Milani as telling a confidant: "If people like Shariati have risen up against Islam now that this regime is still in control, imagine what would happen if there is chaos! I believe that we have to stop our opposition to this regime altogether and focus, instead, on fixing those of us who have gravitated towards sunni Islam [i.e., Shariati's ideas]" (Judaki 2009, 290).

The conservative Islamists released from prison for that reason spread details of their prison debates to the broader society. As a consequence, many religious political activists began to reorganize and recalibrate their political and armed activities in closer coordination with the Islamist clergy. In the absence of the guerrilla organizations, practically destroyed by the secret police, this new wave of Islamist activism took centre stage in the first waves of the Islamic Revolution in January 1978.

In that month, the shah's regime authorized the publication of a newspaper article with insulting contents about Ayatollah Khomeini. Immediately afterwards, some angry seminary students staged a public protest in Qom. The rally led to a clash with the anti-riot police and the killing of a few protestors. A chain of mourning rituals then followed in various cities over the next few months, allowing conservative Islamist activists to declare their presence loudly – the Islamic Revolution had begun.

While this new wave of Islamism was gaining momentum, the shah's government was struggling to understand its causes and goals. Nasr (2015) reports his own numerous interactions with the shah, the prime minister, and other top officials, in which he had advised them to communicate with the grand ayatollahs and high-ranking clerics in the shia seminaries; but they had all declined, citing their own lack of the proper knowledge, skills, even manners to deal with the religious leaders. He observes that since the early 1960s a culturally informed state elite had given way to predominantly secular technocrats, most of them graduates of top American universities such as Harvard, MIT, and Princeton – a group he calls the "Massachusetts circle." In contrast to their predecessors, they had little or no religious training, which explained their almost total lack of understanding of popular religious sentiment and their failure to communicate with the religious leaders.

As the revolution proceeded, the government began releasing political prisoners, many of them nationalists and Marxists. But it was too late for them to sway the course of events, which were in full swing under the leadership of Ayatollah Ruhollah Khomeini (who was in exile in Iraq and then in France) and his conservative, Islamist, and clergy-obsessed allies and foot soldiers. For this group, what mattered most was respect for Islamic teachings and for the clergy as their guardians. While most of the revolutionary masses wanted social justice, this new group of activists sought an Islamic state, enforcing Islamic laws with regards to dress, music, alcohol, gender norms, and sexual practices. Full Islamization was on their agenda.

THE LATE 1970S: THE ISLAMIC REVOLUTION AND ISLAMIZATION

Despite its reputation as "Islamic," Iran's 1979 revolution had many secular objectives, similar to those of other great modern revolutions. In a motto not unlike that of the French Revolution's "*liberté, égalité, fraternité*," mass demonstrations in Iran were chanting "Sovereignty, Freedom, the Islamic Republic." As Amanat (2017) argues, the call for "sovereignty" continued the main goal of the nationalist movement of a quarter-century earlier for control of the country's oil resources against the British, but now targeted against powerful US influence. "Freedom" was a reaction to a half-century of Pahlavi autocracy. The concept of "Islamic Republic," however, was vague from the beginning and, as Halliday points out, had no specific class content (Halliday 1978).

It evolved during revolutionary pushes and pulls and, depending on who was using it, implied anything from a commitment to social justice, through the observance of Islamic cultural norms, through reconstruction of the social and political system according to an Islamic model, to clerical rule (Amanat 2017).

The victory of the revolution in February 1979 gave the Islamists more confidence in pursuing Islamization, i.e., ensuring that political, legal, cultural, and, less dramatically, economic structures complied with so-called Islamic principles. The project started with banning the buy-and-sell of alcohol, an Islamic dress code (*hijab*) for women, and restricting the kinds of music played on state radio and TV. Later, it took new dimensions, such as modifying school curricula, screening out "non-Islamic" materials from publications, and so on. In June 1980, the Islamists launched a "cultural revolution" at the universities, first to expel non-compliant professors and students, and then to revise educational materials, particularly in the social sciences and humanities. Most conspicuously, the graduates of seminaries poured into the courts of law and the justice system and gradually replaced the more secular lawyers, judges, and clerks. Islamization eventually reached its climax by touching on subtle issues such as gender-based seats in public spaces (public transit, classrooms, offices, and so on) and the banning of a wide range of musical products as corrupt and "westoxicated."

On the political front, and with the final approval of the new constitution a year later, the Islamic Republic was taking more definitive shape. While in the initial draft Ayatollah Khomeini seemed content with a supervisory and monitoring function for the clergy, later revisions projected a much more radical "jurist's rulership" (*velayat-e faqih*), which put a grand ayatollah at the top of the state apparatus and allowed for the clergy's widespread and direct involvement in day-to-day government operations. This new interpretation gave Khomeini "an office above the president and above the Islamic Consultative Assembly [i.e., Parliament]" (Amanat 2017, 783). For the next decade, this authority was enforced through a corps of his appointees in administrative units known as "Imam's representatives" (*namayande-ye imam*).

The Imam's representatives were selected from among the clergy and the seminary students of various ranks, depending on the status of their offices. This moved an army of clerics of all ranks away from their traditional roles within the seminaries and at the mosques and into government posts. This was unprecedented for Iran's shia establishment, with substantial economic and political implications.

Economically, in Amanat's (2017, 791) words, it made "the clergy financially autonomous from their traditional sources of income," and, "in doing so, it helped loosen old ties with the bazaar, its major source of economic support, or income from the charitable endowments." About two decades earlier Morteza Motahhari, one of Khomeini's high-ranking clerical lieutenants, had outlined the differences between shia and sunni clerics. In this famous speech, later published as "The Main Challenge in the Clergy Organization," Motahhari ([1962] 2003) reports a long list of problems with the shia clerics and seminaries and attributes them to their finances. The main source of funding, he said, was the voluntary donation known as *khums* – one-fifth of the annual surplus income of individual Muslims, paid directly to the ayatollah whom the payer considers his or her Source of Emulation (*marja'a taghlid*), a cleric authorized to issue *fatwas* and rulings. Half of such donations became the "imam's share" (*sahme-imam*), earmarked for "promoting Islam" – basically whatever the imam chose, including support for clerics and seminaries, in clear contrast to sunni clerics' reliance on state budgets.

For Motahhari, this feature made the shia clergy and seminaries beholden to the needs and demands of their clients, liable perhaps to compromise on some of their own beliefs. The clerics' large-scale exodus into government ended that problem, but made the clerics reliant on the state, like their sunni counterparts.

The political implication of this change related to their new role as lawyers and judges. They now had to forge shia solutions and policies for the state – something completely novel for them. In the past, if they became involved in politics, they acted mostly as critics. But now, they had become policy-makers, dealing with a wide range of day-to-day government issues, from international politics to local culture, from economics to arts, and from military tactics to the environment. While pushing the populace towards a more "pious life" (through Islamization), they moved into the secular realm of state craftsmanship. They needed a whole host of new ideas, guiding principles, and juristic theories; and these began emerging in a few short years.

THE LATE 1980S: ZARURAT AND MASLAHAT AND THE NEW POLITICAL DOCTRINE

In April 1979, the results of a nationwide referendum determined the shape of the post-revolution state. The referendum had one question and two possible answers: "Islamic Republic: Yes or No?" One of the common criticisms in the pre-referendum debates was that "Islamic Republic" was too vague. Its proponents, however, dismissed this objection and blamed the critics' ignorance of Islam. This claim seemed convincing, as most of the critics belonged to the Marxist and secular opposition. The referendum took place as scheduled, and the "yes" camp won an overwhelming majority.

Soon afterwards, the new leaders began running a vast and complex country. The sheer number of the tasks before them, the complexity of each challenge, and the wide range of issues and problems quickly showed the inadequacy of Islamic jurisprudence for the task. The dilemmas facing the new state ran to the heart of the ruling clergy's beliefs: the religious legitimacy of choosing state officials not for their religious credentials but by people's votes; the conflict between enforcing the largely patriarchal jurisprudential and sharia law (including the *hijab* and polygamy) and keeping women engaged in the revolutionary process and maintaining their much-needed support; the incompatibility between Islamic teachings on music and its popularity and usefulness in mobilizing people (particularly during the Iran-Iraq War); the conflict between supporting Muslim causes overseas and the priority of national interests; and so on. The most serious challenge, however, was economic, manifested in the conflict between the jurisprudential positions of the mainstream clergy and the demands of the young revolutionaries to reform ownership of land, incorporate workers in management and ownership of public and private industrial plants, limit private ownership, run an interest-based banking system, and allow the state to intervene in the market. The list of challenges seemed endless.

Khomeini and his associates responded initially by dismissing the problems as superficial and temporary and treating them as the consequences of revolutionary disruption and the clergy's lack of executive experience. In due course, they thought, the shia clergy would develop a more relevant state-centred jurisprudence, and this would fix the problems. Thus these dilemmas received ad-hoc and temporary responses, with the hope that the passing of the post-revolution crises would weaken the demand for solutions, and that maturation of juridical thinking would strengthen the supply, establishing a new balance soon.

But even those temporary solutions needed a jurisprudential (fiqhi) basis. Khomeini's innovative response here was to introduce the notion of "necessity" (zarurat), according to which, in face of unusual circumstances and when necessities dictated, the Islamic Republic could deviate from Islamic principles and adopt policies that were otherwise un-Islamic. This way, the revolutionaries could fulfil the masses' revolutionary demands without worrying about Islamic teachings. Aware of the anxiety of the more conservative shia clergy mainstream, however, Khomeini emphasized that such measures would require approval by two-thirds of Parliament and be enforced only till the causing necessity was gone. Zarurat created a great deal of excitement within the new political establishment, which tended to support the revolutionary demands. Using this new opening, it introduced a wide range of changes, such as pushing for land reform, allowing for more intervention in the economy, confiscating properties associated with the *ancien régime*, and relaxing the rules regarding legitimate music and sports.

For a while, the revolutionaries and the pragmatists seemed to be on the offensive, and the conservative jurists and clergy in retreat. But it soon became obvious that the initial challenges were anything but temporary. This realization pushed the conservative clerics to begin raising their concerns about violations of Islamic principles again. The pragmatists were finding the zarurat-based arrangement too cumbersome, as they had to prove the "necessity," and for each case. Besides, when necessities lingered, the pragmatists had to repeat the same steps, each time risking a conservative reaction. A new, more stable, and more permanent measure was needed.

Under pressure from close associates and state officials, Khomeini introduced a second notion, expediency (maslahat). By doing so, he indeed allowed the zarurat-based measures to become permanent, out of concern for the survival of the Islamic state. In other words, introducing maslahat transformed and elevated zarurat from a secondary measure (*anaveen-e sanaviyeh*) to primary (*anaveen-e avvaliyeh*).

His rationale and justification for maslahat had several attributes. He argued that at a time when an Islamic state – i.e., the Islamic Republic – was in existence and power, safeguarding its stability and future became a "primary" Islamic principle, like prayers, *Ramazan* fasting, the *hajj* pilgrimage, and *zakat* alms. Not only that, safeguarding the Islamic state had veto power over all other primary Islamic principles. In that sense, protection of the Islamic Republic became "more primary" than all other primary principles. A famous and frequently quoted statement by him appeared in a letter, in January 1988, to Ayatollah Ali Khamenei, his eventual successor as supreme leader:

> To interpret my [previous] saying as if it is suggesting that I have said that the [Islamic] state has authority only within the limits of Islamic instructions is totally against what I meant … I should say that [Islamic] state is … one of the primary Islamic principles, and has priority over all other secondary principles, even over prayers and fasting and *hajj* … The [Islamic] state has even the authority to unliterally terminate the very legitimate Islamic contracts that it has signed with people, when it sees them against the expediencies of the country and Islam … The [Islamic] state can even temporarily stop *hajj*, which is one of the most important Islamic principles ordered by the Almighty Allah, if it sees *hajj* harmful to the interests of the Islamic nation. (Khomeini 1990a, 170–1)

The introduction of maslahat, and its later incorporation into the constitution, transformed the state. The state found a new theoretical and jurisprudential basis for the kind of measures that it had to take to defend itself. Its interests became the overriding principle among alternative policies.

This sea change also demoted the religious establishment within Iranian society and vis-à-vis the government in particular. The clergy was no longer expected to solve social problems, as state authorities could now do so and justify their decisions on the basis not of Islamic jurisprudence but of maslahat. The seminaries and the clergy, which had left the society and the people to join in with the government, now became redundant and subservient within the state apparatus. This was a historical development for Iran, for shia Islam, for the clergy, and particularly for the post-revolution state in Iran. According to Ayatollahi-Tabaar (2018, 187), Khomeini, "rather than Islamizing the state … continued to statize Islam … to better protect the state from the clergy." This is a change that I have called "secularism through the merger of church and state" and explore in the following chapters.

SUMMARY

This chapter's overview of the history of Islam in Iran was meant to provide historical evidence for the conceptual pillars presented in chapters 2 and 3. This history shows that the ebbs and flows in the level and nature of religiosity both by the state and in the populace are indeed the products of material forces in each historical period.

In other words, such fluctuations and developments could not be adequately explained by the contents of Islam as a religion (reason-based factors). Rather, they make sense against the background of economy, politics, international environment, and so on (cause-based forces). As a consequence, any discussion of sacred and secular trends since 1979 needs to also follow the same conceptual model. I turn to this issue in parts two and three, by discussing religious developments in the political, institutional, social, demographic, and philosophical realms.

PART TWO

L'État c'est nous: From Democracy to Theocracy to Autocracy

4

Crossing the Trench

Secularism through the Merger of Clergy and State

To the followers of secularism debates within the Christian world, the title of this chapter may seem paradoxical. After all, secularism has been defined by the separation, not the merger, of church and state. Historically, such a separation has curtailed the influence of religious institutions on the state's structure, functions, policies, and decisions. All of those outcomes have emerged in Iran since 1979, not through the distancing of religion and state as two distinct institutions, but through their merger. My argument in this chapter is that this institutional merger, rather than having the expected and oft-cited effect of sacralizing the state, has resulted in an unintended, opposite situation, rendering religion subservient to the state.[1]

This outcome was the result of two developments, one economic, the other political. Economically, the shia establishment (seminaries, mosques, endowments) shifted from reliance on believers' donations to dependence on the government's budget. Politically, the decentralized nature of the shia clergy clashed with the centralized state, which suppressed major elements of the shia establishment. This political transformation made the shia clergy the junior and subservient partner of the state, unlike its traditional independence and its usual dominance in a theocratic system. These two changes forced seminaries to adapt and create a new system compatible with their new position vis-à-vis not only the Iranian state but also all other social institutions.

These unprecedented changes remained under-studied till very recently, primarily because of a lack of reliable data. As Khalaji (2010) argues, Iran's shia establishment was unwilling to reveal its financial workings. Also the state was very secretive about the political struggles in its inner circles, which might illuminate state–religion relations.

Speaking out of their personal experience, Shariati and Razavi (2018) cite paranoia in the seminaries about researchers from outside, their mistrust towards social-scientific research, and a culture of secrecy surrounding the seminaries. Recently, however, new data have begun to emerge – including government data and several memoirs – that permit a more thorough study of the institutional changes over the past four decades.

THE ECONOMIC TRANSFORMATION

Several scholars have discussed the economic dimension of the shia establishment in Iran (see, for instance, Khalaji 2010; Nikfar 2007; Soroush 1998). But many of these works refer to a 1962 article by Morteza Motahhari, whom we met above. A middle-rank cleric and philosopher, a later top associate and adviser of Ayatollah Khomeini, and a key member of the 1979 revolutionary council, Motahhari was the first of the new leaders to be assassinated, three months after the revolution. In "The Main Challenge in the Clergy Organization," Motahhari ([1962] 2003) criticized the way clerics were paid, through the imam's share of believers' donations. According to him, improvements in communication and transportation technologies allowed for these donations to be concentrated in the hands of only a few grand ayatollahs, giving them and the shia seminaries as a whole enormous economic power. This in turn allowed the senior clerics significant autonomy vis-à-vis the state, which facilitated their anti-establishment political orientation.

During the Pahlavi era, their financial independence from the state abetted their ongoing tension with the state over the management of religious endowments. Aware of this, Reza Shah Pahlavi signed a series of laws and set many regulations, including creation of an Endowment Office, to limit such donations and undermine the religious establishment's discretion in the use of such funds. Fischer ([1980] 2003, 117) has proposed that, as a result, in the 1960s and 1970s religious donations began to flow "more informally and less publicly, adding to the ambience of underground resistance to the state."

While viewing this independence from the state as liberating, Motahhari also noted a downside. In contrast to sunni Muslim clerics, whose reliance on governments has made them less critical of the state, the shia clergy's dependence on believers' donations made them more critical politically but also more compliant towards their supporters and hence less adventurous jurisprudentially – a phenomenon Fischer ([1980] 2003, 42) calls "anti-innovative conservatism" – and more likely to compromise on important matters. Shariati and Razavi (2018) cite some examples: followers' sense of entitlement to deviate from the decrees of their Sources of Emulation about certain rituals (e.g., men injuring themselves during mourning ceremonies); the reluctance and resistance of high-ranking ayatollahs to the designation of one of them as the Great Source of Emulation (*marja'e a'azam*); and financial threats by *bazari* (traditional merchant) donors to push their Sources of Emulation towards or away from politics or teaching foreign languages in the seminaries. In all these examples, clerics had to follow their own followers to preserve their financial resources (for an elaborate discussion of these cases, see Razavi 2018; S. Shariati and Razavi 2018).

Motahhari argued that the solution was definitely not the sunni Muslim model, but a centralized system/account within the seminaries, which would collect all the contributions and make all the payments. This way, no cleric would have to rely on direct payments from his followers, or rely on the state budget. Ironically, the path taken by the shia clergy and seminaries after the 1979 revolution was exactly what Motahhari had argued against – i.e., increasing reliance on the state. Not only that, many clerics took on government jobs and joined government payrolls. Ezzatollah Sahabi, the first director of the Planning and Budget Organization after the revolution, remembers the first signs of this shift in 1980. The head of the Islamic Development Organization (*sazeman-e tablighat-e Islami*) had approached him requesting funds to finance the launch of ten thousand clerics to villages and small towns. He denied the request, arguing that "every year, during the months of *Moharram* and Ramazan, many clerics do so … in response to invitations by local people who also cover their expenses; why should we [the government] allocate a budget to them?" (quoted in Ahmadi-Amooyee 2003, 57–8). In the end, however, the applicant obtained one-fourth of what he asked for. This paved the way for more successful attempts in the following years, which led to religious bodies' increasing reliance on the government. Figure 4.1 illustrates this trend for the period 2008–16.

This growing dependence on the state's budget transformed religious bodies from independent social institutions into a subservient part of the government bureaucracy. They no longer produced creative intellectual products in response to people's queries; rather, they began

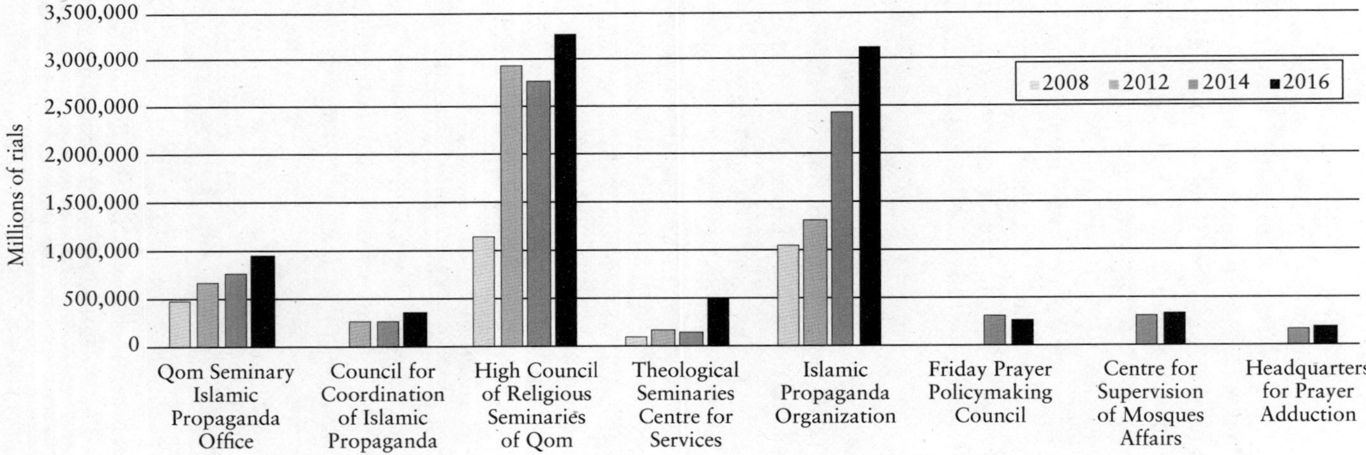

Figure 4.1 State budget allocations (in millions of rials) to seminaries and other religious organizations, 2008–16.
Source: Boroujerdi and Rahimkhani 2018, 38–9.

providing Islamic justification for government decisions and policies, using their religious legitimacy to mobilize people behind state-run projects and, when necessary, even confronting the political opposition, not at the intellectual but at the political level and sometimes even in the streets. This new arrangement gave clergymen access to scarce resources[2] but had powerful secularizing effects on society, and on the clergy itself.

To conceptualize this transformation, I find the rational-choice theory, from the sociology of religion, a real help. This theory addresses the relationship between people, religious institutions, and religiosity, and emerged as a rival for secularization theory. While proponents of the latter attributed the prevalent secularity of the modern world to a decline in *demand* for religion, rational-choice theorists cited the failure of faith institutions to *supply* attractive products for their market. The decline of religion and the rise of secularity reflect religious institutions' unattractive products. These in turn flow from lack of competition, especially where a particular faith enjoys homogeneity or monopoly in the market.

In its genesis, the theory of the religious market emerged to differentiate US religiosity from mostly secular western Europe. The United States was viewed as religiously pluralistic, with various Christian denominations competing for followers, so they had to demonstrate a great deal of vitality and innovation in the religious market. In Europe, in contrast, the monopoly of a single denomination – often a state church – in many countries seemed to blunt the spirit of innovation; hence the rise of secularity (for a detailed discussion of rational choice theory, see Stark, 1999; Stark and Bainbridge 1987; Stark and Finke 2000).

The drastic change in the place of the religious establishment in post-revolution Iran could be likened to a shift from the religiously pluralistic United States to religiously monopolistic European nations – but with a twist. Both before and after the revolution, shia Islam remained dominant in Iran's social space (still a monopoly), but the merger of the religious and political institutions eliminated religion's two major rivals: the state (for public resources) and alternative ideologies such as Marxism (for social acceptance). With their increasing reliance on the state's finances and absorption into the government machinery, the shia religious institutions felt no more need to be responsive to the larger population and/or to recruit supporters and financiers from among them. In other words, this realignment altered the religious market in Iran, so that the clergy no longer faced competition. This, according to rational-choice theory, is the condition most conducive to secularization.

THE POLITICAL TRANSFORMATION

The economic reconfiguration was accompanied by a similar political process that further undermined the autonomy of religious institutions vis-à-vis the state. Throughout the twentieth century, the shia establishment became more active in politics, first in opposition and later with direct claims on the state apparatus. Ayatollah Khomeini and his theory of the jurist's rulership (*velayat-e faqih*) embodied this change, and the 1979 revolution was the last chapter of this long story.

Up until then, the founders of the Qom seminary and most of the grand ayatollahs remained distant from politics and government affairs. Any contacts and coordination involved mostly the very top of the clergy – the grand ayatollahs – and the shah, and only when absolutely necessary and for mutual benefit. The grand ayatollahs occasionally advised governments when they saw something important at stake. In return, the shah interfered only minimally in the clergy's affairs, mostly when the top *marja* (grand ayatollah) had died and his substitute had not yet been determined. In those cases, the shah would send a condolence telegram to one of the remaining grand ayatollahs, thereby indicating the successor. Other than that, as Khalaji (2010, 41) says, "The Shah did not have any direct role in determining the sources of emulation – marja – nor in confirming their *ijtihad* credentials, and had left these to be decided through the internal norms and by the members of the seminaries."

The prime example of this stand off occurred in the 1940s–50s, when Ayatollah Boroujerdi was the supreme marja and head of the Qom seminaries. Boroujerdi faced opposition from several other high-ranking ayatollahs – mostly Kashani and Khansari – along with their foot soldiers, the Fadaian-e Islam, who were challenging this arrangement, arguing that the grand ayatollahs should engage in politics more directly and that the top marja should be chosen not only for his religious credentials but also for his political views (for a thorough discussion of this period, see Rahnema 2005). All those challenges, however, went nowhere until 1961, when Boroujerdi's death created a vacuum and resulted in brief disarray in the clergy's ranks. After a period of intense unrest and riots in 1963, led mostly by Qom seminary students and instructors, things went back to normal.

But Ayatollah Khomeini emerged as a politically active cleric, and rose to become a Source of Emulation (*marja'e taghlid*). As a critic of Boroujerdi's approach and a fan of Kashani's style and Fadaian-e Islam supporters, Khomeini set out to resuscitate the shia clergy in Iran's political landscape.

The victory of the 1979 revolution gave Khomeini a chance to initiate a statecraft process in order to materialize his vision of the jurist-ruler (*velayat-e faqih*), a process that was full of ebbs and flows. In the first phase, the religious establishment claimed a place at the top of the state hierarchy, but Khomeini had to shake up the seminaries to bring them fully into line. The second phase surrounded the appointment in November 1985, and the later the firing, of Ayatollah Montazeri as Khomeini's successor (this is the first succession crisis discussed below). The third phase – the second succession crisis, in June 1989 – was perhaps the most dramatic, through which the current supreme leader – Khamenei – succeeded Khomeini. During the latter two phases, driven largely by political needs of the state, many rules and norms within the shia clergy establishment were violated. The outcome rendered the seminaries inferior to the state. To oversimplify slightly, one may argue that the first phase brought about a theocracy, and the latter two an autocracy.

I analyse these three phases next, but I wish to introduce historical institutionalism first. In chapter 2, I mentioned two of its elements: path-dependency and critical junctures. Here, I discuss another dimension, which relates to institutional transformation. It can help us conceptualize the three phases of the transformation of religious institutions in Iran.

Historical Institutionalism

This perspective emerged to address the need for a comprehensive account of how institutions persist and how they change. Mahoney and Thelen (2010, 19) offer a typology of institutional changes (see table 4.1). As the figure illustrates, the type of institutional change depends on a combination of the level of power – from high to low "veto possibilities" – of the political context that produces the exogenous shock and the amount of discretionary power – from high to low – the targeted institutions enjoy in deciding their own preferences. The combination of these two factors generates four possibilities – drift, conversion, displacement, and layering – as outlined by Mahoney and Thelen (2010, 16–18):

Table 4.1
Contextual and institutional sources of institutional change

		Low level of discretion in interpretation/ enforcement	*High level of discretion in interpretation/ enforcement*
Characteristics of the political context	Strong veto possibilities	*Layering*	*Drift*
	Weak veto possibilities	*Displacement*	*Conversion*

Source: Mahoney and Thelen (2010, 19). Reproduced with permission.

Displacement "is present when existing rules are replaced by new ones," resulting in a radical institutional shift. The "rapid, sudden breakdown of institutions and their replacement with new ones that accompanies revolutions obviously involves displacement'" (16).

Conversion "occurs when rules remain formally the same but are interpreted and enacted in new ways. This gap between the rules and their instantiation is not driven by neglect in the face of a changed setting (as is true with drift); instead, the gap is produced by actors who actively exploit the inherent ambiguities of the institutions. Through redeployment, they convert the institution to new goals, functions, or purposes" (17–8).

Drift "occurs when rules remain formally the same but their impact changes as a result of shifts in external conditions. When actors choose not to respond to such environmental changes, their very inaction can cause change in the impact of the institution" (17).

Layering "occurs when new rules are attached to existing ones, thereby changing the ways in which the original rules structure behavior ... Layering does not introduce wholly new institutions or rules, but rather involves amendments, revisions, or additions to existing ones. Such layering can, however, bring substantial change if amendments alter the logic of the institution or compromise the stable reproduction of the original 'core' ... Processes of layering often take place when institutional challengers lack the capacity to actually change the original rules (or, as in displacement, to set up an explicit alternative institution or system). They instead work within the existing system by adding new rules on top of or alongside old ones. While defenders of the status quo may be able to preserve the original rules, they are unable to prevent the introduction of amendments and modifications. Each new element may be a small change in itself, yet these small changes can accumulate, leading to a big change over the long run" (16–17).

Applying the above typology to the changes in the religious establishment in Iran, I find three of the four concepts applicable, and would argue that since 1979 the religious institutions have experienced these three in tandem: *conversion*; then *drifting*; and finally *layering*. In the first stage, when the new state was not yet fully settled and the clergy still enjoyed enormous popularity, owing to their participation in the revolution, the seminaries remained largely intact, despite new interpretations for their old rules, regulations, and teachings; this was roughly *conversion*. In the next stage (*drifting*), the government established itself and made itself and the seminaries almost equally powerful; then inconsistency and conflict emerged. Through a series of actions, however, the power of seminaries and the clergy began to collapse, and the state increased its own power and reduced the seminaries' independence. But it was still useful for the government to keep seminaries in the game, though subdued. This resulted in the third stage (*layering*), in which both parties remained powerful, but with the state in charge. This created a situation that fits Samuel Huntington's (1996, 36) quip about Orthodox Christianity, where "God is Caesar's junior partner."

Historically, the transformation in the place of the shia institutions in Iran went through three phases: the emergence of the jurist-ruler, the crisis surrounding Khomeini's first successor, and the mini-crisis relating to the choice of his final successor. Next we explore these in detail (for a fuller discussion of the specific developments in this regard, see Ghobadzadeh 2015).

Episode One: The Emergence of the Jurist-Ruler (1979)

Shia clerics' engagement in the Islamic Revolution of 1979 was not a natural extension of their beliefs or past practices. Indeed, it represented a break from their long- and medium-term traditions that unfolded gradually as the wave of revolution progressed. This series of events altered their position in Iran.

This occurred because of a long process rooted in the emergence of Ayatollah Ruhollah Khomeini in the early 1960s, when he became both a political opposition leader and a Source of Emulation (*marja'e taghlid*). He obtained the latter through the former.[3] According to Ashraf (1990, 119), "Never before had a member of the ulama risen to the high office of Source of Emulation through political mobilization of the masses." So, from the very beginning, it became clear that his goals, as well as his means of achieving them, differed drastically from those of other two major camps within Iran's shia clergy: the "collaborationists" (who worked closely with the shah's secular state) and the "accommodationists" (who coexisted peacefully with it). Khomeini opened a third, anti-establishment front. This was the beginning of a long process that reconfigured Iranian religion and the place of its establishment in politics and society.

The unexpected nature of his rise is captured by Ezzatollah Sahabi, a long-time activist in the religio-political organizations, immediately after his release from the shah's prison in 1979. After seven years in prison and while reintegrating with society, Sahabi noted two changes in the political behaviour of the shia clergy: a visible move from pacifism to militancy against the shah and a determination to lead the revolutionary movement (Sahabi 2013, 29). He recalled that his father, Yadollah Sahabi, and Mehdi Bazargan – two very influential leaders of the liberal Islamist Freedom Movement (*nehzat-e azadi*) who met regularly with activist clerics and former members of the Nationalist Front (*jebheye melli*) – had noticed that too. The militant clerics, according to him, had begun viewing their old comrades as rivals.

The victory of the Islamic Revolution only increased this tendency. It gave the clerics a new confidence and brought political power so visibly within their reach, encouraging thoughts of the jurist-rulership (*velayat-e faqih*) – that is, a jurist is permitted, even required, to take over the administration and to govern. This was a bold step away from the shia Muslim view that all states were illegitimate till the return of the occulted twelfth Imam, Mahdi. Until such time, jurists could take on only tasks related to the judiciary and the welfare of the poor, orphans, and the sick, if the state neglected them. For most of its history, the shia political philosophy had never developed, because the ruler had to be infallible (i.e., Mahdi), the Imam's occultation had lasted longer than expected, and shia Muslims had had almost permanent minority status (for an elaborate discussion of the various views of shia jurists, see M. Kadivar 2001).

In hindsight, some observers have started viewing this gestalt shift by the clergy as obvious and inevitable, given the ideas that Khomeini had raised in *Rulership of the Jurist* (*Velayat-e faqih*, 1970). There he had considered the wide acceptance of the notion of the apolitical jurist as part of a conspiracy by the colonial powers:

> Colonial powers had made us believe that Islam does not have a theory of state or a design for state apparatus; or that, even if it had a theory, it would not have a mechanism to enforce it. In other words, Islam is just a legislator at most. This is part of their plot to block Muslims from entering politics or building a state. This view is in direct conflict with our fundamental beliefs. We believe in 'rulership'; and we believe that the Prophet must assign a ruler, and he has done that already. To merely state the theories and the rulings, do you need to be a ruler? That does not require a ruler. All those rulings can be simply put in a book and passed on to Muslims. If a ruler is needed, logically, it is needed in order to rule. We need a ruler in order to execute the rulings … In the same way that Islam has offered the rulings, it has also anticipated an executive branch. The ruler-jurist is in charge of the execution of the laws, too. (Khomeini [1970] 1999)

For these "straight-line" observers, this pronouncement of 1970 connects directly to the post-1979 theocratic state. But in reality the route was curved and crooked.

For one thing, Khomeini, often viewed as the uncompromising mastermind behind the shah's overthrow and the jurist-rulership (*velayat-e faqih*), changed his mind many times before solidifying his views. We can see this in his 1972 conversations with representatives of the MKO, who were seeking his support for the group's strategy of armed struggle against the government. Khomeini is quoted as observing:

> Keep this to yourself; but honestly, I do not believe in the armed struggle … The Vietnam War [as an example for the success of such a strategy] is brought about by the Americans and the Soviets, and it has nothing to do with the Vietnamese people; in any of the countries that have succeeded [in overthrowing a government through armed struggle], somebody else [another country] has supported them; and we lack such support in the case of Iran. If there was a king or ruler [to help Iranians] this would be possible; otherwise, nothing will happen. (Quoted in Jafarian 2004, 710–18)

In the same meeting, he warned the MKO about a possible backlash from conservative clerics against its radical interpretations of Islam:

"If you write this kind of stuff, they will denounce you and block your works." He then cited his own experience: "When I gave my lectures on an Islamic state (jurist-rulership), most of them objected and considered it to be a deviation from Islam." This, combined with his recommendation to the MKO to hide its views, can explain his almost-total silence about his own ideas and his lack of insistence after 1979 on implementing jurist-rulership.

Ezzatollah Sahabi (2013), who was a participant-observer of the negotiations on the new constitution, reports that jurist-rulership was not even in the conversation during the early drafts; nor did Khomeini, in his comments on those drafts, ask for its inclusion (for more details, see Ghamari-Tabrizi 2008, 2014, 2016; Rahnema 2014; Zibakalam 2014). Such a proposal arrived about five months after the February 1979 victory of the revolution and a month before the ad-hoc Assembly of Experts convened to discuss the constitution.

The proposal was approved through a peculiar process. First, it was suggested by Ayatollah Montazeri, one of the most progressive, human rights–conscious, pro–social justice, and high-ranking clerics and a leader in anti-shah activism. Second, it received its most enthusiastic support from the most conservative, reactionary, and politically inactive clerics, who supported the shah and never endorsed the Islamic Revolution wholeheartedly. Third, during the Assembly's discussions, the members obtained a strong justification for it through a booklet written by Mozaffar Baghayee, the leader of the *zahmatkeshan*, notorious for his involvement in the 1953 overthrow of Mosaddegh's nationalist government, his connections with the CIA, and his popularity as a potential leader of the country among some of the shah's generals who were in 1980 planning a military coup against the revolution.

These events do not mean that Khomeini did not favour jurist-rulership; after all, he was the first to theorize it and later supported it aggressively. Rather, he was not planning to propose it at that time. Only a few months into the Islamic Republic, while he was still supporting the predominantly liberal interim government that he himself had appointed, he might not have felt prepared and/or confident enough to adopt it. The chaotic environment was too complex for a jurist to manage, and such a system could damage clerics' long-term spiritual image. After this notion was suggested and supported by others, however, he seemed to be gaining the confidence to act.

While the mainstream in the shia seminaries and clergy still opposed jurist rule, its clerical supporters were taking on a host of new and unconventional tasks. The government's Islamization project needed them for a host of new positions, from serving on boards of education to monitoring the contents of state-run TV and radio programs, and from running courts to serving abroad as ambassadors. After some initial hesitation, Khomeini even allowed clerics to serve as president of the Islamic Republic. In return for these services, such clerics started receiving their salaries and other financial support from the government, so they no longer needed the donations of the faithful. The consolidation of the new state suggested a successful institutional rearrangement of religion and state that pulled them together as a united whole. The expectation was that religious teachings would inform state decisions and policies, which may have been Khomeini's initial idea. But soon new challenges appeared, the first of which related to the appointment of his successor.

Episode Two: The First Succession Crisis (1985)

Most of the grand ayatollahs, who were also Sources of Emulation, remained opposed to Khomeini's theory of the jurist-ruler. But they either kept quiet or spoke only privately. The single exception was Ayatollah Mohammad-Kazem Shariatmadari, who threw his weight behind the Muslim People's Republic Party (MPRP), an antidote to the ruling Islamic Republic Party formed by Khomeini's high-ranking clerical supporters. While having voted for an Islamic Republic in an earlier referendum, the MPRP later opposed inclusion of the jurist-rulership in the new constitution.

The later treatment received by Shariatmadari illustrates the extent to which religious institutions became subservient to the state. Accused in 1982 of involvement in a military-coup plot to overthrow the revolutionary government, he was put under house arrest and remained thus till his death in 1986. In an unprecedented move, the state also disqualified him as a Source of Emulation – a decision ratified by a pro-government body within the Qom seminary, not through the gaining or losing of recognition by the community of believers. The unusual nature of this action was acknowledged even by one of Khomeini's most staunch supporters, former president Akbar Hashemi Rafsanjani (served 1989–97), who called it something "unprecedented in *shia* history" (Hashemi Rafsanjani 2007c, 53)

This highly unusual demotion was followed a couple of years later by another, during discussions about the religious credentials required for the supreme leader, taking place in the background behind speculation about Khomeini's potential successor. For almost a decade after the revolution, and while the seminaries and most of the high-ranking ayatollahs still opposed an Islamic Republic and Khomeini's theory of the jurist-ruler, most of the new revolutionary leaders had a very clear idea about who should replace Khomeini: Hosseinali Montazeri, a middle-ranking *mojtahid* who had spent a few years in prison for his anti-shah activism.

Selling Montazeri to the conservative camp in the seminaries, however, was difficult. He was not yet a Source of Emulation, not having published a *resale-ye amaliyyeh* (the practical manual for followers on how to live as a devout Muslim). Also, his economic views trended left, opposed to the more conservative, capitalist or petit-bourgeois views dominant in the seminaries and among the grand ayatollahs. These had made him unpopular in the religious establishment and among the apolitical yet very powerful Sources of Emulation. To place him in the running, the revolutionaries started a quiet yet aggressive campaign to undermine the seminaries' opposition. These efforts intensified in the lead-up to the November 1985 meeting of the Assembly of Experts, which chose Montazeri as the next supreme leader.

Long before this selection, the leaders of the state had realized that Montazeri should publish a practical manual (see Hashemi Rafsanjani 2007a, 26; Sadri-Nia 2017, 18:28). They also started calling him "ayatollah," instead of the lower-ranking *hojjat-ul-Islam*. Former minister of the interior Aliakbar Nategh-e Noori remembers urging Khomeini to start addressing Montazeri as an ayatollah to facilitate the latter's promotion (Sadri-Nia 2017, 18:49), a request that Khomeini indirectly declined.

Ironically, a similar campaign had been launched about fifteen years prior, for Khomeini himself. In June 1970, after the death of Grand Ayatollah Muhsin al-Tabatabaei al-Hakim, both the pro- and the anti-government clerics in the Qom seminary rushed to name their candidates: Grand Ayatollah Abu al-Qasim al-Musawi al-Khoei for the former, and Khomeini for the latter. As a part of the latter's campaign, an open letter recommending him and his qualifications was published, signed by 12 high-ranking instructors at the Qom seminary, including Montazeri (Saleh and Javadzadeh 2007, 260).

What is important is that Khomeini's reluctance in 1985 to endorse Montazeri was based not on jurisprudential grounds but on purely political and practical ones. He argued that people would be suspicious of such support, as they would notice the overnight shift and would likely wonder about the how and why of it. Minister Nategh-e Noori's impression of Khomeini's response was that such a move was permissible in principle but should start with people other than Khomeini.

As a result, soon a countrywide campaign was launched for "Ayatollah" Montazeri, spearheaded by official radio and TV. The state even planned to prosecute a high-ranking ayatollah, Seyed-Sadegh Rouhani, for his objection to Montazeri (Hashemi Rafsanjani 2008, 346). Hashemi Rafsanjani, Khomeini's most powerful lieutenant, opposed such a prosecution, but realized that some kind of action was indeed necessary to bring the clergy establishment into line. In his memoirs, he favourably cites a conversation with some officials and high-ranking clerics about "the need to control the seminaries, to block the entrance of inappropriate individuals and spies" (Hashemi Rafsanjani 2008, 318). Later, in its meeting with Khomeini, the same group complained about the presence of anti-revolution clerics in the Qom seminary, in hopes of obtaining his approval for harsher measures against them. Besides all these political manoeuvres, the state ensured, in the months leading to the elections for the Leader-Selection Assembly of Experts (*majlis-e khobregan-e rahbari*), that all provincial governors were on board, as they oversaw the electoral process – hence a series of new governors was appointed to be sure.

This well-orchestrated and politically driven campaign eventually bore fruit. In November 1985, Hosseinali Montazeri, now elevated to ayatollah, was named Khomeini's deputy and successor as supreme leader. This resembled the earlier disqualification of Shariatmadari but in the opposite direction – one being a politically driven disqualification, the other a politically driven accreditation.

Coincidentally, in 1989, when Montazeri's political views started diverging from Khomeini's and he became more critical of the state's policies and decisions (particularly over treatment of political prisoners, including widespread torture and mass executions of thousands of prisoners), he experienced the same fate as Shariatmadari. This time, too, through another politically driven process, widely believed orchestrated by Khomeini's son (Ahmad) and the intelligence minister (Mohammad Mohammadi-Rayshahri), Montazeri was disqualified from having any political position and was allowed to practise only as a jurist (faqih) without any political designation. In references to him, the state-run media and pro-government personalities stopped using the label "Ayatollah" and began referring to him simply as "Mr."

This put an end to the Montazeri affair – at least for as long as Khomeini was alive – but transformed the Islamic Republic's relation to religion and the shia establishment. Through these three major decisions – disqualifying Shariatmadari, selecting Montazeri, and later disqualifying him – by 1989 the government had undermined the shia establishment and its centuries-old traditions. The Pahlavis too, as secular rulers, had pushed the shia establishment into opposition; the difference, however, was that this time it was done by a state ruling in the name of the shia establishment. A consequence was to undo the politicization of the shia institutions, which had started before the revolution and been championed by Khomeini himself. It showed that in the Islamic Republic members of the shia seminaries could participate in government only so long as they did not challenge or criticize its policies. When they did so, they would be asked to do what Khomeini asked of Montazeri in his last letter to him: "In Islam, the expediency of the state has priority over everything, and we all should be committed to that. As for you, Allah willing, you will give vitality to the seminaries and the state *by focusing on your teaching and research*" (Khomeini 1990b, 112, italics added).

This series of events reshaped relations between state and religion. The transformation displayed itself fully in early June 1989, when Khomeini died and state officials assembled to select his successor.

Episode Three: The Second Succession Crisis (1989)

By 1989, political events had solidified a new place for the *shia* establishment in Iran and rendered seminaries subservient to the state. After Khomeini died in 1989, high-ranking clerical state officials, pressed to find his successor immediately, faced a threefold challenge: the existing grand ayatollahs with the right religious credentials (such as Golpayegani, Mar'ashi-Najafi, and Sistani) were anti-revolution and/or pro-capitalism; the only one with the credentials and a revolutionary past (Montazeri) was out of the picture; and none of the politically acceptable clerics was a Source of Emulation.

In a crucial session of the Leader-Selection Assembly of Experts in June 1989, Akbar Hashemi Rafsanjani, Speaker of Parliament and the most influential statesman after Khomeini, convinced members to lower the religious credentials required, to accommodate more candidates. He then talked them into selecting Ali Khamenei, the next most influential revolutionary leader, who was a middle-ranking cleric serving as president of Iran at the time.

Showing a mixture of reluctance, disbelief, and humility, Khamenei soon rose to the demands of his new position. To consolidate his power, he launched a twofold project: to solidify his own authority both within the ranks of the army, law enforcement, and the security and intelligence services and, more important, within the religious establishment. On the latter front, he began to adopt the roles and tasks of a Source of Emulation – e.g., accepting the title of ayatollah given to him by the state media, teaching high-level jurisprudence courses, issuing religious decrees (*fatwas*), and accepting religious donations.

These efforts rattled the upper echelons of the clergy. Still ambivalent about Khomeini's role and authority, it now faced someone much more junior and with inferior religious credentials. The strongest opposition came from "Mr" Montazeri. He wrote Khamenei in 1994: "The Shia establishment has always been an independent spiritual authority. This independence should not be undermined by you, and the shia seminaries should not become subservient to the state, as this would not be good for the future of Islam and Shi'ism" (Montazeri 2001, 669). Three years later, in a public speech, Montazeri reiterated the same points, this time more harshly and directly: "I have warned him before that he was not qualified to act as a Source of Emulation … I had sent him a message [to that effect] … Is the meaning of these acts anything other than undermining the shia Sources of Emulation and making them irrelevant?" (Montazeri 2001, 669). In response, government-provoked vigilantes ambushed his offices, and he was put under house arrest in 1997 and kept there for six years.

Unable to count on the high-ranking clergy, Khamenei increased his reliance on the military and intelligence community. One reflection: the proportions of clergy and military commanders in high-ranking political offices shifted. Boroujerdi and Rahimkhani (2018, 63) report the incumbency rate for the Expediency Discernment Assembly during the period 1988 through 2022, comparing the relative proportion of clerics and of former Revolutionary Guard commanders. The clergy had about 85 per cent of the members in 1988–89, and slightly more than 30 per cent in 2017. The proportion of former Revolutionary Guard commanders rose from 0 per cent in 1988 to 30 per cent in 2017.

These economic and political changes reversed centuries of past religious practice and the institutional independence of the shia establishment. To adapt, the seminaries had to alter their organization, their mindsets, and their curriculum.

THE ORGANIZATIONAL SHAKE-UP

The post-1979 economic and political remaking of the shia clergy redefined relations between religion, state, and civil society. To be effective and to work smoothly, those macro-level changes had to match intra-institutional adjustments at the micro- or meso- level. Indeed, the continued presence of opposition voices within the higher ranks of clergy had made it clear that only radical alterations in the seminaries' structure and functioning would silence them and achieve complete state control.

The organizational changes had begun right after the revolution, through a series of reforms intended to centralize the constitutive elements and increase their dependence on the government. Historically, seminaries were decentralized, which, while making them extremely inefficient, rendered them difficult targets for any state keen to tame them. Aware of this reality, clerics often commented, "Our orderliness is in our disorderliness." Under the benevolent guise of streamlining this mayhem, the Islamic Republic indeed aimed to bring the seminaries under its control through extensive organizational reforms.

An eight-volume history of the Qom Seminary's Instructors Society (*jame'eye modarresin-e howze-ye elmiye-ye Qom*), published by the Centre for Islamic Revolution Documents (*markaz-e asnad-e enghelab-e eslami*), details this process (see, specifically, volumes 2–8 of Saleh and Javadzadeh 2007; Saleh 2007a, 2007b, 2007c, 2007d, 2007e, 2007f, 2007g). The issue of "reforming the seminaries and bringing order to it" was raised in February 1980 (Saleh 2007a, 463). The first tangible outcome, after a series of meetings and discussions, was a management council, consisting of three representatives from Khomeini and three from Grand Ayatollah Mohammad Reza Golpayegani.

The inclusion of Golpayegani, and the exclusion of several other high-ranking ayatollahs, was not a coincidence. Golpayegani was known for his apolitical approach, similar to that of Ayatollah Boroujerdi two decades earlier. Some other grand ayatollahs, like Shariatmadari, were too involved in politics, and their politics differed from Khomeini's; Shariatmadari had founded the MPRP as a rival to the Islamic Republic Party set up by Khomeini's top clergy associates. In a sense, the message of the government's move was that, while before 1979 Khomeini had strongly urged the seminaries and the clergy into politics, now he wanted them to be either politically active for the government or entirely apolitical. Golpayegani preferred the latter stance: "The seminaries should not be expected to quickly have all the answers for all the needs both inside and outside the country ... We should act without haste and while maintaining all the spiritual aspects of the seminaries ... even if the results appear fifty years from now" (Saleh 2007a, 468).

This nuanced position was reflected clearly in Khomeini's first message to the Qom Seminary's management council: "The Qom seminary should pay close attention to the education of Islamic subjects and particularly to jurisprudence; and they should continue with the thousand-year old style of shia jurists" (Saleh 2007a, 465). Note that his own jurist-ruler innovation was a complete break from those ancient ways. A year later he commented: "One of the important issues ... is to create order and discipline in seminaries ... which is of utmost importance for the purpose of preventing the deviates – in terms of both beliefs and ethics – from entering the seminaries" (Saleh 2007a, 465). In these epistles, he used certain words as code: "order" and "discipline" connoted centralizing the seminaries (and making them easier to control); and "deviates" referred to ridding them of internal opposition.

The next decade witnessed a series of trial-and-error measures to create a workable model. First, the management council was expanded from six to nine members, to add three other high-ranking clerics; this, plus a two-thirds majority required to approve motions, limited the influence of Golpayegani's representatives. Second, Khomeini suggested ignoring the seminaries in the provinces and focusing on Qom, both because it was complex and because the provincial seminaries would be easier to handle when things were in order at the centre. Third and perhaps most important, Khomeini brought into the reform process the young seminary students, particularly the revolutionaries who later volunteered during the Iran–Iraq War (1980–88). His repeated emphases on this last point resulted in new ways to incorporate younger, revolutionary clerics in the reform processes. This was indeed an antidote to the grand ayatollahs' insistence that Sources of Emulation should run the seminaries. The latter group opposed a greater role for the younger clerics because the time and energy they spent on political issues hampered their education. The concern was that this combination of high political aspirations and low religious credentials would increasingly allow political necessities rather than theological considerations to guide the seminaries.

Khomeini of course blazed this path, but his death in 1989 left the bulk of the work to his successor, Ayatollah Khamenei. Lacking the appropriate religious credentials (as we saw above), he initially proved reluctant about this process and merely offered some broad comments, but even they hinted at his vision for the seminaries – they should be "productive," "an unproductive seminary would not be worth keeping," and they needed "centralized management … and that is what makes [them] productive" (Saleh 2007a, 503–5). In the 1990s, as he gained more confidence, he made centralization a theme in his communications with the management council. When other grand ayatollahs such as Golpayegani and Araki were consulted, they stressed safeguarding the seminaries' "independence," their "traditional jurisprudence," and the "spiritual development" of the clerics. With every new slate of members at the management council, Khamenei's influence increased (for details, see Saleh 2007a, 513–57).

Khalaji (2010) offers an exhaustive list of the operations that transformed the seminaries:

- A new management system, several new regulatory bodies, and a multitude of teaching-research centres.
- Substantial government funds for these new bodies.
- Centralized granting of clerical degrees and standardized exams under state supervision.
- Political requirements for clerical promotion.
- Subsidized health insurance and housing for students.
- Centralized procedures for paying fellowships and bursaries.
- Centralized dispatch of students and clerics to proselytize.
- Centralized procedures for appointing leaders of collective prayers (*imam-e jama'at*) in mosques all across the country.
- A new military brigade of clerics under the command of the Revolutionary Guard.
- A special court to prosecute clerics (which, according to one set of statistics, employs more than 2 per cent of the nation's clerics).
- More state involvement in managing donated properties (*oghaf*), or endowments.

As a result of all these measures, according to Khalaji (2010), more than half of all clerics in the country have ended up on government payrolls.

Intellectual and Curricular Consequences

This revolution in the seminaries has altered their curricula and theoretical perspectives as well. Tabatabayeefar (2015) outlines the major jurisprudential (fiqhi) camps in the Qom seminary today. Using his data and the information offered in the current book, we can depict the intellectual changes at Qom.

Up until the early 1960s, the Qom seminaries followed traditional jurisprudence (*fiqh-e sonati*), with three defining features. First, it was largely individual-oriented, concerned mostly with the piety of individual believers, rather than with Muslims as a society or a polity. Second, it sought to maximize the correspondence between believers' daily lives and religious teachings, which removed it from many areas of modern life for which there were no explicit religious teachings. Third, of the four conventional sources of fiqhi reasoning – the Quran, the *sunnah* (the Prophet's words, deeds, and writings), *aghl* (reasoning), and *ijma'a* (consensus) – it emphasized the first two, ignoring rational thought and social necessity. Some young, junior clerics, however, thought seminaries should become more involved in the political opposition.

In the early 1960s there emerged what was later called "dynamic jurisprudence" (*fiqh-e pooya*). Its advocates looked to society-based thinking and greater involvement in politics. Khomeini became their symbol, loudest voice, and unifying figure. For the next fifteen years, and in the lead-up to the revolution, this approach was gaining strength, leaving the traditionalists in almost total isolation in society – but not in the seminaries. The new Islamic Republic brought a historically unprecedented challenge to the "dynamic" agenda, i.e., to develop a "jurisprudence of governance" (*fiqh-e hokoomati*). Given traditionalists' ascendancy in the seminaries, the dynamic clerics tried first to address the new challenge with the old theories and methods, including Khomeini's concept of necessity (zarurat), which allowed the state to deviate *temporarily* from Islamic principles in an emergency. But the challenges and crises proved anything but temporary; hence the calls for a more lasting solution, and

Khomeini introduced state expediency (*maslahat-e hokoomat*) (see the next chapter). These innovations helped the dynamic camp become the new mainstream during the 1980s.

Soon after securing dominance, however, the dynamic camp faced an inherent paradox: jurists' opinions and recommendations were typically diverse, yet the state needed a single stance for policy-making. The presence of alternative voices would not only create confusion but also undermine the legitimacy of the view adopted by the government. The state therefore began suppressing those alternative voices and pushed them away from politics and back into the seminaries.[4] This move included jurists on both left and right, such as Ayatollahs Montazeri (left) and Azari-Ghomi (right). Particularly illustrative is Khomeini's farewell letter to Montazeri (quoted above, 86), urging him to stick to teaching and researching legal theories – quite the opposite of his advice to clerics a decade earlier.

Realizing the state's new expectations of them, the seminaries had two options: to put their own legal views aside and go with the government's or to remain independent and seek refuge in traditional jurisprudence. Ayatollah Mesbah-e-Yazdi was among those who chose the first option; hence, he and the institutes he managed were given extraordinary resources for development and expansion almost continuously from the 1990s on. Another, perhaps larger group chose the second path and remained quietist vis-à-vis the state.

The presence of these two options has affected some basic, centuries-old concepts and methods of shia jurisprudence. One example is a recent, celebrated textbook published by the seminaries' Research and Textbook Planning Unit – an *Introduction to Fiqh*, by Reza Islami (2015). This tome revises the dynamic among the four conventional sources of fiqhi reasoning – the Quran, the *sunnah*, *aghl*, and *ijma'a* – emphasizing the first two and discrediting the others. Its rationale is that shia scholars accepted the four principles because they were reluctant to oppose this dominant sunni position. Political considerations may have played a role back then, but may help explain the book's own discrediting of reason and consensus. Could this be due to the great schism between Iran's shia establishment and sunnis elsewhere, or at least in the Middle East? Perhaps jurists' new mandate from the state relieved them of the need for critical thinking and intellectual innovations? With the state's need for only one legal view, why seek the agreement of all jurists (hence consensus)?

During the 2010s, another unusual concept surfaced: *secular seminaries*. It emerged along with the government and the supreme leader's grievances about growing isolationism in the seminaries. Rahimpour-Azghadi, a state-favoured speaker, offered a clear critique:

> A jurisprudence unrelated to people's lives [generates] a life unrelated to jurisprudence … *kharij* courses [high-level courses on Islamic jurisprudence] that, instead of theorizing for a religious state, for a religious society, and for a religious civilization, are in reality generating a secular jurisprudence; a jurisprudence that focuses on individual prayers and rules around personal cleanliness, but is silent on economics, politics, international affairs, banking system, etc. ... that is exactly what secularism is … Indeed, the root of secularism is in the seminaries. What is secularism? It is the separation of religion from state and governance … They [the high-ranking seminary instructors] are still discussing whether our banking system is usury-based or not … Forty years have passed already … We keep criticizing the *sunni* Muslims that they have closed the gates of *ijtihad* [creative reasoning in finding sharia-based answers for contemporary questions] … What have you [seminaries] done? You have done the exact same thing. (Rahimpour-Azghadi 2018)

This proposition was then followed by intense discussions and multiple rebuttals showing the relevance of such a concept for seminaries today.

SUMMARY

The increasing reliance of the shia establishment on the government's budget, as we saw above, marked a turning point in the history of shia Islam and a reversal of an arrangement initiated by the seventh Imam, Musa al-Kadhim (term 765–799). According to Modarresi (1993), he required that shia Muslims pay a yearly tax to their leader, collected through an extensive network of representatives that he had created across the eastern Middle East. Its success made him and his successors independent from governments and allowed followers to criticize their rulers. But events in Iran after 1979 altered this set-up and made the shia establishment dependent on state support. As well, Khomeini introduced the notion of jurist rule (*velayat-e faqih*). This new interdependence of religion and government robbed the former of its independence and deeply secularized the shia establishment.

As Khalaji (2010, 147) argues, "The more the shia jurists warm up to the notion of an Islamic state, the more they distance themselves from the traditional shi'i intellectual perspective … and, in a sense, the more this-worldly and secular they become." This intellectual realignment has been reinforced by a generational one as well: over the past three decades, younger seminary students have been brought up and socialized as government employees and have benefitted from economic rewards flowing from jurist rule. Their education and work have moved towards providing government-friendly materials and products, rather than religious content. While in the 1980s the seminaries' mainstream opposed Khomeini's jurist-ruler, there has been almost no opposition to it since (with a couple of notable exceptions).

During these four decades, the seminaries have almost entirely stopped producing any new ideas and have failed to respond to the intellectual challenges directed at religion in general, or at Islam and shi'ism in particular. Moreover, many of their previous, adamantine teachings were easily replaced with new pronouncements in sync with the state's needs. In effect, they have become an extension of the government apparatus, a part of its propaganda machine. The religious functions traditionally the purview of seminary-educated religious authorities are now conducted by state-appointed clerics on government payrolls. The ultimate result has eviscerated the sacred element and the spiritual dimension of seminaries, turning them into secular institutions with an extremely thin religious veneer.

These changes in the structure and functioning of the religious establishment went hand in hand with a similar alteration in the state. Facing the challenges of running a vast country in a very complex political and economic world, and free from the pressures of the traditional jurisprudence of the seminaries, revolutionary government adopted a pragmatic approach to problem-solving. While it justified this *volte-face* initially on the basis of short-term necessity, over time it redrafted its own political philosophy. Such a reorientation occurred gradually, and through a series of innovative concepts from Ayatollah Khomeini, but the theoretical part of the process was completed within the 1980s. I turn to this in the next chapter.

5

Secularizing the State

Maslahat, *Memoirs, and Minutes*

The shia clergy's direct involvement in daily government operations after the 1979 revolution was, as we saw above, unprecedented in shia history, but only the beginning of a much deeper and more consequential process. Chapter 4 explored the reshaping of the shia clergy and seminaries after 1979. That process triggered a chain of innovations, both theological and jurisprudential, intended to justify the new arrangements.

Shia theologians and jurists had a wide range of theoretical resources to draw on. Had such needs emerged for sunni Muslims, they would have had to look into the political conduct of the Prophet Muhammad for the answers. But shia Muslims had many more options, because they believed the Twelve Imams who succeeded the Prophet were infallible, so their behaviour could offer inspiration and ideas. Previously, as Fischer ([1980] 2003) argues, shia Muslims had drawn on only two models of political behaviour, one centred on the headship of the state, the other revolving around the opposition to governments (corresponding to shia's first and third Imams, Ali and Hussain, respectively. But the Twelve Imams provide a much wider and more diverse set of possibilities, including: armed opposition to an established regime (in the cases of Hussain [no. 3] and Musa-Kazem [no. 7]); quiet opposition (Mohammad-Taghi [no. 9], Ali-al-Naghi [no. 10], and Hassan-al-Askari [no. 11]); giving up their claim to authority and signing a peace treaty with the enemy (Hassan [no. 2]); almost complete pacifism and full subscription to scholarly activities (Ali-ibn-al-Hussain [no. 4], Mohammad-al-Bagher [no. 5], and Ja'far-al-Sadegh [no. 6]); participating in the government as a ruler-select (Ali-ibn-Musa-al-Riza [no. 8]); and, finally, forming the government and serving as the head of the state (Ali [no. 1]).

Before Iran's 1979 revolution, Ayatollah Ruhollah Khomeini had chosen the militant-opposition model (nos. 3 and 7), and afterwards he opted for the head-of-the-state model (no. 1). While prior to 1979 he sought principally to justify the clergy's political activism in theological terms, later he looked for the jurisprudential basis for an Islamic state. This latter goal he accomplished, first, through the concept of the jurist-rulership (*velayat-e faqih*); and later, by invoking necessity (zarurat) and state exigencies (maslahat) (see chapter 4 for all three concepts). His overriding purpose throughout was to give the state's needs and necessities priority over Islamic teachings. This was a direct consequence of shia clerics' new roles in government after the revolution.

Iranian history is replete with eras in which shia dynasties took over the state and ruled in the name of the shia faith – most notably the Bouyids (932–1055), the Safavids (1501–1722), and the Qajars (1789–1925). But the post-1979 experience was different in at least two ways. First, the previous shia rulers were largely secular – most of them military commanders; whereas most of the Islamic Republic's were shia clerics. Second, while the earlier ones were only observant of shia sensibilities and never claimed to govern by shia jurisprudence, the republic aimed to create a social system based on Islamic teachings and principles. The secularizing consequence of this new dispensation lay exactly in these two distinct features of the Islamic Revolution – rule by clerics and Islamization.

This unprecedented jurisprudential state of affairs started of course before 1979, with clerics' political activism against the shah, in their new urge to lead the anti-shah movement, and in their call for an Islamic state (for a discussion of these unexpected changes see Sahabi 2013). At the time, however, and in the first months of the Islamic Republic, the proposed "Islamic state" (*hokoumat-e eslami*) would have given clerics only a supervisory and monitoring role. Khomeini informed members of the Guardian Council (the government body responsible for ensuring Parliament's passed bills were consistent with Islam and the constitutions): "Do not leave the impression that you are interfering in all affairs ... The clergy should only guide, not rule. We should be careful not to be too rough on people so that they withdraw from the [public] scene" (quoted in Hashemi Rafsanjani 2007b, 196). Starting from this point, the debates were largely about whether such a supervisory role should remain advisory or involve some kind of veto power. This debate intensified in summer 1979 during the lead-up to the discussion of the new constitution, in which the latter position triumphed.

This political-theoretical victory was reinforced, inadvertently, by the interim cabinet of Mahdi Bazargan. As a supporter of a limited advisory role for the clergy, but unhappy with its constant criticism of his ministers, Bazargan suggested inserting clerics more directly into day-to-day government operations. This, he thought, would make these ivory-tower thinkers more realistic and reduce their criticism. Hence, he proposed that clerics on the Revolutionary Council become deputy ministers, so they could grasp the complexity of executive affairs. He meant thereby to reduce the tensions between the clergy and non-clerics on the council, and he succeeded (see Sahabi 2013, 75–6). However, and unintended: the new dispensation raised clerics' confidence in their own ability to run the country and to handle executive affairs. This process carried on through to the end of 1981, with the appointment of clerics first as ministers, then as prime minister, and finally as president.

Khomeini's increasing involvement in state policies and decisions aided and abetted the clergy's role. While in the first few months after 11 February 1979, he had resided in Qom, not Tehran, and had opposed proposals for a clerical president, he later moved to Tehran and warmed up to the idea. From that point on, he was active in a wide range of government decisions – from economic to political, from military to foreign affairs – on a daily basis. As a result, this man, who had once opposed his son Ahmad taking on any government position, made him a de-facto fifth member of the decision-making circle that consisted of the heads of the three branches of the state (executive, legislative, and judicial) and the prime minister (for details of his extensive role, see the journal of daily activities of one of the members of this council, the parliamentary speaker and the later president Akbar Hashemi Rafsanjani 1998, 2007a, 2007c, 2008).

The clerics' intense, senior-level making of policies and implementing them altered their views about how state and religion interacted. While they started operating by assuming – the repeated claim before the revolution – that Islam had an answer and a policy solution for every social and state challenge, they soon grasped that general Islamic principles could not help them create good policy. Early on, they thought this was a function of their inexperience, and that more theoretical work would extract solutions embedded in the corpus of jurisprudential rulings. As parliamentary Speaker Akbar Hashemi

Rafsanjani observed, "This is a serious problem that the seminaries have not done much work on the issue of the connection between *velayat-e [faqih]*, the Islamic-style administration, and the Islamic state of Imam Mahdi. This has left some negative impacts in the history of Islam and, if it continues like this, it will result in great harm for Muslim, and particularly *shia* Muslim, societies" (Hashemi Rafsanjani 2008, 89).

Besides the paucity of macro-level jurisprudential rulings, Khomeini worried about personal and personality conflicts among the clergy apparatchiks. Initially he offered them moral advice, mostly about maintaining revolutionary unity in the face of a wide array of enemies. He also warned that such conflicts could threaten the popularity of the clergy, the religious establishment, and Islam itself. Hence, he discouraged clergy-based organizations from offering nationwide electoral lists in the elections, fearing that this might suggest a power-hungry clergy. Both of the proposed solutions – more theoretical work on jurisprudence to arrive at applied rulings, and avoidance of personal conflicts – showed that the problems were diagnosed as temporary and easy to fix. As more years passed, this stance was severely challenged.

In dealing with day-to-day economic problems, clerics high up in government were increasingly realizing that most of their Islam-based initial responses conflicted with accepted economic wisdom and current political necessities. For instance, they soon grasped that insisting on making an interest-based banking system compatible with the Islamic ban on usury would simply cost the state control over the economy. As well, confiscating the properties of big businesses to reflect the revolutionary demand for economic justice went against Islamic respect for private property and ownership, and the need to encourage economic growth through the private sector.

In other words, clashes between power and principles, and among principles, started to emerge, and Khomeini began making comments that now seem like setting the stage for a radical departure from traditional jurisprudence. In one of his speeches in 1983, he reacted to people proposing to replace civil taxes with Islamic donations: "Someone has written that people should not be paying state taxes, only the religious donations. How ignorant can one be [to say this]? How would you pay for the several hundred millions of Toomans of daily expenses of this war [Iran–Iraq War] through religious donations?" (Khomeini 1986, 186). Such statements suggest differences between the state's needs and Islamic principles. Careful examination of Islamic history reveals several conflicts between principles and power. Bernard Lewis refers to at least two in the medieval Islamic Caliphate:

> The Umayyad caliphs accomplished this task [maintaining the Islamic state and society during dangerous internal struggles] through a series of compromises and interim arrangements … They did this at the cost of some dilution of the pristine Islamic message … by creating what has been called an 'Arab kingdom' … Only true Arabs, those who were of pure Arabian descent on both sides, were admitted to the highest levels of power and privilege … By another of the compromises for which the Umayyad are blamed by a later historiographic tradition, some Islamic percepts in such matters as administration and taxation were tacitly set aside, and a system of government established … that relied more and more on the structure, the methods, and above all the personnel of the empires which the Islamic caliphate had overthrown and superseded. (Lewis 1995, 65–6)

Faced with a similar problem, the Islamic Republic came up with a similar solution: put aside Islamic principles to stabilize the state, and let pragmatic concerns override religious teachings. This shift resulted in government decisions, policies, and actions largely unprecedented in shia history. The historical enormity of this sea change made it long and painful, stretching through the 1980s, with phases of premature confidence, deep confusion, and final settlement.

DATA

There are excellent analyses of this process already (see, for instance, Ghamari-Tabrizi 2008; Hajjarian 2000, 2001); but newly available data allow us to map it out in much higher resolution. Two recent sources of data are particularly illuminating. The first is the daily journals of Akbar Hashemi Rafsanjani, Khomeini's second-in-command and a mid-ranking cleric who served as variously parliamentary Speaker, president, and commander-in-chief. Three years into the Islamic Republic, he started keeping daily journals, which dealt with people with whom he met, the state's main challenges, and his talks with Khomeini and heads of government branches, and offered his general reflections as he was maturing as a statesman. The twenty volumes already published and/or being readied provide a rare glimpse into the work and thinking of the innermost circles of the Islamic Republic. They also sketch the new state's evolving visions and political philosophy.

The second recent source of data consists of all the decisions made so far by Iran's Guardian Council of the Constitution (GCC), which ensures that legislation is compatible with Islamic principles and the country's constitution. Its blessing is required before a bill becomes law. It consists of twelve members, six high-ranking clerics appointed by the supreme leader and six lawyers selected by the judiciary and Parliament. In addition to reviewing and approving bills, the GCC can interpret the constitution, decide (both pre- and post-election) whether parliamentary candidates are fit for office, and approve the integrity of the electoral processes. Its crucial gatekeeping authority places it uniquely to both reflect and guide the thinking behind the state machinery; hence, its decisions provide valuable supplementary insight into the evolution of the Islamic Republic's political philosophy. Luckily, in an atypical move by a government body, the GCC has published the minutes of all its meetings and the details of all its decisions vis-à-vis parliamentary bills. The nine thick volumes cover the first three decades of the GCC's operations, with more recent ones being made available on its website (see Markaz-e tahghighat-e shora-ye negahban 2006a, 2006b, 2006c, 2007, 2009, 2010a, 2010b, 2010c, 2012).

CHALLENGES AND THE EMERGENCE OF NECESSITY (ZARURAT)

Through the daily journals of Akbar Hashemi Rafsanjani, we can see that the main political and intellectual challenges to the new revolutionary state started surfacing about 1983 – after it had spent four years consolidating the new government, putting out the existential threats from both domestic opponents and the invading Iraqi army, and establishing the components of the state structure. Having kept the immediate threats at bay, the authorities now turned inward and started building the ideal Islamic country that they wanted – and that was when the trouble began and serious challenges arose. Hashemi Rafsanjani (2007a, 9–18) lists about a dozen such challenges, including gradual corrosion of the unity among the political figures and the ranks of the Muslim revolutionaries; the rising eagerness of a more mature Revolutionary Guard to play a more active political role; the emergence of factions within the ruling Islamic Republic Party; the transfer of political conflicts in Parliament to the broader society, as a result of live coverage of its debates; deciding how to integrate the revolutionary courts within the broader judicial system; and keeping a nationalistic foreign policy alongside solidarity with an international revolutionary and/or Muslim movement.

Two new challenges particularly affected the role of religion in both society and the state: the split within the clergy and conflicts around the role of the Guardian Council. On the first, Hashemi Rafsanjani (2007a, 12) writes: "The [politically active] clergy, which in the past had rarely shown any signs of disagreements over political matters, witnessed internal conflicts that resulted in a split between the Militant Clergy, which was formed before the revolution, and the Militant Clerics [that branched out of the former] ... This split has persisted till now, and is probably the most important and fundamental split within the cadres of the Islamic Revolution." This division both deepened and made more visible how incompatible religion and state policies were. One could no longer argue for one coherent set of Islamic principles on which everyone agreed and behind which all clerics could unite. The second, somewhat-related conflict divided Parliament and the Guardian Council over fundamental goals of the revolution, such as the state and the market's shares in the economy, limits on private property, and enforcing religiously informed moral standards and cultural norms. Long-simmering disagreements, according to Hashemi Rafsanjani, became more intense and more frequent in 1983.

On the divide within the clergy, Khomeini allowed the Militant Clerics (*Majma'e rouhanioun-e mobarez*) to branch off from the older Militant Clergy (*Jame'e-ye rouhaniat-e mobarez*). Some observers felt that he even favoured the new group, as he considered its views on revolutionary social justice closer to his own; he probably thought it more capable of relating Islamic principles to the demands of the revolutionary masses. As for the stalemate between Parliament and the GCC, he ruled that if a bill had the support of two-thirds of MPs, it should automatically become law (Hashemi Rafsanjani 2007a, 14). This gave an upper hand to Parliament, whose members had a much stronger urge for social justice than the conservative GCC.

To justify this latter measure, Khomeini introduced the innovative concept of necessity (zarurat) (for a discussion of this and later developments in the context of ayatollah Khomeini's political philosophy, see Ghamari-Tabrizi 2008, 2014; Hajjarian 2000, 2001;

Rahnema 2014). In a nutshell, his argument was twofold. First, he distinguished primary from secondary jurisprudential rulings (*ahkam-e avvaliyyeh* versus *ahkam-e sanaviyyeh*) – corresponding, respectively, to those mentioned in religious scripts and on which scholars have some consensus, and emergency measures to address urgent practical considerations. Second, when a secondary ruling was needed, the primary rulings were to be suspended, at least for as long as the justifying necessities last. This conceptual innovation opened a new path for the Islamic Republic: its decisions and policies had no longer to be compatible with primary Islamic principles but be only effective and supported by Parliament as representative of the society. In other words, the centre of gravity of state decisions and policies shifted from religion to politics, and from religious principle to secular necessities.

The supremacy of political considerations over religious principles shaped many decisions from 1983 on. For example, it allowed a banking system based on interest, despite Islam's ban on usury (*reba*). Also, the government established a Central Council of Friday Prayer Leaders to set criteria for clerics qualified to lead Friday prayers. While this body focused initially on candidates' seminary credentials, it gradually became a tool for appointing politically aligned clerics. Similar state discretion also underlay a wide range of decisions, such as launching missile attacks on Iraqi cities during the Iran-Iraq War, developing closer relations after 1991 with Russia, legislating state taxes, and even stopping religious rituals like holding collective prayers at government buildings or wounding oneself during religious mourning ceremonies.

One of the most telling examples related to how the judiciary enforced Islamic penal law. While the initial ruling was that, according to Islamic jurisprudence, judges could base verdicts on their understanding of Islamic principles, the inconsistency between judges soon became a major problem. In exchanges between Parliament, the Guardian Council, and Khomeini in 1985, the MPs had asked for state intervention to create more consistency, while the GCC had emphasized the initial ruling. To break the stalemate, the case was referred to Khomeini, who responded: "At this time, when the majority of our judges are not qualified and have been allowed to judge only out of necessity, the judges do not have the right to decide about the rulings on their own and without the permission of a qualified *mujtahid*. Therefore, there should be a committee … to standardize the permissible rulings, and no judges should be allowed to disobey them. Of course, this is only a temporary and emergency solution, until the qualified judges are found, God willing" (quoted in Hashemi Rafsanjani 2008, 306).

Hashemi Rafsanjani, who helped convince Khomeini to devise zarurat-based secondary principles, saw this as the beginning of a process to develop more state-friendly shia jurisprudence. In 1985, he said:

> [One of our biggest challenges is that we have to work according to the classic jurisprudence that is taught in seminaries and is written in books and without engagement with practical realities; and such a jurisprudence is not perfect. However, *the jurisprudence that is currently being written in the company of the state* could be very solid; because, while a portion of it comes from the Quran and the Narrations [of the Prophet], a big part of it is arrived at through *ijtihad* [critical thinking in religious sources], discussion, and reasoning. (Hashemi Rafsanjani 2008, 204, italics added)

The introduction of zarurat broke the impasse but did not remove the underlying problem. Viewing this provision as a way to bypass its authority, the GCC accepted it reluctantly but repeatedly emphasized that any such legislation was temporary. Thus Parliament had to renew the law frequently, every time with a new termination date, a task that became increasingly difficult as the legislative body's composition was constantly changing or the political zeitgeist shifted. A new, more sustainable solution was needed.

THE EMERGENCE OF MASLAHAT-E NEZAM (STATE EEXPEDIENCY)

Noticing the constant resurfacing of the old conflicts between the traditional jurists in the Guardian Council and the majority of MPs and the ministers with every new issue, a decade after the revolution Khomeini suggested a universal formula: state expediency (*maslahat-e nezam*) as a permanent foundation for the Islamic Republic. This principle had two components: maslahat (expediency), whereby practical necessities could override Islamic principles permanently, a concept from sunni Islam that allowed its legal theory to adapt constantly; and *nezam* (the state), whose survival and sustenance must serve as the ultimate maslahat, which transcended all the others. The combination of these two elements meant that the stability of the state – here, the Islamic Republic – superseded all Islamic principles, even the pillars of Islam, as well as all other maslahats.

Maslahat-e nezam transformed the political philosophy of the Islamic Republic. From this point on, state policies did not have to comply with Islamic principles so could be driven by purely secular forces so as to stabilize and protect the government at any price. Khomeini, when suggesting the notion of maslahat, had in fact an entirely different set of practical considerations in mind than the ones he adopted towards the end of his life and also those adopted by the next supreme leader, Ali Khamenei (still in power in 2021). In the same letter to the state officials in which he suggested this concept, Khomeini (1990a, 176) also wrote: "The interests of state and people are of utmost importance, the resistance against which may result in the defeat of ***the Islam of the poor and the victory of the American Islam of the wealthy*** and the arrogant" (italics added).

Hajjarian (2001) offers many examples in which the maslahat principle was invoked, and these include: laws to create consistency in judicial outcomes, overriding the fiqhi principle allowing judges to rule according to their understanding; permitting the playing of chess, overruling faqihs, including Khomeini himself, who previously considered it forbidden; and allowing the state to regulate labour relations. The most telling example, however, was probably the permission given to banks to charge and pay interest (*reba*) right from the outset, despite a clear Islamic ban. Despite constant opposition from the conservatives, the banking system has to this day operated on the basis of interest. Usury had a similar history of being overridden by practical consideration in the Christian world. Medieval Christianity considered usury illicit, but, according to Bertrand Russell ([1946] 2005, 568), that was because "church property was almost entirely in land, and landowners have always been borrowers rather than lenders"; so, paying interest was detrimental to the church's wealth. However, "when Protestantism arose, its support – especially the support of Calvinism – came chiefly from the rich middle classes, who were lenders rather than borrowers. Accordingly, first Calvin, then other Protestants, and finally the Catholic Church, sanctioned 'usury.'" Similar practical considerations were at work in the Islamic Republic, too.

In another example, Saeed Emami, the deputy minister of intelligence, commented: "The intelligence forces do not need to do daily prayers;

their labours themselves are prayers" (Emami 2006). A few years later, he was arrested and put in jail, where he allegedly committed suicide, due to pressure from his former employers to confess to something he had not committed, for the sake of maslahat-e nezam.

In yet another instance, Deputy Minister of Foreign Affairs Mohammad-Javad Larijani suggested that the Realm of Islam (*dar-ul-Islam*) had an epicentre (*omm-ul-ghora*, referring to Iran), and the latter's stability and interests took precedence over the former. The conflict closely resembled one in the early Soviet Union between Leon Trotsky (proponent of international communism) and Joseph Stalin (promoter of Soviet national interests), and Larijani's proposition was almost identical to Stalin's response.

Such dynamics shaped not only domestic affairs, but foreign relations. A clear example appears in state authorities' excitement in the mid-1980s over the possible conversion of some Middle Eastern militant groups to shi'ism, but only because of political considerations and without any implications for centuries-old theological differences between shia and sunni Muslims. A classified document published in Ayatollah Montazeri's memoir contains a briefing report on exchanges between Iranian authorities and the representatives of an Egyptian militant Islamic organization (see appendix A).

This letter reports the readiness of some sunni clerics to switch to shi'ism, because it more readily mobilizes people to achieve political goals. The letter quotes one of the sunni clerics: "I have come to the conclusion that shi'ism is the only faith that has the capacity to resist the oppression ... and to lead people ... I am ready to convert to shi'ism and to declare that publicly." In another place, someone else is quoted as saying: "We in Egypt have encountered a fundamental problem, which is the fact that people do not follow their religious leaders the way that shias do ... So, we raised this idea in our [leadership] council that we all convert to shi'ism ... so that the exact same thing that led to the victory of the Iranian revolution can also happen in Egypt" (Montazeri 2000, 1185–93). The Iranian representative recommends that they convert discreetly, following the shia principle of *taghia* (secrecy in declaring one's true beliefs when that involves risk). These quotes say nothing about the most fundamental disagreement between shia and sunni Muslims, over the legitimate successor of the Prophet Muhammad. Rather, the proposal is made strictly for practical reasons, and this logic resembles Khomeini's maslahat.

One can find similar moves in the history of early Islam. After the Prophet Muhammad's remarkable success (622–32) in uniting the warring tribes of the Arabian Peninsula and establishing a powerful state, several other leaders tried to imitate his movement. Aslan (2011, 112) describes this rise of "false prophets":

> Muhammad's vision of a divinely inspired state was proving so popular that throughout the Arabian Peninsula other regions had begun to replicate it using their own indigenous leadership and their own native ideology. In Yemen, a man named al-Aswad, who claimed to receive divine messages from a god he called Rahman … had set up his own state independent of Mecca and Medina. In eastern Arabia, another man, Maslama (or Musaylama), had so successfully imitated Muhammad's formula that he had already gathered thousands of followers in Yamama.

In all these examples, the encounter between religion and politics creates a unique environment in which the needs of the polity undermine religion. The diversity of these examples shows that post-revolution Iran was not unique; nor was that type of arrangement limited to the 620s.

Naturally, such a drastic shift inevitably affects all of the state's activities,[1] but particularly the content of its laws and the structure of its law-making, and Iran since 1979 is no exception. In the following section, I analyse the contents of all the acts of the Iranian Parliament from 1981 to 2009, and propose that the GCC's changing way of assessing them reflects changes in the state's political philosophy.

CHANGES IN LEGISLATIVE SENSIBILITIES

Shortly after its introduction in 1988 by Ayatollah Khomeini, maslahat-e nezam found a place in the nation's law-making system, through a constitutional reform approved in the summer of 1989 and the installation of the Expediency Council (*majma'e tashkhis-e* maslahat-e nezam), which would decide which practical necessities might override Islamic principles. It could also apply the same consideration to settle disagreements between Parliament and the Guardian Council of the Constitution (GCC), which ensured bills' compatibility with Islamic principles. Impasses had arisen frequently after the GCC rejected a bill as un-Islamic, and Parliament had refused to revise it. Now, in such cases, the Expediency Council could refer to the principle of what best served the state: the GCC's Islamic principles or Parliament's bill. In many such cases, and because of maslahat, Parliament won.

But maslahat changed how the two bodies operated, as they were both instructed to treat state interest as the "ultimate Islamic principle." Logically, this would downplay concern for religious compatibility. To capture this dynamic and test this hypothesis, I have analysed the contents of all the GCC's decisions from 1981 to 2009. These rulings are documented in nine volumes and published in print or online by the GCC (Markaz-e tahghighat-e shora-ye negahban 2006a, 2006b, 2006c, 2007, 2009, 2010a, 2010b, 2010c, 2012).

When assessing a bill, the council, which consists of six high-ranking clerics and six experts on constitutional law, determines whether it is one of the following four: passable; impassable as un-Islamic; impassable because unconstitutional; or impassable because it is both. Accordingly, for each decision, I have documented the council's verdict. Also, when, in the case of the second, third, and fourth scenarios, a bill is returned to Parliament for revisions, I have documented whether or not such changes were made and whether the bill was eventually passed by the council or not (in which case, it would be referred to the Expediency Council for a final settlement).

How could the legal and administrative machinery be influenced by the introduction of maslahat-e nezam? To answer this question, I offer an assumption and a hypothesis. I assume that the GCC's dual task – i.e., ensuring bills' compatibility with Islam and with the constitution – creates two sets of concerns: religious and secular/administrative. When Islam is a bigger concern than the constitution, we should expect to see a higher proportion of the rejected bills corresponding with the first concern; and vice versa. Based on this assumption, I hypothesize that after the introduction of maslahat-e nezam as the ultimate criterion, and after its incorporation into the constitution in 1989, fewer bills should be rejected as un-Islamic and more as unconstitutional.

Figure 5.1 allows for an examination of this hypothesis. The y axis reports the number of bills rejected for each of the years between 1980 and 2009. The two trendlines represent incompatibility with Islam and with the constitution. The lines show a turning point about 1988, when maslahat was introduced, before it entered the constitution. Prior to then, the two lines dovetail each other almost perfectly; that is, the numbers for the rejected bills on the two grounds are fairly

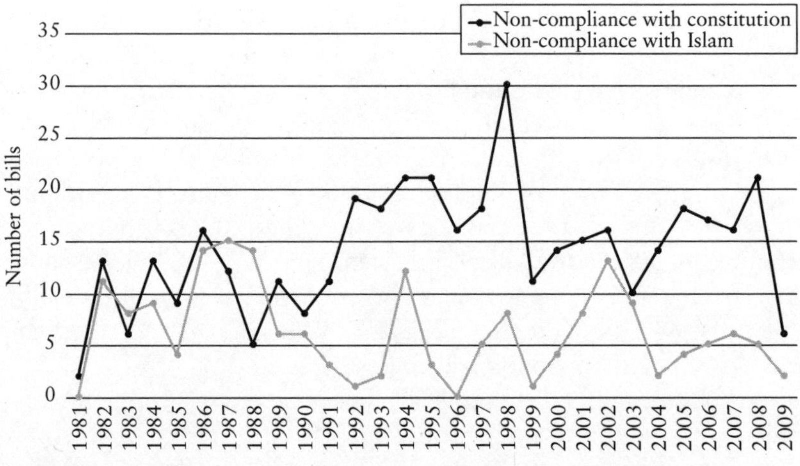

Figure 5.1 Distribution of the Guardian Council's reasons for rejecting parliament's bills, 1981–2009.
Source: Author's calculations, based on Guardian Council's publications.

close, and their patterns of year-to-year change are fairly similar. About 1988, the two lines start diverging, with religion-based rejections declining and the constitution-based rejections rising. This new pattern seems to have continued till 2009, three decades after the establishment of the Islamic Republic. The information included in this figure confirms my hypothesis, as religion declines notably in the council's reason for rejections after 1987, while unconstitutionality rises.

The years 1981–88 are the most conflictual in the whole period. The revolutionary goal of social justice was high on the agenda, resulting in many bills to reduce the income gap, restrict private property, facilitate workers' participation in management, and introduce egalitarian land reform. The constitution had been written and approved during this period of high fervour for social justice, and it contained many of the social-justice ideals of the time. But the same constitution had also anticipated formation of the Guardian Council, to ensure laws were compatible with Islam and the constitution. To appease the conservative seminaries, Khomeini selected the clerical members of this council from among the most conservative high-ranking clergy, a convention that has continued to this day. For these conservative clerics, many of the social justice–oriented bills were simply too "socialistic" or "communistic"; hence many rejections – on both Islamic and constitutional grounds. This tension led to many of Khomeini's "temporary" solutions before he finally settled for maslahat, which placed a pragmatist philosophy not alongside Islamic principle but above them.

This change in 1987 marked the beginning of a second era in 1989. The subservience of Islamic principles to pragmatic reasons of state reduced the former's relevance for disputing Parliament's bills. The two trends in figure 5.1 began to diverge, with religion-based rejections on a decline and constitutional ones on the rise. But something else happened too: the almost-complete elimination of the social-justice faction from the government and Parliament, replaced by a group of neoliberals. Little concerned with economic justice, this group pushed for economic growth by restricting the state's regulatory role in the market and by opening the national economy to foreign investment and international loans. The removal of economic justice from the agenda certainly eliminated many sources of tension between the GCC and Parliament, but not all, as the number of constitution-based rejections grew.

After 1997, with the election of the reformist president Mohammad Khatami, who favoured expansion of civil liberties over economic growth, rejections started rising again. This trend accelerated when, two years later, like-minded reformists won a majority in Parliament. This two-stage victory shattered the power of the conservatives, who now had to fight an aggressively "offending" camp promoting democratic ideals and political freedom. For conservatives, this was no longer a functioning system, so they reacted with everything in their artillery, including rejection of bills for any reason that would work, religious or constitutional. This reaction was the force behind the record high number of rejections in 1998 and the start of a convergence between the two trends.

During the years 1997–2003, the GCC, along with conservative allies, took it on themselves to prove that the reformists were not as committed to religious values as the conservatives were. Despite legal prohibitions, GCC members actively participated in political campaigns against the moderates, which brought a great deal of criticism towards them. Undaunted, the council used its legal position to reject many reformist bills. Most of these rejections were religion-based, to portray moderates as having an uneasy relationship with Islam. Despite this religious façade, however, it was clear that the GCC was driven by politics – more evidence of the practice of overriding religion for political and state-related considerations.

In 2005, when the extremist-conservative Mahmoud Ahmadinejad became president and the conservatives retook Parliament later on, the trendlines seemed to have bounced back to their previous tracks.

Once again, bill rejections occurred mostly vis-à-vis the constitution, rather than Islam. Data after 2009 are not yet available, but the trends seem to have only intensified. In 2018, the Expediency Council was further elevated, to act as a second GCC. These modifications illustrate the secularism that maslahat has engendered.

The maslahat transformation has sometimes generated confusion about its meaning, particularly as it relates to democracy. As for "the absolutist rulership of the jurist" (*valayat-e motlaghe-ye faqih*), a term Khomeini used to justify maslahat, many often consider this a great leap towards totalitarianism. Others, rightly identifying the secularism embedded in it and, assuming an inherent connection between secularism and democracy, consider it a step closer to democracy. I believe both of these views are misleading and based on faulty assumptions; the former incorrectly equates "absolutist" (as the adjective to describe jurist rule) and "dictatorial/totalitarian," while the latter improperly sees secularism and democracy intertwined.

Those who perceive it as a move towards dictatorship are misled by the term "absolutist" (*motlaghe*). In the bulk of later discussions about this term, many took it to mean totalitarian. They then argued that this notion was a stepping stone on the state's way to total dictatorship and the undermining of political liberties and human rights (see, for instance, Amanat 2017). This interpretation is not totally irrelevant; during the debates on this concept, some participants clearly understood it as giving the jurist-ruler (faqih) extra-constitutional authority. But, for others, this term did not refer to the political nature of the state but was rather a statement about its religious nature and about whether the jurist-ruler was limited only to jurisprudential issues or, alternatively, could deal with all socio-political issues (for an excellent discussion of the details of these debates, see Ghamari-Tabrizi 2008).

In other words, the debate was happening not between political foes but between religious rivals. By calling the jurist's rulership "absolutist," Khomeini was indeed trying to challenge the conservative clerics who believed in the jurist's limited authority in state affairs and his primary duty of safeguarding Islamic principles. Khomeini meant thereby to expand the jurist-ruler's role from advisory to direct and full activity in all of the state's affairs. In other words, he expanded his authority horizontally, rather than elevating it to a higher power. So, in theory, it was possible to combine an "absolute" jurist-ruler with a more democratic form of government (indeed, this seems to be a position taken by Hajjarian 2001). In this sense, the term "absolutist" here meant total and comprehensive, rather than totalitarian and dictatorial, and Khomeini (1990a, 176) wanted, initially, to use this expanded authority to prevent "the defeat of the Islam of the poor and the victory of the American Islam of the wealthy and the arrogant" (although, in his last year of life – he died in June 1989 – he used maslahat in the removal of Ayatollah Montazeri as deputy leader and in the mass execution of political prisoners in the summer of 1988). That was why the fiercest opposition to Khomeini's concept of maslahat came not from the pro-democracy or justice-oriented forces, but from the conservative, anti-democratic, and inegalitarian camp (for an example, see a famous exchange between Khomeini and Khamenei, on 67 above).

Hajjarian (2001) viewed maslahat as a stepping stone to national sovereignty and democracy. Acknowledging that it secularized the state, he commented: "The deeper the process of secularization, the higher the capacities for democracy" (147). While this could certainly be a possibility, such a process could equally result in a dictatorship. Hajjarian seems to assume that maslahat is normally invoked for the public good, which is a possibility, but the state could equally suspend Islamic teachings to safeguard its own interests vis-à-vis the public. Hajjarian seems to generalize what occurred when Khomeini introduced the concept. The main issue at the time was economic policy, around which existed two camps, one in favour of social justice and economic redistribution, the other keen to maintain private property. While the former was citing revolutionary goals, the latter was calling on Islamic principles. Introducing maslahat, Khomeini entered this debate in favour of social justice. But, as the still-ongoing era of his successor, Ali Khamenei, showed, one could easily use an authoritarian and anti–social justice agenda to override Islamic teachings.

SUMMARY

This chapter gave an overview of the changes in the political philosophy of the Islamic Republic. Faced with running a vast and complex country and the inadequacy of Islamic teaching to inform their responses, state authorities initially used a series of short-term measures. Most such measures were meant to remove the conflict between state plans and Islamic principles. Over time, however, Khomeini gravitated towards a more radical and sustainable solution, by introducing the concepts of necessity (zarurat) and state exigencies (maslahat). The transformation that these concepts unleashed allowed the state's practical and political interests to override or harness religious principles as appropriate. This made the contents of Islamic jurisprudence irrelevant, except to justify, not to inform, state decisions and policies. Regardless of its façade, this arrangement is nothing but secularist in spirit.

In part three, I continue to examine the secularizing trends in post-revolution Iran, but shifting from state apparatus and philosophy to religious beliefs and practices among ordinary people.

PART THREE

Backlash: Streets, Young People, Women, and Demography

6

Secularization on the Streets

> Oh, my dear children, hear this from your dying father: Observe the Ramazan fasting every year; it's only for one month and it will come and go; it is also good for your health. But, do not get even close to praying; this will stick with you for the rest of your lives, day and night, in health and sickness, at home or away; there will be no way out!
>
> A humorous folk story in western Iran

The previous two chapters analysed secularization at the institutional level, in chapter 4 by focusing on the relationship between state and religion, and in chapter 5 by exploring the state's political philosophy. In this chapter, we turn to religious changes among ordinary people. This is a crucial aspect of the religious dynamics in Iran since 1979, because the Islamic Revolution is often cited as evidence of the return of religion in the modern age and the return of people to religion. Also, the Islamic Republic made it a primary goal to thoroughly Islamize the populace, through aggressive Islamization. To assess the validity of the observation on religion's resurfacing and the success of Islamization in Iran, we should analyse the level of religiosity among Iranians both before and after the revolution and any possible changes in their religiosity.

At the risk of giving away the findings prematurely, let me offer two brief, tentative answers to these two questions: religiosity has declined significantly among Iranians, particularly among the young, since 1979; and the entrance of politics into religion and of religion into politics has transformed the contents of religiosity in Iran. Such findings are notable for another, more theoretical reason as well. As we saw in chapter 2, the success of secularism as a state ideology often requires the presence of a secular populace; and vice versa. So, against this background, the examination of Iran's religious trends – sacralization/secularization – will enable us to predict the degree of the success of theocratic/secular trends at the state level.

THE CONCEPTUAL BACKDROP: RELIGION AS A MULTIDIMENSIONAL PHENOMENON

The early analyses of religiosity in the nineteenth century treated the concept simplistically, based on either a dichotomy of presence/absence or, at most, a continuum ranging between the two extremes. Later scholars acknowledged that religiosity has more than one dimension, and that these do not always go together and can move in different, sometimes opposite directions. The initial step in treating religion as multidimensional was taken by Émile Durkheim ([1897] 2013, [1912] 2008), who considered religion to consist of beliefs, rituals, and communities. Later, Glock and Stark (1965) suggested five possible dimensions for religiosity: experiential, ritualistic, ideological, intellectual, and cognitive. They noted that "being religious on one dimension does not necessarily imply religiosity on other dimensions" (22). For example, "those who scored high on ritual observance and biblical literacy tended to score low on religious belief and religious feeling, and vice versa" (22).

Despite other studies on this topic, including critiques (see, for instance, Clayton and Gladden 1974), little has been added to Glock and Stark's ideas. The recent emergence of the "rational-choice theory" as a "new paradigm" in the sociology of religion has created a theoretical framework that can accommodate the multidimensionality of religiosity more easily. Its basic premise is that individuals approach religion in a calculated and rational way, trying to maximize their benefits and minimize their costs, and that they analyse cost-benefit in reference to their own preferences and within their limitations. Thus religious behaviours are likely to be diverse and multi-faceted, and individuals emphasize various facets based on their perception of the potential costs and benefits of their choices.

To what extent does this concept of multidimensional religiosity – as one originally developed in reference to Western Christian societies – apply to the dynamics of religiosity in Iran? How has the occurrence of the Islamic Revolution and the establishment of the Islamic Republic possibly affected this dynamic? Until very recently, answering these questions would have been extremely difficult, due to the lack of proper data. But this problem has eased, thanks to some rich new data on the post-revolution period and the rediscovery of some old data on the years before 1979.

DATA

Two unique sets of data allow us to address the questions of concern in this chapter. The first comes from a large-scale countrywide survey called the National Survey of Values and Attitudes (NSVA) in 2000 (NSVA 2001). As an equivalent to the General Social Surveys in other countries, the NSVA contains the responses of more than eighteen thousand men and women in the country's twenty-four provinces to a wide range of questions, including about twenty on religion. The large size of the sample, along with its random-sampling design and its national coverage, gives us a great deal of confidence in the representativeness of the information it contains.

The second source of data is another nationwide survey in 1974 – i.e., about five years before the revolution – that included several questions about religious behaviour and attitudes. This survey was conducted under the auspices of the Iranian National Broadcasting Organization's Centre for Public Opinion and Social Research as the first phase of an ongoing longitudinal study of opinion trends in Iran. During the four weeks it was conducted, five thousand respondents (fifteen years of age and above) in twenty-three cities and fifty-two villages were interviewed, using a questionnaire containing 126 questions and a multi-staged cluster sampling (Asadi 1977, 2). Unfortunately, I could not locate the micro-data for this survey; however, Ali Asadi (1977) reported the findings in a series of descriptive frequency tables, which have recently been republished by Abdi and Goodarzi (2017). To the best of my knowledge, this is the only large-scale survey of attitudes in Iran before the revolution, and it provides a unique window into the psyche and the pulse of Iranian society at that time.

The less-than-perfect match between the two surveys employed here limits our ability to zoom in on many details of interest, but it does not seriously hinder a grasp of the general trends. Out of more than a hundred questions in each survey, I use only a few relating to religious sentiment and/or behaviour. Appendix B lists the questions I used from these surveys, along with the aspect of religious sentiment/behaviour that I think each question captures.

CHANGES IN RELIGIOSITY: ITS FOUR DIMENSIONS IN POST-REVOLUTION IRAN

To decompose religiosity into its constituent dimensions, I applied a series of statistical measures to the NSVA survey of 2000, for which the microdata were available. Before discussing the results, let me provide an overview of the statistical process. First, I applied a statistical procedure called multidimensional scaling (MDS), whose function is to examine the degrees of compatibility among a number of variables and then put those having a high degree of correlation into one cluster. The application of MDS to the religion variables in the NSVA survey of 2000 resulted in four distinct clusters (or dimensions). Second, for each of these four dimensions, I developed a composite index, which varied from 0 to 1 (representing the weakest and the strongest degrees of religiosity, respectively). Third, I then harnessed the indices as new variables and applied the statistical procedure called correlation to examine the internal relationships among the various dimensions of religiosity.

The MDS procedure generated a fascinating pattern of relationships among the fourteen religion-related variables (see figure 6.1). In general, MDS produced a conceptual space on two axes, resulting in the generation of four quadrants. In each quadrant there is a relatively distinct cluster of variables, each suggesting a dimension of religiosity. The vertical line divides the graph into two areas, with the variables capturing the social/collective aspect of religiosity clustered on the right half, and those capturing the individual dimension on the left. Likewise, a horizontal line splits the perceptual map into two sections, with the upper half containing the variables related to practices and/or experiences and the lower half those related to beliefs. Based on these configurations, and for ease of discussion, I suggest the following labels for each cluster of variables: zone A: individual practices/experiences; zone B: collective practices/experiences; zone C: collective beliefs; and zone D: individual beliefs. These four zones or clusters can be understood as representing the four dimensions of religiosity in post-revolution Iran.

Out of the four aspects (or dimensions) of religiosity identified above, A, B, and D are close to what the existing literature on the multidimensionality of religion has already found. Variables clustered in area A correspond roughly to individual practices/experiences, such as observing prayers, experiencing the divine, or finding solutions in religion. Those in area B correspond clearly to collective practices,

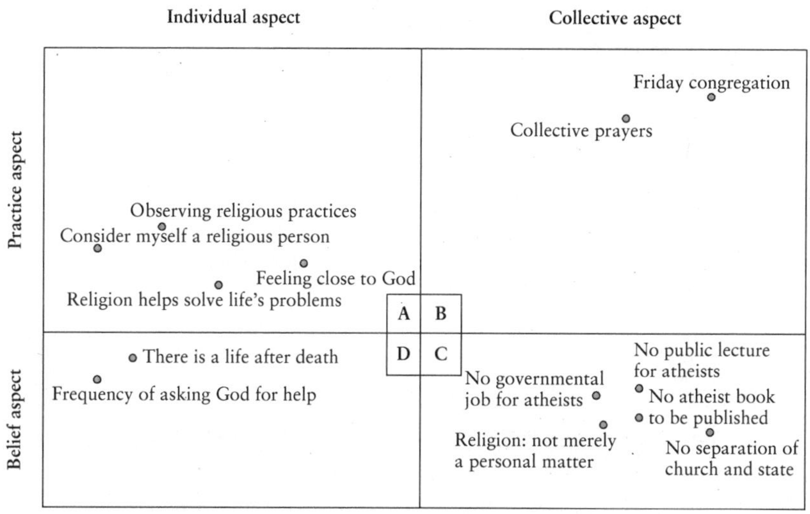

Figure 6.1 Euclidean distance model of dimensions of religiosity.
Source: NSVA 2000.

such as group prayers in the mosque and participating in Friday congregations. Items in area D point to either a belief or a state of mind, as opposed to practices and rituals captured in zone A. The closer proximity of clusters A and D makes them, in a sense, parts of one broader cluster that captures the individual dimension of religiosity, whether it is related to beliefs or to practices.

The most important and interesting part of figure 6.1, which seems to be speaking to something quite unique to post-revolution Iran, is zone C. This cluster includes variables that point to the societal implications of religious beliefs, such as: whether atheists should be allowed to hold government jobs and run for office; whether they should be permitted to deliver public lectures and publish their views in books and in the press; whether religion (mosque) and state should be separate; and whether religion should be treated as a purely private and personal affair or something public. The close proximity of the items in zone C indicates a strong correlation among them.

Zone C is clearly a unique feature of the religious landscape in a country in which the government rules in the name of religion. Those who oppose secularism – defined as separation of religious institutions and state – seem to also have strong views about who should or should not enjoy the advantages associated with government jobs, as well as who should be granted such basic civil rights as freedom of expression. There seems to be a strong political element present in these religious beliefs; hence, I have called this particular dimension the "religio-political" set of beliefs. Its content is probably the closest to what is nowadays called "political Islam" or "Islamism." The defining feature of Islamism is a strong connection between religion and politics, and a claim on the part of the faithful on state power. This particular cluster of variables has a noticeable distance from all the other clusters, indicating that they are not necessarily predicated on the basis of other, more individualistic and more conventional aspects of religiosity.

Using the clusters identified through MDS, I have developed four composite indices, in order to quantitatively gauge the level of each dimension and the internal relationship of all four. I have standardized each index, so that it varies from 0 to 1, representing the lowest through highest degrees of religiosity, respectively. Table 6.1 shows the average values for each of these four indices. It is clear that, unlike the popular belief about the predominance of collective practices among Muslims, individual beliefs and practices register the highest average values (0.91 and 0.72, respectively), with the lowest value reported for collective practices such as participation in group prayers and/or Friday congregation (0.33). The political-religious dimension reports a middle value of 0.60.

The average values of these four indices aside, the correlations among them, reported in table 6.2, point to a number of unique patterns. First, the strongest correlations occur between individual beliefs and individual practices (although in absolute terms the correlation coefficients are moderate). Second, the weakest coefficients appear between the religio-political index and all the other indices of religiosity. Third, and crucially, all the correlation coefficients between the conventional dimensions of religiosity and the religio-political dimension are negative, meaning that the stronger one's attachment to the religio-political beliefs dimension of religiosity, the weaker the attachment to all other, more conventional aspects of religiosity; and vice versa.

This latter finding is invaluable in explaining the religious landscape of Iran today. The negative correlations above indicate that the source of political or politicized Islam is not necessarily conventional religiosity and the strength of one's attachment to the faith. This speaks against a very popular belief in global debates about the Muslim world that political Islam or Islamism is a natural or logical extension of the faith

Table 6.1
Mean of four indices (dimensions) of religiosity, 2000

	Mean	*Standard deviation*	*N*
Index of individual beliefs	0.91	0.12	18,314
Index of religio-political beliefs	0.60	0.01	16,880
Index of collective practices	0.33	0.26	17,880
Index of individual practices	0.72	0.15	18,162

Source: NSVA 2000.

Table 6.2
Correlation coefficients for four dimensions of religiosity, 2000

	Index of individual beliefs	*Index of religio-political beliefs*	*Index of collective practices*	*Index of individual practices*
Index of individual beliefs	1.00	–0.05	0.17	0.47
Index of religio-political beliefs	–0.05	1.00	–0.08	–0.08
Index of collective practices	0.17	–0.08	1.00	0.39
Index of individual practices	0.47	–0.08	0.39	1.00

All correlation coefficients are significant at the 0.01 level.
Source: NSVA 2000.

(for a discussion of this debate see Gilsinan 2015; Wood 2015). This negative correlation implies that one cannot find in Islam the sources of Islamism or the solutions to it. A closer examination of the contents of the questions included in the religio-political index shows that they are mostly about access to societal and/or political resources and opportunities. A strong and widespread belief in this dimension of religiosity would limit opportunities available to the non-religious/more-secular segments of the population and hence raise the chances of success for the remaining contenders.

In terms of the implications for secularization, the above finding suggests that an ideologized subscription to religion, which has emerged in post-revolution Iran, would indeed suppress conventional religiosity and replace it with more secular political and economic considerations.

Changes in the Level of Religiosity

I now turn to possible changes in the level of religiosity, using data from two surveys that cover a quarter-century, including both pre- and post-revolution periods. Two large-scale, nationwide surveys conducted in 1974 (Asadi 1977) and 2000 (NSVA) provide a glimpse into the changes in religiosity during the last quarter of the twentieth century. The only limitation is that the questions asked do not perfectly match, hence a less-than-perfect comparison (see appendix B for details).

In the two surveys, there are questions on the frequency of observance of individual religious practices and participation in religious functions. Table 6.3 shows, for individual practices, little change in the levels of religiosity, as virtually the same proportion of people (83 per cent) that were practising daily prayers – *namaz* or *salat* – in 1974 were doing the same in 2000 (82 per cent). Some may argue that the reported level of religiosity for 1974 could be exaggerated due to the presence of a larger proportion of rural, as opposed to urban, population and the fact that the former show higher degrees of religiosity in almost all countries. Breaking down the 1974 percentage of those who "always" observe prayers by urban/rural designations gives the values of 77 per cent and 87 per cent for urban and rural areas, respectively (Abdi and Goodarzi 2017, 233). So, even the lower value of 77 per cent indicates only a 6-percentage-point increase in this category over a quarter-century. That is to say that, overall, the intense Islamization since the revolution has not significantly touched this dimension of religiosity among Iranians.

Unlike individual daily practices, however, rates of participation in collective religious practices paint an entirely different picture. Table 6.4 shows that in 1974, 59 per cent of the sample participated in collective prayers "always" or "most of the time." In 2000, this proportion has dropped to 20 per cent, a downward trend also apparent for those who "sometimes" participated. The opposite trend can be seen for those who "never" or "seldom" participate in collective prayers, jumping from 0 to 49 per cent. This is in clear contrast with the trends observed earlier for the individual dimension of religiosity.

There is yet another variable that captures the longitudinal aspect of changes in religiosity over this period. In both surveys, respondents have been asked to share their impressions of whether the influence of religion or the strength of people's religious sentiments and beliefs will go higher or lower in the near future. The results, presented in

Table 6.3
Frequency of practising daily prayers[1] (percentage), 1974, 2000

	Never[2]	Sometimes	Always[3]
1974	6	11	83
2000	6	12	82

Significant at 0.05 level; N (1974) = 4,420, N (2000) = 16,821.
1 The question in the 2000 survey asks about "the frequency of practising daily prayers and Ramazan fasting."
2 This category combines both "Never" and "Seldom" responses in the 2000 survey.
3 This category combines both "Always" and "Most of the time" responses in the 2000 survey.
Source: 1974, Asadi 1977; 2000, NSVA 2000.

Table 6.4
Frequency of participating in collective prayers[1] (percentage), 1974, 2000

	Never	*Seldom*	*Sometimes*[2]	*Most of the time*	*Always*
1974	0	0*	39*	23*	36*
2000	23*	26*	31*	14*	6*

* Significant at 0.05 level.
1 In the 1974 survey, "frequency of visiting the mosque."
2 For the 1974 survey, this category combines two groups of responses: "two or three times a month" and "once a week."
Source: 1974, Asadi 1977; 2000, NSVA 2000.

table 6.5, yield two very interesting findings. The first is the change in the proportion of those who were "not certain" or simply "did not know" how to answer this question. In 1974, the absolute majority of respondents (61 per cent) belonged to this category; in 2000, only 3 per cent, indicating that people have become more aware of, or sensitive to, the future of religion in their surroundings. It seems that religion has changed from being a "non-issue" to "an issue," around which clear views and opinions have been shaped. The second trend in table 6.5 is even more revealing. The numbers show a noticeable drop between 1974 and 2000 in the proportion of those who believed that people would be *more* religious in the future – from 26 per cent to 16 per cent. Instead, more than 50 per cent of the respondents in 2000 thought that people would become *less* religious, significantly higher than the 9 per cent who believed so back in 1974.

Taken together, the above findings indicate that the establishment of the Islamic Republic has resulted in three changes: more sensitivity

Table 6.5
Influence of religion, or strength of people's religious sentiments, in the future[1] (percentage), 1974, 2000

	More	*Same*	*Less*	*Don't know/ undecided*
1974	26	4	9	61
2000	16	29	53	3

Significant at 0.05 level.
1 In 2000 survey: "… five years from now."
Source: 1974, Asadi 1977; 2000, NSVA 2000.

among people about the role of religion in their society; greater awareness about its possible influence in the future; and, for an overwhelming majority, a stronger conviction that its influence will decline. The general connotation of these findings is that in 1974, when institutional secularization was in full swing, a high proportion of people had strong religious beliefs and followed their individual religious practices; and that this situation did not change much in the next quarter-century. However, the degree of commitment to collective religious practices, and views about the significance of religion in the future, have shifted noticeably, and mostly downward.

To what extent are these changes generational, rather than indicators of social change? That is to say, to what extent are they the products of an older generation giving way to a younger one that has been growing up in the last quarter-century; and how much is due to a sweeping alteration in the feelings, views, and beliefs of the existing population? The breakdown of the data by age, shown in table 6.6, allows for a tentative examination of these two scenarios. The value of considering age here stems from the fact that the future of the society can be predicted, to some extent, on the basis of the sentiments of the younger generations.

Table 6.6 shows that in 1974 a larger proportion of the younger age groups believed that people were becoming *more* religious and that, with only one exception (those sixty-five and older), these proportions decrease as age increases. In 2000, however, this trend was completely the reverse, as a smaller proportion of younger age groups felt that people would demonstrate stronger beliefs in the future, and these proportions rise with age. In contrast, the proportion who thought that people were becoming less religious jumped from single-digit numbers to values between 41.7 per cent for the oldest group

Table 6.6
Influence of religion, or strength of people's religious sentiments, in the future[1] (percentage), 1974, 2000

Age groupe	*More*	*Same*	*Less*	*Don't know/undecided*
1974				
15–24	37*	2*	10*	51*
25–34	25*	4*	11*	60*
35–44	21*	4*	9*	66*
45–54	20	5*	6*	69*
55–64	16*	5*	7*	72*
65 and older	21*	2*	10*	67*
2000				
15–24	11.1*	28.5*	60.4*	0*
25–34	15.6*	31.7*	52.7*	0*
35–44	19*	29.9*	51.1*	0*
45–54	21.6	28.9*	49.5*	0*
55–64	22*	29.2*	48.7*	0.1*
65 and older	27.1*	27.2*	45.7*	0*

* *Significant at 0.05 level.*
1 In the 2000 survey: "... five years from now."
Source: 1974, Asadi 1977; 2000, NSVA 2000.

(sixty-five and older) and 59.5 per cent for the youngest (fifteen to twenty-four). Here again, the proportion of those with no answer dropped from a range of 50–60 per cent to virtually zero. The noticeable changes along the columns of table 6.6, combined with those along the rows, signify both social and generational shifts: not only have the younger generations become less optimistic about religion's future significance, but also the older generations themselves have changed attitudes drastically.

The above finding that in 1974, under a secularist state, a larger proportion of young adults believed that people were becoming *more* religious is particularly telling. This phenomenon is probably the outcome of two factors. First, this could have been a natural reaction to a secular state that was oppressive, anti-democratic, and gradually losing its winning economic cards. The increased oil prices of 1973, while greatly increasing government revenues and creating many opportunities for people, had also caused an economic shock and led to wildly high inflation rates in the range of 20–40 per cent. The state's oppression and the decline of its economic power might well have created a reaction to those factors but also to its secularist posture and ideology.

Second and probably more important, the state was tolerating, even promoting, some degrees of mild religious vitality, as an antidote to its mostly Marxist or Marxist-leaning armed opposition. As a step towards that goal, the government freed some political prisoners who were traditionally religious and held strongly negative views towards the other, Marxist-leaning opposition groups, because it hoped that such individuals would help weaken those groups by revitalizing religious sentiment. This was about the time of the MKO's ideological jump from political Islam to Marxism (see chapter 3).

As part of its efforts to shore up religion in order to undermine the Marxist opposition, the government began a series of initiatives to improve the position of religion in universities. Homa Nategh, then a professor of history at the University of Tehran, recalled:

> [About 1976–77] The regime began a series of TV programs promoting Eastern civilization vis-à-vis the West ... Ehsan Naraghi ... wrote a book in which he said that we have mysticism as a philosophy that can replace Marxism ... At the University's [of Tehran] faculty council, Mr Fardid said that ... "if the students were taught the authentic Islam and the White Revolution [of the shah], they would no longer revolt; and that the Quran is a treatise against the West ..."; and Ehsan Naraghi wrote a letter to the University and requested that the *hijab* be allowed at university campuses ... Dr Seyyed Hossein Nasr in 1977 [attended] the Congress of Mecca in Saudi Arabia, which in its statement had called for the closure of universities and strengthening of the seminaries; and the Iranian government had supported that ... The members of the royal family also began hosting religious ceremonies ... Attending *khaneghahs* [sufi circles] became fashionable ... The whole point [of these activities] was to provide an antidote to the Islam of the Mojahedin [Khalgh Organization] ... In his address to the attendees of the New Year's visit with the statesmen, the shah said, "Yes to Islam, but no to the Marxist Islam!" (Nategh 1983, 5:11–22:00)

This commentary indicates that, just when state oppression and the new economic challenges had started alienating the younger generation from the state-promoted secular culture, the government's relaxing of restrictions on religious activities had provided young people with an alternative worldview, a cultural frame of reference, and, eventually, a political discourse.

SUMMARY

We started with two major questions: First, what are the dimensions of religiosity in Iran, and do they correspond with those found in societies with official separation of church and state? Second, has post-1979 institutional (de)secularization been accompanied by a similar trend at the individual level, which is known as individual or subjective (de)secularization?

With regard to the components of religion, two patterns stood out. First, Iranians do not treat religion as a package; instead, they break the package into smaller pieces and have expressed differential levels of loyalty towards each piece. People of various ages, genders, and other social characteristics value aspects of religion quite differently, depending on whether that aspect is more belief- or practice-centred, and whether it is individually or socially/communally oriented. In this regard, the religious behaviour of Iranians seems to be evolving along the lines suggested by the market model of religious adherence (see the epigraph at the opening of this chapter, 115). Second, the religious opinions of those surveyed in 2000 underscore the presence of a uniquely Iranian component of religiosity, which, in the absence of a better word, I call "religio-political beliefs." This aspect of religiosity involves views about whether or not people's religious commitments should serve as a basis for allocating social privileges and public opportunities. This component, all by itself, singles out a group of believers for whom religion is not a private and personal matter but a means for allocating vital resources and/or warranting certain rights (which turn into "privileges" in this context). Since the levers for allocating such resources are clearly in the hands of the government, one may argue that this aspect of religiosity in Iran is strongly related to the presence of a state that rules in the name of religion.

As for the relationship between institutional and individual (de)secularization, the data reveal an interesting and unexpected trend. Contrary to the implications of the secularization thesis, a half-century of institutional secularization in pre-revolution Iran did not yield a similar trend at the individual level; people had remained noticeably religious, and, as late as 1974, they were expecting religious sentiment to intensify in the near future. In a similar fashion, more than two decades of institutional Islamization did not strengthen individual religious sentiment: in 2000, people reported virtually the same level of religiosity as their peers twenty-six years prior. In contrast, those dimensions of religiosity that involve collective practices witnessed a dramatic decline. Moreover, the general perception, especially among younger people, was that religiosity was in decline in Iran.

Before offering any definitive conclusions based on the religiosity trends discussed in this chapter, I would like to focus, in the next chapter, on Iranian youths. Whatever future trends in religiosity look like, the younger generations are their bearers. To better understand those trends, I compare the Iranian situation with that of a few other countries.

7

Religiosity among Young People

International Comparisons

When it comes to a society's socio-cultural profile, young people provide a sneak preview of the future. This is particularly true for societies that have simultaneously experienced a major social change and a sudden burgeoning of their youth population – and post-revolution Iran has had both, with the Islamic Revolution and a baby boom soon afterwards. A close examination of religious faith among young Iranians therefore offers us a window into the future of religion in the country.

Let's begin with the demographic change! As Iran's population pyramid presented in figure 7.1 shows, in 2019 there was a bulge in the numbers of people in their thirties and forties. This corresponds to a jump in birth rates during the 1980s, which rapidly rejuvenated the population. Iran's fertility rate (the average number of births per woman) reached as much as 6.5, one of the highest figures in the world (World Bank 2021). Faced with the challenge of supporting such a large and extremely young population, the government launched an aggressive family-planning campaign, which proved so successful that the country's fertility rate dropped to about 1.8 in 2007, far below the replacement level of 2.1 needed for the population to remain stable.

In recent years, fertility levels have begun rising slowly, reaching about 2.13 in 2018, though falling to 1.94 in 2020 (for estimates on various demographic indicators, see CIA 2021; World Bank 2021). Certainly the authorities, anxious over the rapidly ageing population, encouraged couples to have more children, but also at play was the "baby-boom echo," whereby couples born in an earlier baby boom also have more offspring. The relative increase among groups at the bottom (youngest groups) of the population pyramid in figure 7.1

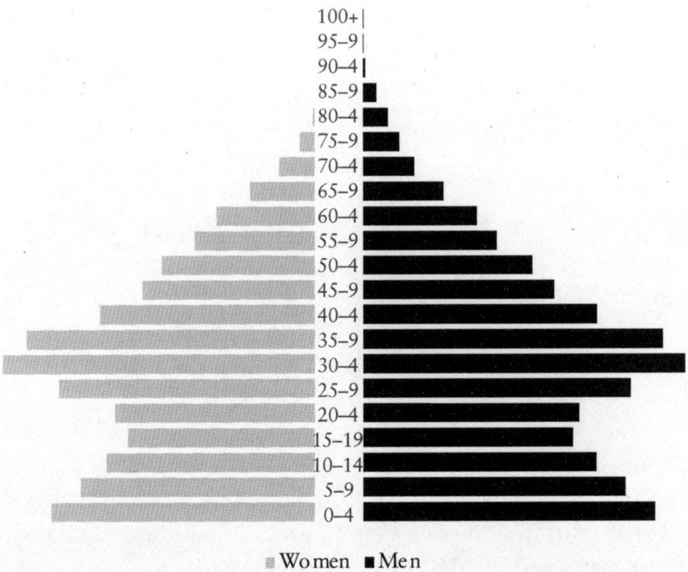

Figure 7.1 Population pyramid for Iran, 2019.
Source: www.populationpyramid.net/iran-islamic-republic-of/2019.

could be the "echo" of the 1980s' baby boom. Despite all these demographic ups and downs, Iran's population remains relatively young, with close to 40 per cent under 24 (see CIA 2021), and a median age of 31.1 (*Financial Tribune* 2017), indicating that half are still younger than 31.

What is the religious profile of this large group born since 1979? It shows a unique pattern of attachment to certain components of religion and detachment from others, a combination that sets it apart from its counterparts elsewhere. In this chapter, I focus on young Iranians' experiences with religion and religiosity, while comparing them with their peers in five other countries, two Muslim nations in the Middle East (Egypt and Turkey) and three non-Muslim Western countries (Canada, the United Kingdom, and the United States). In addition, I compare various Iranian youth cohorts. This method permits comparison between not only young Iranians and their peers elsewhere, but also with earlier generations of young Iranians.

I chose the five countries above for two reasons. First, the Western nations selected belong to the "Anglo-Saxon" world, which, unlike parts of continental Europe, has an easier time with religion. As we saw in chapter 1, the model of secularism in these countries seems to have been put in place historically to protect religion from state intrusion, as opposed to protecting the state from religion, as in places like France, Italy, and Spain. The more extremist secularism in the latter countries makes them too dissimilar to Iran for useful comparisons. Second, Egypt and Turkey are the only countries in the greater Middle East, besides Iran, that have distinct and continuous historical trajectories as nations. Most other Muslim countries in this region have been formed through international pacts and diplomatic agreements, especially at Versailles in 1919, as Britain and France carved up the Ottoman Empire with little regard for historical, ethnic, and cultural commonalities of their populations. Also, over the past fifty years, Egypt and Turkey have seen religious changes, with Egypt moving from a soft secularist state to a short-lived religion-friendly one in the wake of the Arab Spring, and then back to secularism, and Turkey switching from French-style secularism to a more religion-friendly state. This diversity of experiences, alongside the major commonalities, provides a rich framework for comparative analysis.

THE CONTEXT

As social demographers have long shown, demographic patterns in societies affect their cultural, economic, political, and social experiences. In the case of Iran, young people have been frequently cited as major players during and since the revolution. After 1979, they made up the overwhelming majority of the volunteers for the 1980–88 war with Iraq and of the rural-development campaign, or "construction *jihad*" (for more details, see Hooglund 2009). Young voters apparently were a major factor in the victory of the reformist Mohammad Khatami in the 1997 presidential election (Rezaei and Abdi 1998), and in the uprising (the "green movement") after the controversial presidential election of 2009. The predominance of issues such as youth education, housing, marriage, and unemployment in policy debates speaks to their continuing major role in Iranian society (for more details, see Memarian and Nesvaderani 2015).

The full impact of such a sudden population increase on the country's infrastructure was felt only years later, when the baby boomers reached school age and put pressure on the education system, initially at the primary level, and later at the secondary and university levels as well. These pressures began to cast doubts on the wisdom of the revolutionaries' encouraging larger families. As economic conditions started to deteriorate, even some of the families themselves began to wonder. As a result, by about 1990 there emerged a nationwide family-planning campaign, which reduced birth rates and overall population growth during the 1990s and afterwards (for an assessment of Iran's family planning program, see Hoodfar 2009).

This youth bulge was a mixed blessing for the government. On the one hand, it allowed the Islamic Republic to solidify the foundations of its Islamist view and way of life, through public education, the print media it subsidized, its monopoly over radio and TV, and its gradually increasing control over secondary socialization sites such as mosques. Its enormous financial resources, thanks to oil revenues, were crucial for financing such projects. On the other hand, cheaper international travel and better communication technology during the 1980s and 1990s exposed many younger people to other cultures and ways of life, which challenged the value system and way of life preferred by the state. The significance of such exposure cannot be overemphasized. Indeed, the influence of the internet and satellite TV on shaping young people's outlook has been so great that some scholars speak of the emergence of a relatively homogeneous and global youth culture (Bibby 2001; N. Howe and Strauss 2000).

In the post-revolution era, young Iranians were operating between two sets of forces with entirely different agendas and modes of operation: the government, which insisted on a religiously informed culture and way of life, inculcating this through education, mainstream media, and formal structures of authority (e.g., family, state machinery, workplace); and their global youth peers, with a much more secular outlook, operating largely through social media and informal social interactions. The constant negotiations between these two forces have created a unique religiosity profile among young Iranians, different from their peers in many other countries. In the remainder of this chapter, I analyse this unique profile, but after I introduce the underlying data.

DATA

I use two sets of data here. The first includes findings from the World Values Survey, conducted by Ronald Inglehart and Pippa Norris in many countries and in seven waves so far, with the first in 1981–83 and the seventh under way 2017–21. This is an extremely rich source, in which inclusion of several countries allows for useful international comparisons, and the collecting of data over time permits monitoring of changes. However, not every country included appears in every wave, and Iran is in only the fourth, conducted 2000–04 (Inglehart et al. 2018), which also encompasses the five other countries I have selected. The overall size of the samples for each country, and the size of the youth sub-samples (age fourteen to twenty-four), are provided in table 7.1.

The second set of data comes from a series of four surveys undertaken by Iranian scholars and government agencies in 1974, 1996, 2000, and 2003:

- Asadi (1977): Ali Asadi, *Gerayesh-haye Farhangi va Negaresh-haye Ejtema'ei dar Iran* (Cultural Trends and Social Attitudes in Iran), conducted 1974 (Asadi 1977).
- Mohseni (2000): Manouchehr Mohseni, *Barresiye Agahi-ha, Negaresh-ha va Raftar-ha dar Iran* (An Examination of Knowledge, Attitudes, and Behaviours in Iran), conducted 1996 (Mohseni 2000).
- NSVA 2000: Dafare Tarh-haye Melli-ye Vezarate Farhang va Ershad-e Eslami (Office of National Projects of the Iranian Ministry of Culture and Islamic Guidance), *Paymayeshe Melliye Arzesh-ha va Negaresh-ha* (National Survey of Values and Attitudes [NSVA]), conducted 2000 (NSVA 2001).
- NSVA 2003: Dafare Tarh-haye Melli-ye Vezarate Farhang va Ershad-e Eslami (Office of National Projects of the Iranian Ministry of Culture and Islamic Guidance), *Paymayeshe Melliye Arzesh-ha va Negaresh-ha* (National Survey of Values and Attitudes [NSVA]), conducted 2003 (NSVA 2003).

For the size of the sample for each of these four surveys, and of their youth sub-samples, see table 7.2.

The first survey, by Asadi, was conducted in 1974, five years before the Islamic Revolution, and the other three in 1996 (Mohseni), 2000 (NSVA), and 2003 (NSVA), seventeen, twenty-one, and twenty-four years, respectively, after the revolution. Collectively, they cover a period of nearly three decades. However, given their irregular timing, they reveal general trends only.

The biggest challenge for me was to find a way to make these surveys comparable. Even more problematic, access to their raw data is

Table 7.1
World Values Survey (wave 4, 2000–04), sample size

Country	*Total sample size*	*Sub-sample aged 15–24*
Canada	4,915	765
Egypt	3,000	657
Iran	2,532	952
Turkey	7,544	1,694
UK	4,744	807
US	6,906	1,147

Source: World Values Survey (wave 4, 2000–04).

Table 7.2
Iranian surveys, sample size

Survey year	*Total sample size*	*Sub-sample: 15–24 age group*
1974 (by Asadi)	1,238	765
1996 (by Mohseni)[1]	718	657
2000 (NSVA, cycle 1)	5,889	1,694
2003 (NSVA, cycle 2)	1,705	1,147

1 Age group: 16–25.

Source: 1974, Asadi 1977; 1996, Mohseni 2000; 2000, NSVA 2000; 2003, NSVA 2003.

limited, and one has to rely on published aggregate tables. To create such compatibility, I collapsed categories of responses to some survey questions into broader and more inclusive answers. In other instances, when the survey questions differed, I have included the various wordings to allow readers to judge the possible influence of their wording. As well, the surveys differed in sampling procedures and target populations. These challenges call for caution in interpreting the results and care in drawing conclusions based on small differences in the results. None the less, the information in the data allows us to sketch a broad picture, against which to interpret smaller and narrower findings more effectively and accurately.

Given the structure of the data, I explore the results in two sections, one on international comparisons, the other on changes over time. As in chapter 6, I treat religiosity as a multidimensional concept but with the understanding that its dimensions do not always operate in tandem with each other.

INTERNATIONAL COMPARISONS

Together, the data on the levels of attachment to various dimensions of religiosity set young Iranians apart from their counterparts in both the Western and the Muslim countries in the study. Let's start with the first dimension of religiosity (presented in figures 7.2 to 7.5), based on the World Values Survey (wave 4, 2000–04) (Inglehart et al. 2018) – belief in a set of relatively abstract ideas, such as God, heaven, hell, and life after death. In all these measures, the pattern remains the same, with Iranians and Egyptians almost tied at the maximum, followed by Turkish, American, Canadian, and British youths, in that order. In all of these dimensions, British score the lowest, a pattern consistent with extensive research suggesting higher secularization in Europe than elsewhere, and the Americans score the highest among Western countries, again, consistent with the literature.

The second group of dimensions (figures 7.6 and 7.7) shows an entirely different pattern. These graphs report the distribution of answers to questions about aspects of religiosity as spiritual/religious experiences and the connection between individuals' religious beliefs and their rights and privileges (e.g., whether non-believers should be allowed to run for office). In these two areas, Egyptians remain at the top, but Iranians drop significantly, in the magnitude of 40–60 percentage points. On one measure – that non-religious politicians are unfit for public office – Iranian youths score only 34.3 per cent, about the same as the Americans. As for ever praying or meditating, Iranians score 59 per cent, even lower than Americans and Canadians and almost as low as British (56 per cent), who are the most secular of all.

An often-mentioned indicator of religiosity is the extent to which one places one's religious identity over other, competing identities, such as nationality, race, and gender. Nationality has attracted more attention recently, particularly after some young Westerners left their countries to join ISIS in the Middle East, which suggested that they were abandoning their national identity in favour of an extremist religious one. Table 7.3 reports on whether young people in three Muslim nations emphasize religious or national identities. More than 80 per cent of young people in Egypt prioritize their Muslim identity over being Egyptian or Arab, but in both Iran and Turkey just above 60 per cent put their Muslim identity ahead of their national identity. Noteworthy in these trends: Iran has the lowest percentage of those who prioritize religion, despite the Islamic Republic since 1979, while both Turkey and Egypt have been under secular rule.

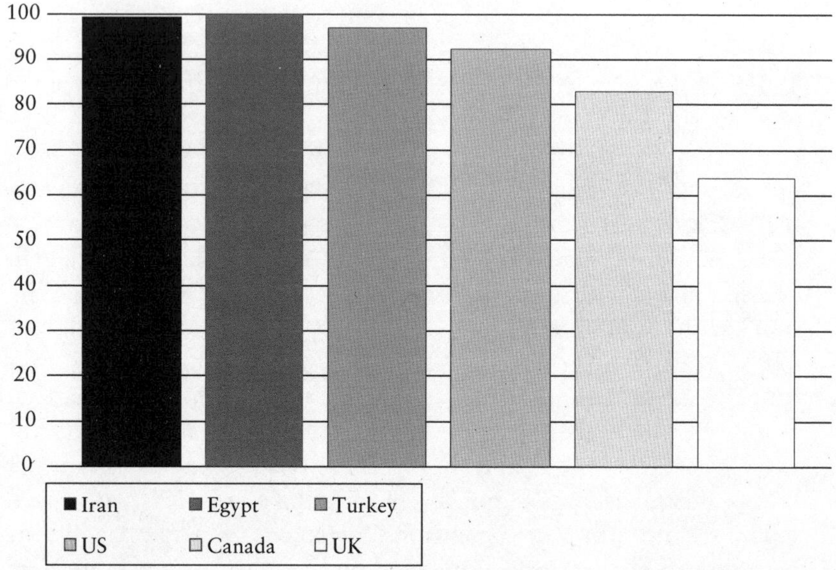

Figure 7.2 Belief in God (percentage of youths 15–24).
Source: Inglehart et al. 2018.

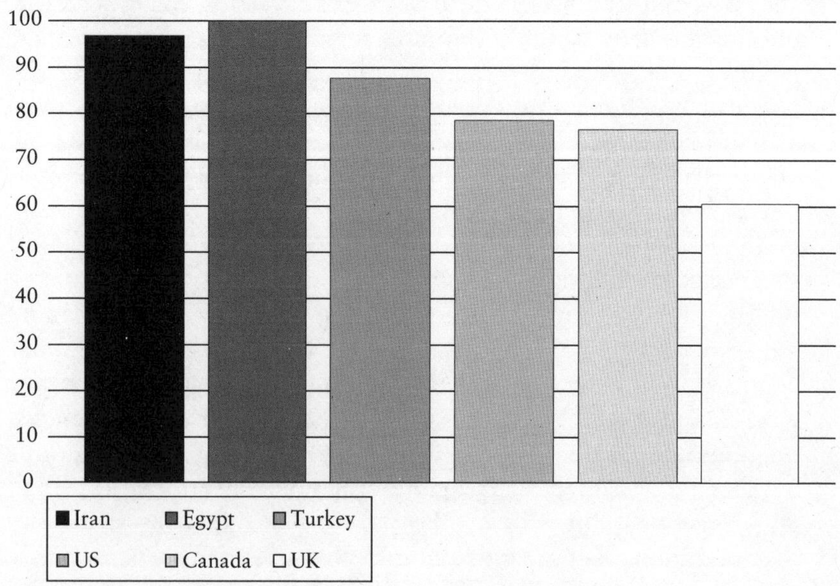

Figure 7.3 Belief in life after death (percentage of youths 15–24).
Source: Inglehart et al. 2018.

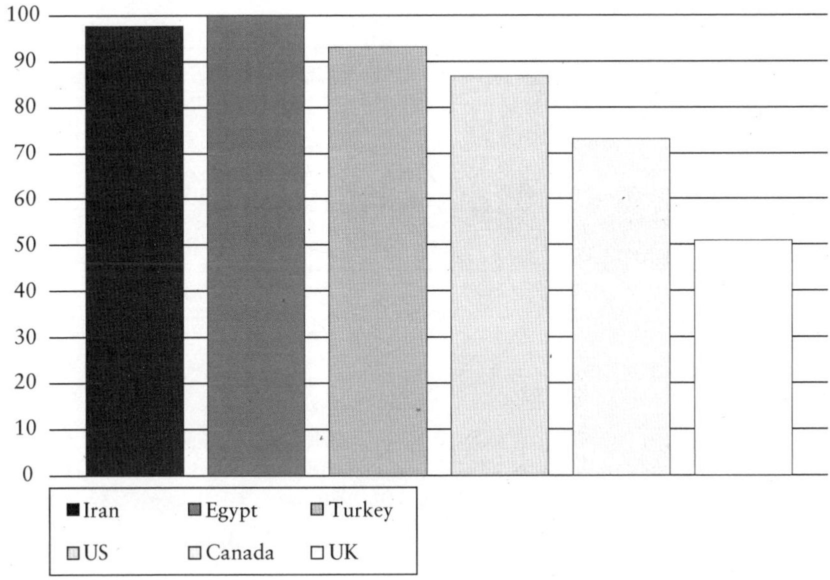

Figure 7.4 Belief in heaven (percentage of youths 15–24).
Source: Inglehart et al. 2018.

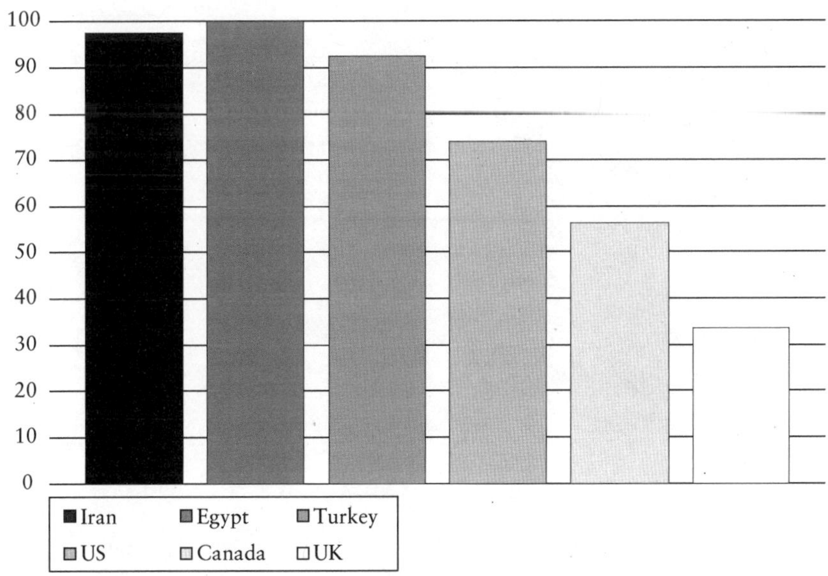

Figure 7.5 Belief in hell (percentage of youths 15–24).
Source: Inglehart et al. 2018.

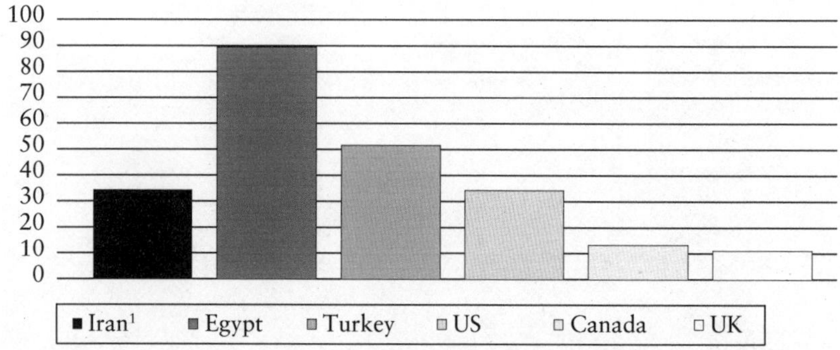

1 The percentage shows the proportion who have given the answer "disagree/strongly disagree" to the question "to what extent do you agree with the need to separate church and state?"

Figure 7.6 How much do you agree with the statement that "those who do not believe in God are unfit for public office"? (Percentage who agree.)
Source: Iran, NSVA 2003; other countries, Inglehart et al. 2018.

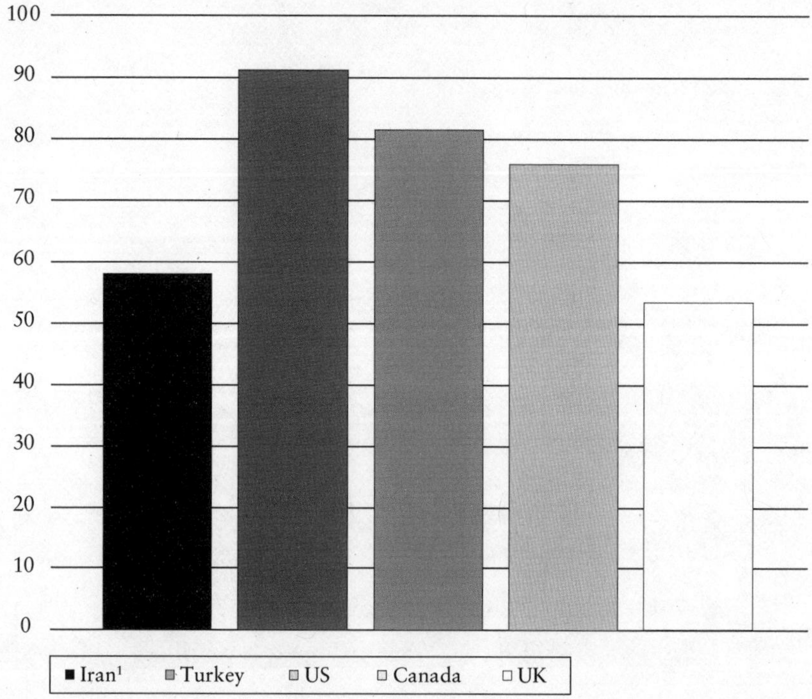

1 The percentage shows the proportion who have given the answer "always/often" to the question: "how often have you done your prayers in the last year?"

Figure 7.7 Have you had spiritual moments (prayers, meditation, etc.)? (Percentage who said "yes.")
Source: Iran, NSVA 2003; other countries, Inglehart et al. 2018.

Table 7.3
"To what extent do you agree with the following statements?"
(Percentage who agree)

Iran	Before anything else, I am an Iranian	34.3
	Before anything else, I am a Muslim	62
Egypt	Before anything else, I am an Egyptian	8.1
	Before anything else, I am a Muslim	82.5
Turkey	Before anything else, I am a Turk	33.9
	Before anything else, I am a Muslim	64.7

Source: WVS 4.

Combining this difference with these three countries' relative similarity on abstract beliefs reveals a distinct pattern: for more concrete dimensions of religiosity – either personal or social – Iranians score lower than Turks and Egyptians and in some cases compare with the most secular Western countries included here. Has this lower rate always been the case in Iran, or does it have anything to do with the 1979 revolution and its aftermath? This takes us to changes over time and the second set of results, which illustrate longitudinal changes between 1974 and 2003.

A CHANGING RELIGIOUS PROFILE

Before discussing the results, I should reiterate an earlier point that the four surveys I use here were not generated by the same researchers or as part of one broad study. Rather, they had different foci, so are inconsistent in the questions they asked and the answers they received. As a result, the following section does not include all four surveys in all the graphs; hence figures cover a longer or shorter period, depending on the questions asked.

Figures 7.8 to 7.11, based on Asadi's 1974 survey (published 1977) and NSVA 2003, illustrate the distribution of answers given by young Iranians to four questions about: the frequency of their doing daily prayers; the extent to which they consider themselves religious; the frequency of their participation in congregational prayers; and the extent to which they fast during Ramazan. Over the thirty-year period of the surveys, the first three measures show a drastic decline, from about 70 per cent to less than 60 per cent for daily prayers; from about 40 per cent to about 20 per cent for considering themselves religious; and, most significant, from about 50 per cent to about 10 per cent for regular attendance at

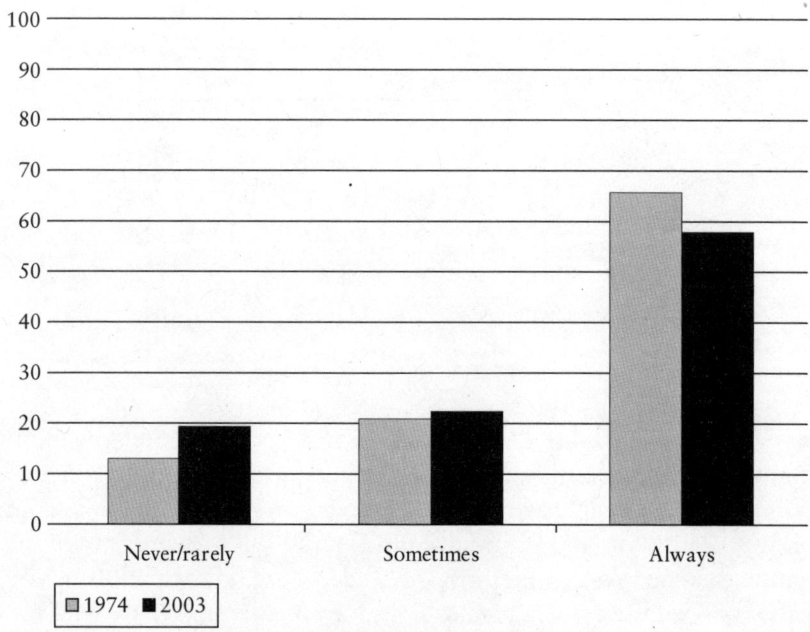

Figure 7.8 Do you do daily prayers? (Percentage.)
Source: Asadi 1977; NSVA 2003.

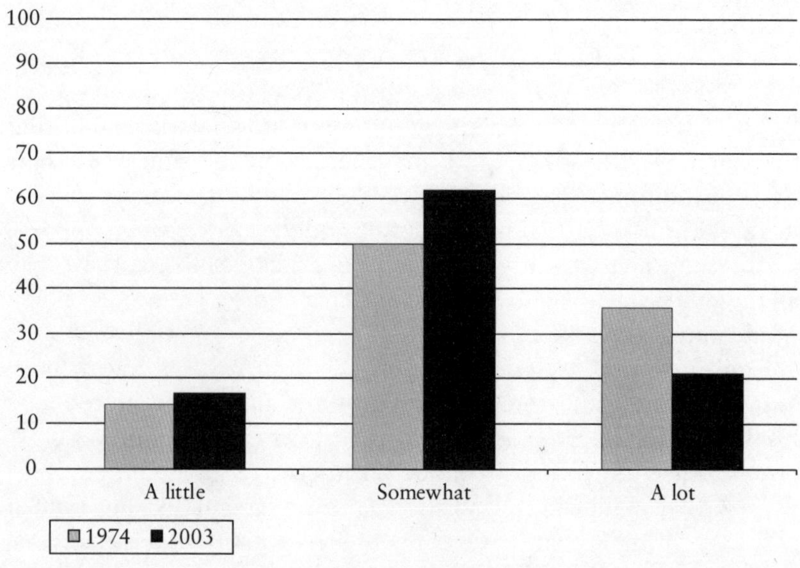

Figure 7.9 To what extent do you consider yourself a religious person? (Percentage.)
Source: Asadi 1977; NSVA 2003.

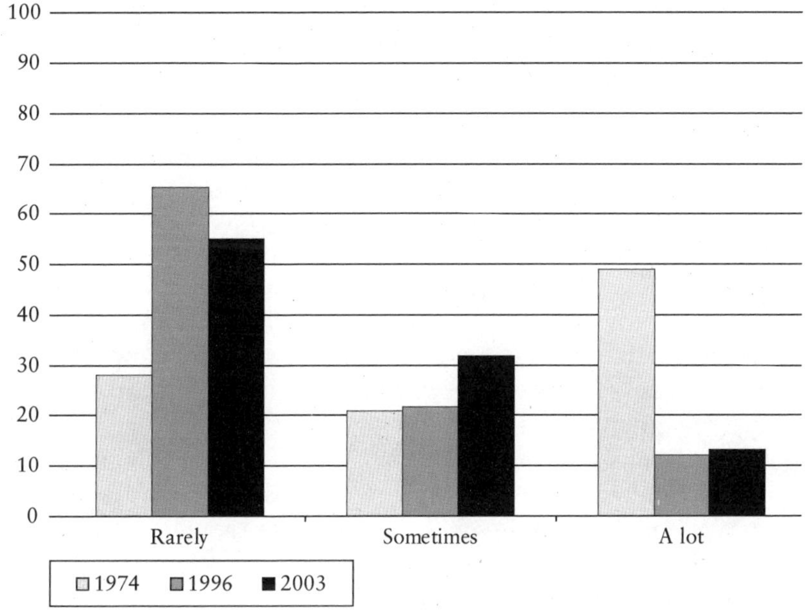

Figure 7.10 How often do you go to mosque (for congregational prayers)?
Source: Asadi 1977; NSVA 2003.

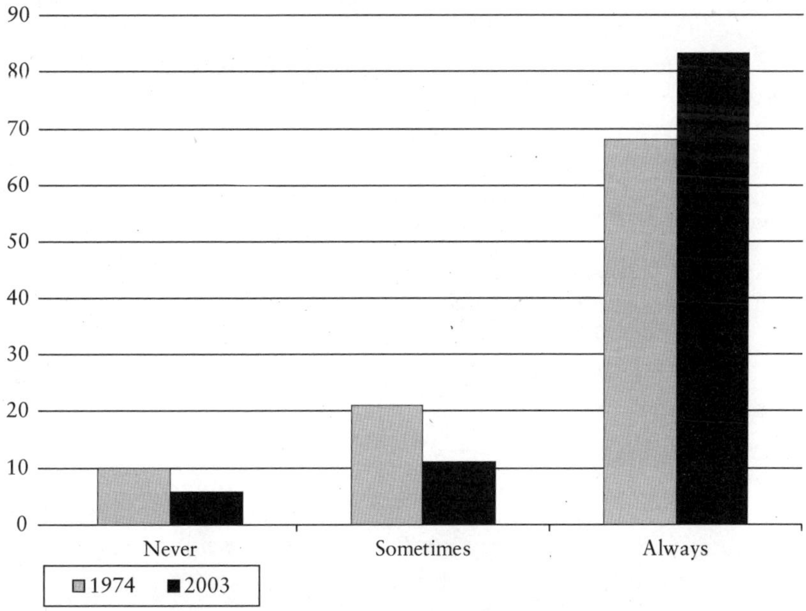

Figure 7.11 How often do you do Ramazan fasting? (Percentage.)
Source: Asadi 1977; NSVA 2003.

congregational prayers. However, as figure 7.11 illustrates, between 1974 and 2003, the proportion who fast during Ramazan rose by about 15 per cent. How to explain this unique and unexpected combination of answers?

Making sense of these trends would require a broader conceptual understanding of how one embraces or rejects a religion or a particular dimension of it. This is a complex process that involves both intellectual and socio-political elements. These two sets of elements correspond roughly with the concepts of reason and cause, which we discussed in chapter 2. I find this distinction particularly helpful for the kinds of religious behaviour adopted by Iranians both before and after the revolution. Below, I use them in the discussion about the religious profile of young Iranians.

Even a cursory look at religious debates among Iran's young people on social media today shows this relative absence of reasons and the heavy presence of causes in their positions on religion. Most of the current debates on religion among Iranians focus on religion's social and political consequences, as opposed to purely religious elements or philosophical and intellectual reasons. In the absence of free media in Iran for such discussions, a good place to see these trends is in the cyber world (for an excellent report on the contents of the "Persian Blogosphere," see Kelly and Etling 2008). This is a significant contrast to the situation before the Islamic Revolution, when lively debates on fundamentals of religious beliefs were common.

One interesting manifestation of the above-mentioned shift away from purely religious elements can be found in the debates on creation versus evolution, which were prominent before the revolution but largely absent afterwards. Those debates led some prominent religious authorities and activists after 1979 to try to resolve the perceived conflict as a starting point for promoting religion among young people. Such efforts included Yadollah Sahabi's *Khelghate Ensan* (The Creation of Humans), Ali Meshkini's *Ghor'an va Takamol* (The Quran and Evolution), and the Mojahedin-e Khalgh Organization's *Takamol* (Evolution). Today, such issues are still being debated in the West, but even a cursory look at the swath of religious publications in post-revolution Iran reveals not even one single title on the subject, nor does it appear in the freer blog world. The only exception is a 2017 translation of Adel Ziadat's (1986) *Western Science in the Arab World: The Impact of Darwinism: 1860–1930*. To the best of my knowledge, no similar book has been published in Iran in the past four decades.

SUMMARY

Young Iranians seem to possess a unique profile of religiosity. The new roles of religion in the Islamic Republic, which we discussed in chapters 4 to 6, have created an environment in which causes have overridden reasons. Given the state's self-defined mandate to Islamize Iran, and the subsequent entrance of religion into the public sphere, an individual's decision about their relationship with religion or dimensions of it is now shaped by its social and political implications, rather than its theoretical merits. Young Iranians seem to be withdrawing from those dimensions of religion that have been more directly subjected to policy-making, an indication of their dissatisfaction with the newly assigned social roles of religion. Yet in more personal and/or abstract areas – such as belief in God, heaven, and hell – the level of commitment to religion seems to have remained either high, or to have declined little, compared to the other nations examined here, both Muslim and non-Muslim.

This conclusion, if correct, implies two further hypotheses. First, the universe of religious beliefs and rituals in post-revolution Iran seems to have been developing along two separate lines, one gearing towards more private, personal, and socially inconsequential beliefs and rituals; another towards those with more visible socio-political functions. Second, the adoption of the latter elements seems to be more heavily influenced by secular and social concerns, as opposed to purely religious ones.

In the last two chapters, we examined the state of religiosity among the Iranian population in general, and among young people in particular. In the next chapter, we turn to Iranian women and their experience with religion since 1979.

8

Women

Gender and Demography as Secularizing Forces

The government has ... given women the right to vote.
This is of utmost concern to the Muslim *ulama.*

Ayatollah Khomeini (in a letter to the shah, 1963)

Denying women's suffrage is against Islam.

Ayatollah Khomeini (in a letter to MPs, 1980)

"Why don't they enroll women [as volunteer fighters for the war fronts]?"

"Because they are more effective in civil support in the back."

"What are you talking about, brother? We have women who are like lionesses; they fight better than you and me."

Ahmad Mahmoud[1]

The issue of women's rights had a central place in both pre- and post-revolution politics in Iran. During the more than half-century of Pahlavi rule, the shahs were trying to present themselves as champions of women's civil rights. Their two major and controversial actions were prohibiting women's Islamic dress – the *hijab* – during the 1920s–30s and granting women the right to vote and to run for office during the 1960s. While there were some secular and leftist opposition forces who were critical of the Pahlavis' policies on women – mostly calling them inauthentic and undemocratic – the major opposition came from the Islamist wings of the opposition.

In 1962, when the shah introduced the "White Revolution," which included women's rights to vote and be elected, one of the loudest voices of opposition came from Ayatollah Khomeini. Immediately after the law was introduced, he issued two letters, to the prime minister and to the shah. To the latter he wrote: "As the media have reported that, in the [new] election law, the government has ... removed 'Muslimness' as one of the required conditions for the voters and the candidates; and has given women the right to vote. This is of utmost concern to the Muslim *ulama* as well as to the rank-and-file Muslims" (quoted in Barzegar 2014). He informed the prime minister: "The election of women to the parliaments and to provincial and city councils is against the pillar rules of Islam ... and the sources of emulation have declared such a measure Islamically illegitimate" (quoted in Barzegar 2014). Despite the centrality of this issue, however, it was virtually buried in the political debates of the next fifteen years, only to resurface before the revolution, and particularly after it.

In the lead-up to the revolution, Khomeini and his aides found themselves caught between the implications of a visibly patriarchal corpus of religious teachings on women, as well as their own earlier opposition to the shah's proposals of 1962, and the demands of building a popular political movement against the monarchy, which needed the participation of women in social and political affairs. They had to come up with an innovative way to reconcile the two; and Khomeini's words during the autumn and winter of 1978–79 seemed to do the job, particularly for younger people, who didn't have a vivid memory of the events of 1962. The task became much more urgent and complex, however, after the revolution, as the new Islamic Republic began to devise and implement new policies and programs. With the promise of building a new society on the basis of Islamic principles, the ruling clergy needed definitive measures and a clear position on women's rights; hence a process of revisiting, and revising, some deep-seated earlier religious beliefs and statements.

The revisions included not just expanding women's suffrage but increasing their access to education and work and their rights under family law. While falling short of giving women full equality, their concessions were visibly distant from, and in some cases even in conflict with, the long-held traditional religious positions of the shia establishment. They were not, however, the outcome of epiphanies and moments of sudden enlightenment; rather, they indicated that, underneath the surface of a conservative, gendered order, a quiet women's movement was shaping up, and that it had bulldozed through the thinking and practices of the conservative clergy. It seriously challenged the dominant patriarchal ideology of the post-revolution state and has been one of the most powerful forces at work in secularizing Iranian society and government. The outcome transformed the state, moving the Islamic Republic away from its ideological and religious principles and towards a pragmatist state doctrine vis-à-vis women's rights.

The sea change flowed from two forces – one political, another demographic – that operated in two episodes about two decades apart. The political force surfaced during 1979–80, when hundreds of thousands of women took part in political rallies and revolutionary activities, first in support of the revolution and later in backing the Islamic Republic. The government's concern to maintain this high level of women's engagement helped push it to revise its positions on women and resulted in several new laws clearly at odds with traditional Islamic principles.

The second episode came during the 2000s, when the post-1979 baby boom (see figure 7.3) reached marriage age. Faced with the a "marriage squeeze" – an imbalance of numbers of men and women at marrying age (discussed below) – Iranian society had to relax traditional norms about women's marriage, divorce, education, employment, and so on, to allow them more flexibility and diversity in their life paths. This reality triggered a chain of reactions and responses by the state that were informed more by practical socio-political considerations than by Islamic teachings; in some cases, they were even in direct contradiction to the latter (see Zibakalam 2014). In the following pages, I discuss these two developments in detail.

WOMEN TRANSFORM POLITICS: THE 1980S

One of the outstanding and defining features of the 1979 revolution in Iran was the high level of women's participation in the anti-shah protests. Obviously, these women were not a homogeneous group, nor were they equally attached to religion. The more religious ones were more traditional and less educated and came from lower-class or traditional middle-class backgrounds, particularly in smaller towns. They saw in Ayatollah Khomeini a high-ranking *marja'a* (Source of Emulation) and a *seyyed* (a descendant of the Prophet Muhammad), with a deep commitment to empowering *mostaz'afan* (the underprivileged) and a plain language rich in religious symbolism. The more modern and better-educated middle-class women were drawn to the revolution by its declared goals of independence from foreign interference, political freedom, and social justice. Some of the latter went as far as adopting religion and becoming devout Muslims, while others remained non-religious but fairly tolerant of religion and religious expression around them.

The latter group's complex relation with religion is captured in the memoirs of Ezatollah Sahabi, a member of the Revolutionary Council (which lasted January 1979–July 1980). He reports a meeting with a group of educated middle-class women of Marxist persuasion three months before the victory of the revolution (in February 1979), in which some indicated they were ready to observe such religious practices as wearing the *hijab* as a small price for earning greater freedom and justice:

> One day, a group of women with leftist tendencies came to our house. They were well-dressed and wore no scarves. They were discussing amongst themselves what would happen to them now that [Ayatollah] Khomeini and the clergy were about to become the new rulers ... One of them said, "Dear ladies, it is not such a big deal! Let us get rid of the shah's dictatorship and have the country in order, and we will agree to be wearing this little scarf. This is better than having my daughter drawn into [social] corruption." (Sahabi 2013, 30)

He also remembers that a few months after the revolution, when he was the head of the Budget and Planning Organization, the female employees who were sympathetic to Marxist groups had taken the initiative and designed a uniform for themselves consisting of the long tunic and scarf. Their rationale was that each country and each working place has the right to require its employees to wear a uniform, "in the same way that there are uniforms in the Soviet Union and [Communist] China" (30). These examples show the direct ways in which women's lives and ways of life were affected by the religious dimension of the revolution, but also how some women accepted these religious requirements without necessarily believing in them (for some lively discussion and differing views on this, see Afary and Anderson 2005; Ghamari-Tabrizi 2016; Honig 2008; A. Sadri 2006).

While the new religiously informed restrictions on women were imposed on them largely from above, such impositions were facilitated by women's stronger attachment to religion, which phenomenon is more or less universal; in almost all societies and in all faiths, women show a stronger commitment to religion than men do. Berger et al. (2008, 109) maintain that, at least in the Christian world, this has been "one of the most pervasive findings in the literature" and "shows on almost every indicator (practice, belief, self-identification, private prayer, etc.) and is found in almost every denomination – large or small, traditional or innovative, Orthodox, Catholic, or Protestant." Systematically gathered empirical data on Muslim societies are fairly limited, but the existing data point to a similar tendency in the Islamic world, including Iran (see, for instance, Abdi and Goodarzi 2017, 227–48). During the revolutionary period, it helped religious leaders recruit female supporters.

But the active recruitment of women for, and their participation in, the revolutionary movement came into conflict with another, almost universal feature of religions: their patriarchal teachings. While some degree of patriarchy and gender inequality is present in all major religions, the research shows that it is particularly pronounced in Muslim societies (for some international comparisons, see Inglehart and Norris 2003; and see Fish 2011). Depending on the religion and the society, this patriarchal bias shows itself in many ways: it may limit and/or discourage women's paid employment; deny educational opportunities to young girls; restrict married women's rights to divorce and child custody; allow polygamy; and oppose women's participation in political and electoral processes. All of these elements were present, to varying degrees, in the traditional and more religious segments of Iran's population both before and after the revolution; they were also encouraged, explicitly or implicitly, by the shia clergy.

It did not take long, however, before the new rulers identified this fundamental contradiction between patriarchal religious teachings and women's anti-patriarchal involvement in the revolutionary movement; and they felt the need to be creative and flexible in addressing this dilemma. Women's suffrage was among the first vexing issues, complicated of course by Khomeini's stated opposition to women's suffrage in 1962. In the aftermath of the Islamic Revolution, he found himself face to face with this matter again; but this time he was in charge of the state. His response was remarkably similar to what the shah had done, including rejection of the conservative Muslim clergy's position. There is a reference, in Hashemi Rafsanjani's memoir, to their encounter:

> Ahmad [Ruhollah Khomeini's son] brought me the letter written by 11 members of the Parliament, in which they had asked Imam [Khomeini] to abolish the rights of women to vote/elect and be elected in the parliamentary elections. He added that, earlier, somebody else had asked for a similar thing and had requested Imam [Khomeini] to order the Guardian Council to implement this ban, but Imam had discouraged him, and had told him that taking positions like this is harmful. Anyhow, Ahmad took the letter to Imam and when he came back, he said that Imam has ordered me [as Speaker] to gather these 11 MPs and tell them that *denying women's suffrage is against Islam*. What we said during the shah's time was because anything they/he did was against Islam, including giving women the right to vote, and not because there was anything wrong with women's electing and being elected. But, today, our Parliament is operating according to Islam, and *giving women the same electoral rights as men's is Islamic, rational, and humane*. (Hashemi Rafsanjani 2007a, 358–9, italics added)

Informed by Khomeini's revised position, the Islamic Republic recognized women's suffrage in its constitution.

Soon afterwards, women's educational, cultural, and occupational demands emerged as the next set of challenges. A letter issued by "a group of [revolutionary] sister students in the holy city of Qom" during the 1980s clearly shows how these women expected more rights and opportunities in return for supporting the revolution:

> Does it suffice for an Islamic government to every once in a while put up a show, in the form of a seminar, and praise the status of women, and not pay attention to the needs and demands of … half of the population? Shouldn't the educational, cultural, and recreational facilities such as libraries [and] gymnasiums … be fairly and equally accessible to the public? Considering sisters' contribution to the victory of the revolution, their instrumental role in nurturing the martyrs, and their invaluable service behind the frontlines, which does not need a reminder or an elaboration, we expect the regime's officials to genuinely work toward the fulfillment of sisters' needs. (Quoted in Shahrokni 2019, 18)

Hashemi Rafsanjani's memoir reveals the intensity of the behind-the-scene disputes. On one occasion, he reports: "The religious devotees should learn that there is no honour in denying education to their girls; the time that this was considered a source of pride is past history now. It is exactly because of those misguided ideas that today our society faces a shortage of female skilled workers" (495). Another time, he emphasizes that "in sharia, there are no restrictions on the kind of positions that women can take [in society]. They can become ministers, governors, members of Parliament, managers of industrial plants, advisers to ministers, university presidents, and so on" (496). That issue, too, was put to rest quickly in favour of women's rights.

The fiercest dilemma for the new ruling clergy, however, was polygamy – an explicit sharia ruling, with a clear reference in the Quran,[2] allowed men up to four wives. Addressing a group of women concerned about a rumour that Parliament had legalized polygamy, Hashemi Rafsanjani replied defensively:

> Parliament has not passed any such law. In principle, such a law would not be against sharia, and Islam has allowed it under some very particular conditions. But, we neither encourage that practice, nor do we facilitate it. Indeed, even the Quran does not encourage it. Those who do this [i.e., polygamy] make miserable both their own and their families' lives. It is not good for society; and our society does not tolerate it, either. It causes hardship for women and children. The Quran makes it very clear that if you fear that you may not be entirely fair in treating multiple wives you should not have more than one; and this fairness is difficult to achieve, and the Quran has shown that difficulty. (2011, 496)

The theoretical assurances by leaders in speeches and meetings soon proved inadequate; hence the introduction of a series of policies and programs, most differing from conservative Muslims' patriarchal way of life and/or patriarchal understanding of Islamic teachings. In many cases, according to some scholars, those policies and programs simply reinstated pre-revolution laws, and sometimes they went beyond them (Keddie 2007, 2008; Zibakalam 2014). Keddie provides a long list of such reforms:

> The accessibility of schools made it easier for girls to attend, as did the enforcement of single-sex primary and secondary schools …

> [with] religious leaders' endorsement of girls' education … the percentage of females among university admissions continually rose, until they were about 66 percent by the year 2003 … female literacy rose from 36 per cent in 1976 to 72 per cent in 1996 … birth rates have fallen from among the highest in the Middle East to among the lowest … limits [were put in place] on a husband's right to stop his wife from taking a job … a new marriage contract was introduced that spelled out husband's behaviour that would give the wife the right to divorce … These and later changes moved in the direction of restoring aspects of the annulled [pre-revolution] Family Protection Law. (2003, 286–92)

These changes, which happened under the pressure of women's demands for gender equality and the state's need to keep women's support, reconfigured the official understanding of religion. In essence, the ruling clergy seemed to move away from its own conventional Islamic teaching towards more secular, pragmatic positions. As Keddie (2006, 293) comments, "Sometimes provisions once denounced by clerics as secular heresies passed Parliament as Islamic reforms." She also argues that, while it may be true that an Islamic government may never be truly gender-egalitarian, "the possibility of evolution to something parallel to Christian democracy, a largely secular and democratic form of rule[,] should not be ruled out" (296).

The secularizing effect of women's political involvement in the revolutionary process on the state's religiously informed policies similarly altered religiously informed traditional ways of life in Iranian society. This latter result flowed, above all, from a demographic shift related to accelerating birth rates soon after the revolution.

THE NEW DEMOGRAPHICS OF THE 2000S: BABY BOOM, MARRIAGE SQUEEZE, TRADITIONAL LIFE CYCLE

Arguing that a society's demographics can affect its religious character may seem a stretch. For students of sociology, however, the connection between demography and culture goes back to the discipline's emergence, with Émile Durkheim's ([1893] 1984) *The Division of Labour in Society*. Explaining the transition of societies from *mechanical* solidarity (i.e., where people perform more or less similar functions) to *organic* solidarity (i.e., where they perform different, supplementary functions), Durkheim postulates that this process usually starts with growing "density" of population. Such density would increase residents' interactions – "moral density" – creating heightened rivalry and competition over resources. This may generate out-migration as a way to ease the pressures; and when that is not possible, it would result in an organic division of labour, in which each person would need the services offered by everybody else in the community. Durkheim proposes that the type of solidarity a society has would inform its moral character, social conscience, legal system, and so on.

A similar dynamic has been suggested for the post–Second World War "baby boom." After the war, for about two decades, fertility rates – defined as the average number of children per woman – in many countries in the western hemisphere rose noticeably. Rapid decline in birth rates followed, known as the "bust period." The initial boom and bust generated corresponding echoes in the following decades – a similar rise and fall in birth rates, only on a much smaller scale. These fluctuations in fertility rates have had enormous social, economic, and political consequences (for an example of a demography-based social analysis, see Foot and Stoffman 1996).

The demographic changes in Iran since 1960 suggest similar booms and busts, creating four distinct demographic periods (for details, see World Bank 2021). From 1960 to about 1975, fertility rates gradually declined, from 6.9 to 6.2. This period coincided with the global introduction of family planning and, in Iran, urbanization and more women in the workforce, all retarding population growth. In the second period, 1976–82, Iran's fertility rate rose back to about 6.5, and it remained above 6 till 1986. This is the period in which the 1979 revolution took place, and this cohort was the source of the post-revolution baby boom.

The economic impact of this increased fertility rate revealed itself quickly. Soon, the baby boom of 1976–82 raised demands for child-care services and elementary schooling, thereby placing significant economic and logistical demands on the government. Post-revolution administrative disarray and instability, and later the Iran-Iraq War (1980–88), exacerbated the problems. Those pressures began to cast doubts on the wisdom of encouraging larger families, as happened after the revolution, and altered policy-makers' attitudes (for reports on population statistics, see Markaz-e Amar-e Iran [Statistical Centre of Iran] 1999, 2012; World Bank 2021).

Changes in family policy in the mid-to-late 1980s ushered in a third period (1982–2007), in which the fertility rate fell from 6.5 to 1.8. This drastic drop earned Iran international recognition as one of the biggest success stories in family planning and population control (for a review of Iran's family planning program, see Hoodfar 2009). The new fertility rate of 1.8 was noticeably lower than the replacement level of 2.1, needed for a population to remain stable, and is on par with the fertility rates of some Western countries whose populations are ageing rapidly.

Concerns about a population decline soon began to emerge. Reports from Iran's 2011 census showed the scale of population ageing and raised new concerns over the economic and political fallout, so much so that, in a rare occurrence, Iran's supreme leader, Ali Khamenei, publicly apologized for the government's failure to foresee the consequences of its family-planning policies. The reversal of the previous measures ushered in a fourth period of slowly rising fertility rates since 2008, which reached the replacement level of 2.1 in 2017.

Overall population aside, such demographic booms and busts generate a "marriage squeeze" – an imbalance in the sex ratio of marriageable men and women. This is a simple demographic feature that has notable social consequences. I now turn to these concepts and their consequences, followed by their impact on religion.

Sex Ratio and Marriage Squeeze: Causes and Consequences

Sex ratio is a demographic index, calculated by dividing the number of males by the number of females. This measure can be determined, for instance, for a whole population, for people of a certain age, or for babies at birth. The world's historical range for sex ratio at birth has been 103–107 boys for every 100 girls born, a number that serves as a baseline for further comparisons. Any major deviation from this historical range signals an unusual social circumstance. For example, in certain parts of China and India the sex ratio has been unusually high, which alludes to a preference for male children and possible female infanticide. Another region with a substantially higher sex ratio is the Silicon Valley in California, which reflects the higher number of males working in high-tech companies, most of whom migrated from elsewhere. The mirror image of this situation is the low sex ratio in certain countries (e.g., Egypt, Mexico), because of male out-migration in search of economic opportunities. Black Americans too have a low sex ratio, apparently because of a higher-than-usual death rate among Black men. One instance of an imbalanced sex ratio that is particularly consequential, and very relevant to our discussion here, is the sex ratio at marriage age.

Given that the bulk of marriages in most of the world still occur in people's third decade, one might expect that the sex ratio at birth would simply carry itself through the next two-to-three decades, so the two ratios should be fairly similar. For the most part, this is correct, but two other factors interact with the initial sex ratio and create a different environment: the age difference between men and women at first marriage and the impact of population booms and busts. In almost all societies, men tend to marry women who are on average two to three years younger. As Wilson (2002) observes, there are both biological and cultural forces at work here. Biologically, the child-bearing years for women normally end at about forty-five to fifty. Given the higher risks associated with pregnancies past thirty, the range for actual child-bearing is even narrower. So a woman marrying younger has a longer time to bear offspring. However, until very recently, and still in many countries, women tend to "marry up": find partners from among more economically established men. Establishing oneself takes time; hence, a "marriageable" man would probably be older. For those reasons, men normally find younger partners, and women the opposite. Therefore, calculating the sex ratio at marriage should take this age difference into account.

An imbalanced sex ratio at marriage age – i.e., very high or very low – has serious social consequences for both men and women. In their influential book *Too Many Women?*, Guttentag and Secord (1983) listed such consequences. In high-sex-ratio populations – more men than women at marriage age – marriageable women are in short supply and hence more "valuable"; they are therefore treated with more respect, are more likely to remain in a long-term relationship, are less likely to participate in the workforce, are more likely to pursue the traditional gender roles of male breadwinner and female housewife, and are more content with those traditional roles. In such populations, the rate of depression and suicide is much lower among women, as is the number of women with great career ambitions. Several studies have shown the robust impact of sex ratio in various contexts (Bolick 2011; Campbell 2004; Courtwright 2008; Dyson 2012; Kruger and Schlemmer 2009; Lloyd and South 1996; Miller and Browning 2000; Rosenfeld and Ward 1991; Stone, Shackelford, and Buss 2007; Ward and Pampel 1985a, 1985b; Wilson 2002).

Low-sex-ratio populations (more women than men), in contrast, have fewer marriageable men, who are more likely to show promiscuous behaviour and avoid long-term commitments. In such circumstances, many women could not follow the traditional path of marrying up and staying in a long-term relationship. Those women will then shift to non-traditional paths and ways of life, such as entering the labour force, pursuing higher education, following a career, settling for short-term relationships with non-committal male partners or longer-term relationships with same-sex partners, joining social movements, and, finally, adopting feminist perspectives. Given the surplus of women in the marriage market in such low-sex-ratio environments, the rates of divorce start rising, especially initiated by men, and the possibility of remarriage remains low for women and high for men. The number of female-headed single-parent families will grow.

In normal circumstances, there is a relative balance between the population of the younger women and the older men in the marriage market. However, such a balance is disrupted when population growth starts accelerating. The base of the population pyramid begins to expand rapidly, making each younger age group more numerous than the previous, older one. Two to three decades later, this imbalance carries itself into the marriage market, by creating an oversupply of women. This is a function of the age difference at marriage that we saw above, so women now have to find their marriage partners from among the men in a much smaller cohort – the "marriage squeeze" – wherein many marriageable women do not find a life partner. Demographic and social trends in Iran in about 2005 began showing all the classic symptoms of such a situation.

IRAN'S "MARRIAGE SQUEEZE" IN THE 2000S

As we discussed above, between about 1976 and 1985, Iran experienced an accelerating birth rate, which became one of the world's highest. Had everything remained consistent all the way through, the children born in that period should have normally reached marriageable age between about 2000 and 2005. However, official government statistics are very revealing: as figure 8.1 shows, the average age at first marriage has also been consistently rising: from 24.9 to 27.4 for men and from 19 to 23 for women during the period 1956–2016. These rising averages pushed back the "marriage squeeze," so it appeared about 2005.

Reflecting these trends, figure 8.2 reports an estimate of the populations of men and women at marriage age in 2006. The data clearly show the low-sex-ratio pattern – i.e., a surplus of about 900,000 marriageable women. The surplus exists for both rural and urban areas, but it is more pronounced in the latter, for the bulk of the early-1980s baby boom occurred in cities.

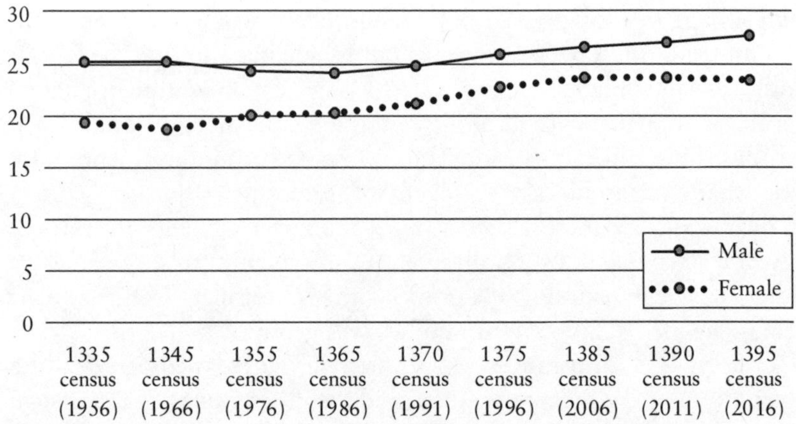

Figure 8.1 Average age at first marriage, by sex, 1956–2016.
Source: Centre of Statistics, Iran, https://www.amar.org.ir, accessed 11 May 2021.

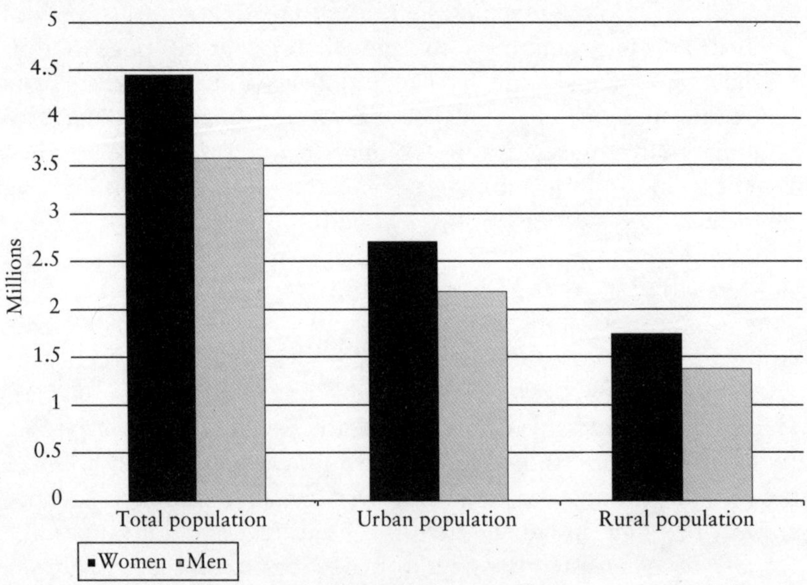

Figure 8.2 Marriage-age population in mid–2000 (estimate), by sex and urban/rural area.
Source: Author's calculations, based on census data from Centre of Statistics, Iran, https://www.amar.org.ir, accessed 11 May 2021.

"Marriage Squeeze" and Religiosity

What would be the likely consequences of this low-sex-ratio environment? Above, I listed some of them. Even a passing look at the news headlines in Iran shows that almost all of them have surfaced, and most have run contrary to traditional religion and the Islamic principles promoted by the state. To be sure, the causal line between a society's demographic features and its socio-economic conditions is far from straight, inevitable, and one-way. Often culture and customs mediate the influences of demography. So it would be necessary to examine each of the above possibilities separately and find out the extent to which they have materialized in the specific conditions of Iran.

A low-sex-ratio population may increase divorce rates and men's remarriage. As in any other society, domestic law could shape these phenomena. Four legal provisions in Iran affect divorce. First, to discourage divorce, the state makes the process so complex and cumbersome that many people choose de-facto divorce. Second, it is particularly difficult for women to initiate divorce. Third, men – on the basis of Islamic jurisprudence – may wed up to four women at the same time. Fourth, men and women may marry on a temporary basis (*mot'aa*) for a limited term that may vary from several hours to several years. These legal complexities influence the ways in which a low sex ratio in Iran may affect marriage.

Thus a low sex ratio may increase divorces (particularly those initiated by men), polygamy, and temporary marriages. Official data on these are difficult to obtain, due to the hesitancy of authorities to admit to their presence; hence we need to rely largely on unobtrusive measures, such as heightened sensibility and intensification of debates on certain issues as a proxy for their increase in frequency.

For divorce, all the evidence points to a sudden increase. According to government estimates, divorce rates in Iran are as high as one for every seven marriages nationwide, and one for every 3.76 marriages in Tehran. A 2016 article in the *Los Angeles Times* quotes reports by the official news agencies that "more than 3 million educated Iranian women over 30 are unmarried" and that "in the last nine months of 2015, the number of registered marriages nationwide dipped by 3.4%, while divorces rose by 4.2% from the previous year" (Bangali and Mostaghimi 2016). Other reports have indicated that the age at divorce is fast declining, as more and more young couples are filing for divorce, and within the first five years of their marriage. The official reasons for rising divorce rates range from "Western influences" to "economic challenges," and from "materialistic lifestyles" to "sexual difficulties." But, according to a *New York Times* reporter, the most influential factor has been "a deep-rooted awakening in Iranian women that is altering traditional attitudes toward marriage, relationships, careers and, generally speaking, women's place in what is still an overwhelmingly patriarchal society" (Yong 2010).

Even though divorce was initially a men's right, some post-revolution laws allowed women to initiate the process in "special circumstances" – that is, extreme physical abuse by a husband, the latter's addiction, or his failure to provide for the family. This change resulted in more divorces initiated by women. To facilitate these, according to Yong (2010), some women gave up their *mahrieh* – the husband's commitment at the time of marriage to pay a lump sum of cash to his wife whenever she requested – which becomes obligatory upon divorce.

This major social change – more woman-initiated divorces – found two symbolic manifestations. The name of a religious day on the Iranian calendar was altered from "marriage day" to "no-divorce day" (Yong 2010). And the first Iranian movie to win the Academy Award (in 2012) was titled *Separation* and narrated the story of a woman-initiated divorce (the same director won a second Oscar five years later). The fact that international movies are nominated by their home governments indicates that such divorces had become frequent enough in Iran to break the previous stigma and to convince the authorities to let a film about such a break-up represent the country on an international stage. Obviously, these officials, always so careful not to let any negative depiction of Iran appear onscreen, must have felt that *Separation* does not reveal much about the country that it is not already known.

Has the low sex ratio in Iran led to an increase in polygamy? Official statistics indicate that it is still rare. In the absence of direct information, one can obtain a sense of its frequency by calculating the sex ratio of those officially married – that is, by dividing the number of married men by the number of married women, multiplied by 100. A score lower than 100 would indicate the presence of polygamy (one man married to more than one woman); a value higher than 100, polyandry (one woman married to more than one man); and a score of 100, just monogamy. The calculated scores for Iran, based on the 1996 census, are 99.3 for the whole country, 99.9 for urban, and 98.3 for rural areas. While these numbers show that polygamy does exist, they also indicate that it is very rare and mostly rural. This is not a surprise, given its highly stigmatized nature in Iranian culture, even though it is allowed by law and sometimes justified by religious and political authorities as socially useful for looking after widows and orphans. This is different from some other Muslim countries in the Middle East, in which polygamy has been mostly a sign of class status and an indicator of high income, showing the husband's financial ability to support multiple wives and families.

Partly as a result of the stigma attached to polygamy, Iran has witnessed an increase in "temporary marriage" and "white marriage." A temporary marriage is a low-commitment, religiously allowed relationship that can be ended at any time through mutual agreement, and without having to go through a lengthy and complicated legal process. The partners spell out the duration of their union at the outset – as short as an hour or a day, or as long as many years. When the union has a longer duration, it comes fairly close to the common-law relationship in Western countries, or what is called in Iran a "white marriage"; when it is too short, it becomes similar to dating, a one-night stand, even prostitution.

The Iranian government has tried many times to formalize all the details of temporary marriage. At times, it has even encouraged the procedure as a healthier and more legitimate substitute for unregulated and free sexual relations among young people. According to one estimate, in the span of only one year (2011–12), the number of temporary marriages rose by about 25 per cent – although authorities prefer not to give any official statistics. Despite occasional publicity campaigns and legal facilitation by the state, temporary marriage continues to face a strongly negative popular stigma. However, such a stigma is attached only to the formal and ritualized version; in the broader society, and particularly among younger people, dating and common-law relationships – "white marriage" – continue to be practised widely.

Pursuit of further education and paid employment by women is another feature of low-sex-ratio environments. The increase in the number of financially independent single women at marriage age will in turn make that a viable option and a sustainable way of life. To what extent has this happened in Iran? The existing data clearly show that educational attainment for women has been rising quite rapidly at all levels, from primary to post-secondary. Some recent government reports have suggested that young women now make up about 65 per cent of university students. Also, some comments from government officials indicate that women are in general more committed to obtaining an education than their male counterparts. The fast increase in the proportion of female university students has recently triggered debate among more conservative elements in government about introducing a gender-based quota to control the male–female balance among students. The Ministry of Higher Education has recently adopted a new policy that expands the list of disciplines that are off-limits to women.

Other indicators of educational attainment also point to rising levels for women. Figure 8.3 reports the level of literacy for both sexes over a four-decade period. While literacy rates have been rising for both sexes, gains for women have been much more pronounced and consistent. In the last two decades reported in this graph, 1976–96, rates remained virtually the same for men, but jumped about 40 per cent for women.

Increasing educational and occupational opportunities, combined with obstacles on the traditional path of marriage, could lead to more women participating in social movements and adopting a feminist outlook. In other words, a low sex ratio encourages feminist movements and heightened emphasis on gender-egalitarian policies and cultures. Empirical verification of whether this has occurred in low-sex-ratio post-revolution Iran is very difficult, because only one or two opinion surveys cover a long period of time. However, the limited data available tentatively confirm that gender-egalitarian and feminist discourses have intensified among women in Iran since 1979.

But, before reporting the statistics on this, I need to make a conceptual point. Feminist and gender-equality discourses are essentially views on how to distribute societal resources and opportunities among men and women. When such resources are plentiful, normally disagreement is absent or does not necessarily result in differential access. When resources are scarce, however, different views or hidden structures of power may determine who obtains access to what. So, assessing the embeddedness of gender-egalitarian views in a given society has to involve both the attitudinal and the institutional dimensions of the issue. Given our focus on the gender-egalitarian views, we focus on the former here.

Figure 8.4 illustrates the proportion of the population who think that, in the case of scarcity of jobs, the priority in hiring should be given to men. The data are reported separately for young men and women (fifteen to twenty-four) in six countries – Canada, Egypt, Iran, Turkey, the United Kingdom, and the United States – in the World Values Survey (wave 4, 2000–04) (Inglehart et al. 2018). We can see

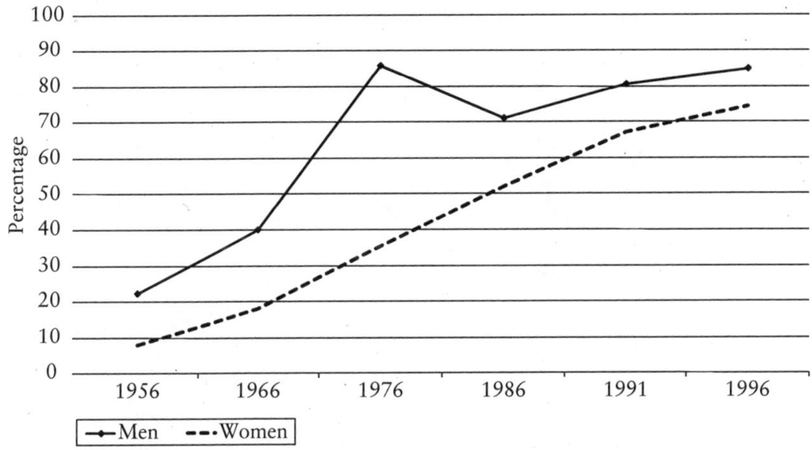

Figure 8.3 Literacy rate of population (six years and older), by sex, 1956–96. *Source*: Centre of Statistics, Iran, https://www.amar.org.ir, accessed 11 May 2021.

immediately the significant difference in the general profiles of the three Western countries and of the three Muslim countries – in the former, less than 20 per cent would give men priority, and in the latter, from 40 per cent to above 90 per cent. Also clear: except in the United States, men in all countries report a higher percentage than women. The combination of these two features confirms a certain proportion of patriarchal views in most of these nations, but significantly higher in the more traditional countries of the Middle East. Breaking down the numbers by gender shows that, in the latter countries, even a large proportion of women would give priority in hiring to men.

Crucial to our questions here, however, is the magnitude of the difference between the rates for men and for women – see figure 8.5. I argue that the larger the difference, the greater the degree of difference between men and women on who should receive scarce societal resources. When the numbers are relatively similar for both genders, one should expect a cultural orientation that is nationwide and not gender-specific. When they differ noticeably, one should expect more gender-specific views. In the latter case, when the percentage is higher for women, a traditional perspective is prevalent; when it is lower, gender-egalitarian and feminist orientation are more prevalent. The magnitude of this difference for the six countries, reported in figure 8.5, shows the largest difference for Iran, indicating that a much smaller proportion of Iranian women share the views of their male counterparts; hence women's wider embrace of gender-egalitarian views.

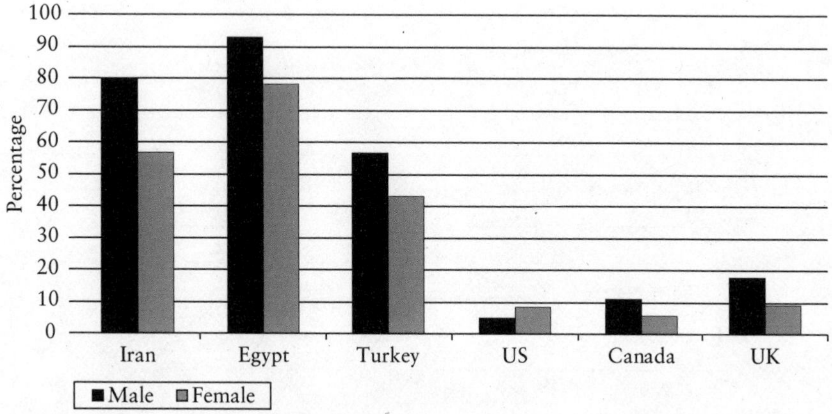

Figure 8.4 Proportion who agree with the statement "when jobs are scarce, the priority should be given to men."
Source: Inglehart et al. 2018.

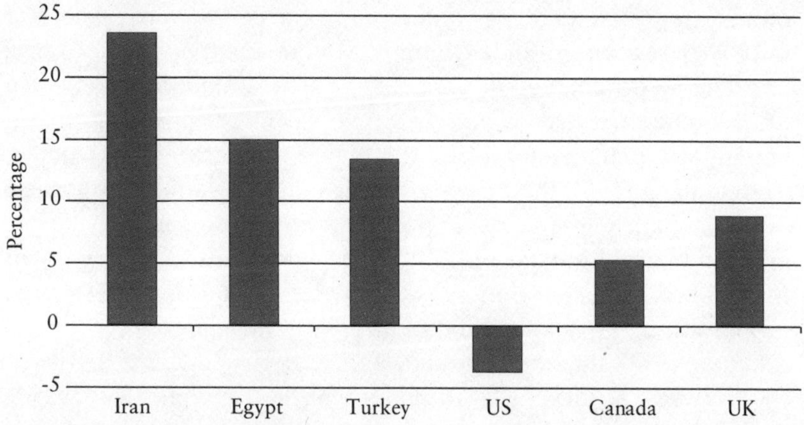

Figure 8.5 The gender difference (men minus women) in the proportions of those who agree with the statement "when jobs are scarce, the priority should be given to men."
Source: Inglehart et al. 2018.

Has the above difference between Iranian women and men changed over time? The data in figure 8.6 report the distribution of responses to the question of whether, "everything else being equal, the priority should be given to male or female job applicants"; the answers are reported based on two surveys conducted in 1996 and 2000 (see Mohseni 2000; NSVA 2001). The reported numbers show a drastic drop in the proportion

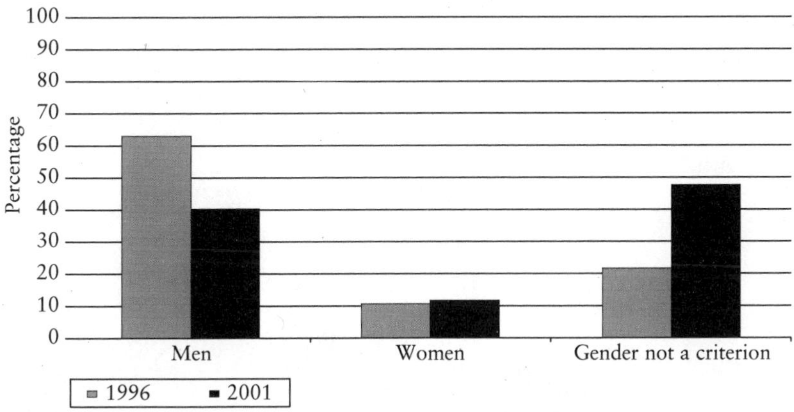

Figure 8.6 Everything equal, would you choose men or women for a specific job? *Source*: Mohseni 2000; NSVA 2000.

who favour men, and an increase of about 30 per cent in the number who think gender should *not* be a factor. This significant increase over a mere five years suggests a seismic shift in the social environment. Unfortunately, data limitations prevent our breaking down the answers by gender.

The views by themselves, however, do not automatically inform daily practice. As we know, there can always be a discrepancy between attitudes and behaviour. A question in two surveys conducted in 2000 and 2003 can act as proxy for the gendered nature of daily practices and policies: "whether men or women enjoy more opportunities for self-advancement." Despite a fairly short time between the two surveys, figure 8.7 reveals an interesting pattern, with an increase of about 30 per cent in the proportion who think women now enjoy more such opportunities and a decline in the other two categories. This trend is consistent with the theoretical expectations of low-sex-ratio environments we discussed above.

As is the case in similar situations, however, a group that is losing out – in terms of opportunities available – tends to argue that more opportunities are available to the competing groups. In this case, it is possible to imagine that men's claims that women have more opportunities are just a way for them to protest the decline of opportunities for themselves. A more refined analysis could come from breaking down the above answers by gender. Figures 8.8 and 8.9 (from NSVA 2000, 2003) report those two sets of answers, and the profiles of the answers given by men and women remain almost identical. In other words, the view that women enjoy more opportunities than men is reported not only by men, but also by women themselves.

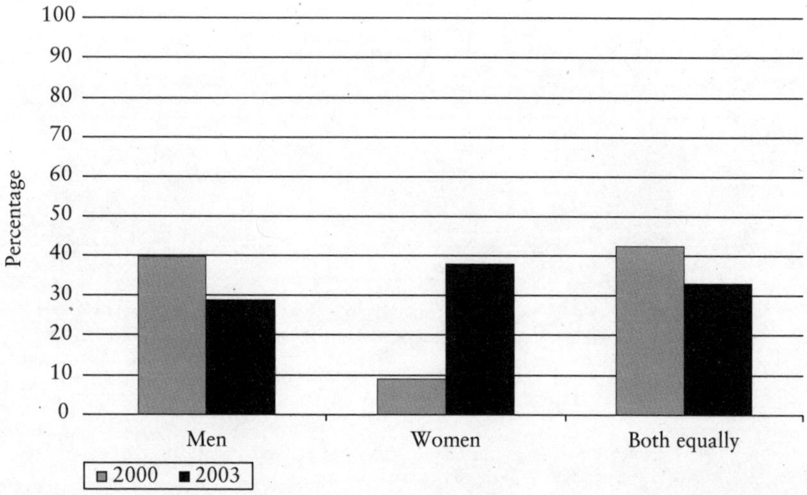

Figure 8.7 In your opinion, which group – men or women – enjoys more opportunities for self-advancement?
Source: NSVA 2000; 2003.

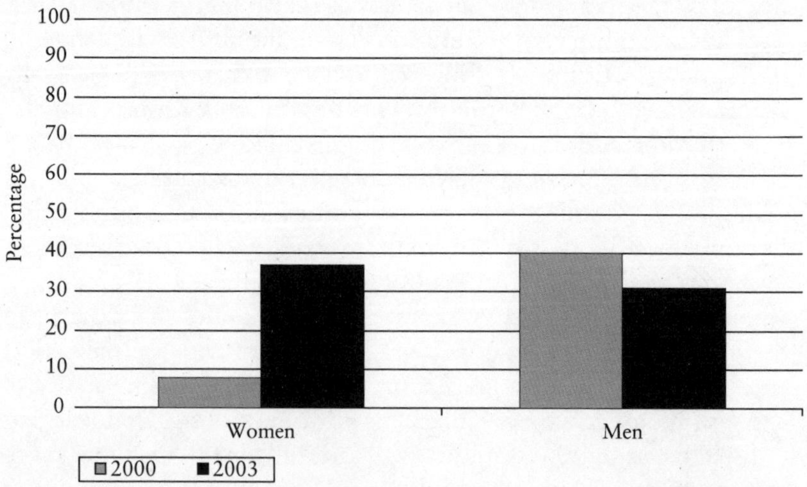

Figure 8.8 In your opinion, which group – men or women – enjoys more opportunities for self-advancement? Women's responses.
Source: NSVA 2000; 2003.

This finding could be taken as suggesting a major change in attitudes – and to a lesser extent in practices – with regard to gender (in) equality. More gender-egalitarian and feminist outlooks seem to be emerging among both men and women, particularly among women.

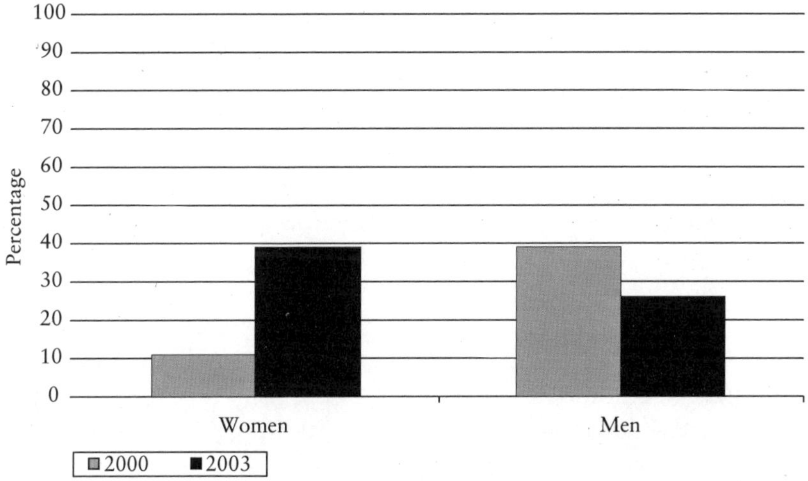

Figure 8.9 In your opinion, which group – men or women – enjoys more opportunities for self-advancement? Men's responses.
Source: NSVA 2000; 2003.

Relating this to the discussion above, we can argue that the gender-related changes in Iranian society are compatible with the implications of a low-sex-ratio population.

While no social phenomenon could be attributed to only one factor, the data presented above seem to confirm the general implications of the sex-ratio argument proposed by Guttentag and Secord (1983). The demographic as well as the attitudinal changes in Iran suggest a tectonic shift, creating more demands by women for socio-economic equality, and informing a path and way of life that are almost diametrically opposed to the traditional way of life informed by conservative religious teachings and promoted by the clergy and the Islamic Republic.

SUMMARY

Women have been a strong force in post-revolution Iran pushing for the secularization of both traditional culture and the state's theocratic orientation. This force materialized, first, through women's participation in the social protests of the 1979 revolution, and a resultant new set of demands for equality that could not be granted using the preferred, conventional, jurisprudential approach of the Islamic Republic; and later, due to a demographic transformation that made the traditional, religion-friendly way of life untenable for women.

How did the state respond to these demands and changes? Theoretically speaking, it could either accommodate or oppose them; and its reactions over the past four decades seem to offer a mix of both. While in the 1980s and 1990s women seemed to be receiving concessions that ran contrary to Islamic teachings and traditional culture, in the 2000s and 2010s the pendulum swung the opposite way, towards the most conservative interpretations of Islamic scriptures and an obvious preference for the most traditional ways of life. This is reflected in a lot of programs on state-run media as well as some recent policies, programs, and laws proposed in family planning and education that reinforce the traditional status of women as wives, mothers, and homemakers. The latter approach has been reinforced further, owing to authorities' realization of population ageing and their consequent campaign to promote larger families.

Why was there such a sudden, reactionary change of heart by the state after about 2000; and what are its possible consequences, particularly for secularization? As for the possible causes, one may think of a socio-political shift among Iranian women, from involvement in government-organized activities to activism in opposition politics. This change surfaced during the 1997 presidential election, which brought political reformists and the moderate President Khatami to power, but showed its full force during the protests against the results of the controversial presidential election of 2009. The massive participation of young adult women in the nationwide demonstrations after that election – many captured in the widely circulated pictures of that year – was a big announcement that the ground had moved with regard to women's place in society. The state's adoption of more traditional gender views during the past decade was a reactive response to that tremor.

As for the implications of the women's movement for secularization trends, the 2009 uprising seems to have also acted as a turning point. As I mentioned above, during the 1980s and 1990s, the state's need to keep women engaged in politics posed some serious challenges to conservative readings of Islamic jurisprudence. This resulted in several legislative changes in favour of women, most of them through re-interpretation, and undermining, of widely accepted Islamic teachings. Secularization of Islamic teachings by the ruling clergy marked this period. In the 2000s and 2010s, as women became more involved in opposition politics, many of the above revisions either remained or were rolled back. But this time the women's movement began to affect the broader society and culture. Rather than secularizing the state's Islamist ideology, it started to secularize the society's Islamic culture.

But even then, the government's return to a more traditional and conservative interpretation of Islam should not be taken as a reversion to a purely Islamic mode of operation, because this change has been triggered more by pragmatic considerations than by religious ones. For one thing, faced by an energized political opposition in the aftermath of the 2009 presidential election, the state had to now rely more heavily on its more conservative religious supporters, so it moved towards more traditional Islam to satisfy and energize this social base. Meanwhile, demographic forces have been at work. As we saw above, after the baby boom following the revolution, the government put in place rigorous population-control policies that collapsed the fertility rate in the early 1990s. This decline, in turn, set in motion a process that would generate, twenty-some years later, a high sex ratio in the marriage market, the opposite of what happened in about 2005. As we discussed above, in such environments, societal norms reinforce traditional marriage and ways of life for women. The state's more conservative position in recent years could be considered its strategic response to these new circumstances, not necessarily a more religious outlook.

PART FOUR

Early Warnings and Aftershocks in Philosophy and Religion

9

A Century of Philosophical Battles

An observer once said, "In Iran, unlike everywhere else, philosophical books sell much more than novels" (Shayegan 2013, 143). That makes philosophical publications and debates a good place for reading the pulse of the society. In the conceptual discussions in chapter 2, I made a distinction between "causes" and "reasons" that could be at work expanding or limiting religion's influence in society. Causes were actual social forces and the unintended consequences of social changes that could influence the state of religion in society; reasons involved the conscious efforts, plans, and thoughts that could expand or shrink religion's influence. In chapters 4 to 8, I explored the causes that had undermined religion's influence in post-revolution Iran. In this chapter, I turn to some "reasons" – i.e., some philosophical elements – that correspond with those causative forces.

I view these philosophical elements – reasons – not as triggering social forces but as reflecting them. Consistent with the conceptual framework introduced in chapter 2, while during critical junctures ideas (i.e., "reasons") influence the material conditions on the ground, in other times they rather reflect and express material conditions and actual forces (i.e., "causes"). I find the latter dynamic to be at work in post-revolution Iran, that is, the secularizing forces on the ground have imposed themselves on the philosophical debates of this period and have found an echo in them. With this conceptual point in mind, I now turn to the philosophical debates in Iran that have relevance for our discussion.

These debates on the place of religion in Iran and among Iranians have been under way for most of the past century, though each time with different fault lines and participants. The first debate occurred during the 1920s–30s and resembled that between Voltaire and the Christian church in Enlightenment Europe. The second, during the 1960s–70s, when opposition to the monarchy was surging, resembled that between Karl Marx and Wilhelm Weitling, in which Marx viewed religion as part, or at least a reflection, of the problem and Weitling saw it as part of the solution. The third, after the Islamic Revolution but particularly in the 1980s and 1990s, moved inside the religious camp itself as a conflict between a liberal and an authoritarian interpretation of religion, borrowing elements from the philosophical arguments of Karl Popper and Martin Heidegger. In this chapter, I offer a brief overview of these three philosophical debates, but focus on the post-1979 period.

1920S–30S: VOLTAIRE VERSUS THE POPE

Voltaire is the French philosopher who is known, among other things, for his advocacy for the separation of church and state. He died only eleven years before the French Revolution of 1789, and his ideas greatly informed the establishment of French democracy as a republic free from the influence of the Catholic church, the Vatican, and the pope.

In the 1900s and 1910s, the idea of a secular state had reached countries on the fringes of Europe and beyond it. After the Great War, both Turkey and Iran adopted this model and launched a heavy, top-down project of secularization, under the leadership of Mustafa Kemal Atatürk in Turkey and Reza Shah in Iran. The clashes were most fierce in two main battlegrounds: in the state machinery, which was supposed to free itself from the control of the established religion and the clergy, particularly in education, justice, and ownership of land; and in popular culture, which was expected to abandon some of the most traditional symbols of religious commitment, particularly the women's dress code (i.e., the veil, or *hijab*). In Iran, this project led to a severe conflict between a secular notion of the state, represented by the ideas of Voltaire, and the religious culture and establishment, represented by the shia Muslim clergy (Davari-Ardekani 2011, 356).

But this confrontation in Iran was only a mock version of what happened in Europe. For one thing, the secularizing state was interested only in the separation of religion and state, not in Voltaire's other ideas, such as freedom of religion and freedom of speech. While the French philosopher had considered his ideas part and parcel of democratization, the Iranian state sought only secularization, not democracy. The clerics, who opposed separation of mosque and state, also had a distorted image of Voltaire and his ideas. The comte de Gobineau, French ambassador to Persia (Iran) in the late nineteenth century, reported that his conversation with some Persians revealed that they saw Voltaire as "only the enemy of the clergy and the priests" and that "thinking like Voltaire means hating the mullahs" (Gobineau 2009, 44). Gobineau believed that this perception was mostly because of Russian influence, as none of Voltaire's works had yet been translated into Persian. So the absence of Voltaire's rationalism and democratic ideals reduced those debates, which started out as an Iranian Enlightenment moment, from a philosophical movement to a confrontation between a secularist state and the clergy, with a severely shrunken intellectual component.

Davari-Ardekani (2011, 259–66) confirms that the encounter between the religious philosophers, most of them clerics, and the ideas of the great Enlightenment thinkers never took a deep philosophical turn. He reports many direct or indirect conversations, which show that the philosophically inclined clerics never took the Enlightenment ideas seriously, aborting any meaningful engagement with them. Even some translators of Enlightenment works, he tells us, approached them as part and parcel of a broader modernization project, not out of a special interest in their contents.

In contrast to Enlightenment thought, however, philosophical materialism received much more attention from religious scholars and clerics:

> The new philosophy [that is, the Enlightenment ideas] did not catch much attention and was not strong enough to trigger any opposition … But, the important one [philosophical school] was materialism, whose propagation the clergy viewed as dangerous and lethal and, hence, they were not prepared to tolerate it. [Incidentally] the state authorities also disliked materialism as they viewed it as the ideological backbone of the opposition *Tudeh* Party [Iran's largest communist party during the 1940s–50s]. That was why, for so many years, most of the philosophical discussions of ours [the religious scholars] were with the materialists. (Davari-Ardekani 2011, 204–5)

The conflict with Marxism was in essence competition for the hearts and minds of the younger generation. This rivalry continued, but it took on additional layers and became more complex over time.

1960s–70s: Karl Marx versus Wilhelm Weitling

In the second half of the nineteenth century, when Marx's ideas were gaining traction among European intellectuals and political activists, Wilhelm Weitling appeared as a rival, with whom Marx had a major disagreement over the place of religion in society. While as leftist Hegelians the two men had many things in common – e.g., both belonged to the socialist movement, emphasized the class struggle, and were radical political activists – they differed significantly on the place of religion in the political struggle for freedom and equality. Marx viewed religion as part of the problem, or at least a reflection of the problem; Weitling saw it as part of the solution. Weitling believed, according to Kołakowski (1978, 174), that "the Gospel teachings have been distorted and falsified by kings and priests, who used it to defend their own privileges; but the time has come to unmask their imposture and build a new world of freedom, equality and Christian love."

Commenting on one of Weitling's books, Wittke (1950, 25–6) observed that it "reveals that its author was by nature deeply religious"; that his communism "was firmly grounded in definite moral precepts"; that it was "a vigorous protest against the existing state of society which profited through the support of an organized priesthood"; that "the remedy … was revolution, thorough and complete, not partial or compromising"; and, finally, that such a revolution would involve "the reform of Christianity itself and a return to the original characteristics of its primitive stage, when men loved their neighbors, lived in the happy days of communal property, and professed a religion which was in complete conformity with the law of nature." In short, according to Wittke, "Weitling's little book belongs in the *Christian communist* tradition" (Wittke 1950, 25, italics added).

A similar rivalry appeared in Iran between two groups of activists who were opposing the monarchy: the religiously oriented and the Marxist. During the 1930s and until the early 1950s, this rivalry intensified, mostly in response to the arrival of the communist Tudeh party. Tudeh was particularly careful not to provoke the Muslim populace and clergy activists, as reflected first and foremost in its name – Tudeh (masses, or people), without any explicit references to the party's Marxist ideology.[1]

The 1953 military coup against the nationalist Prime Minister Mohammad Mosaddegh snuffed out the political and intellectual vitality of Iranian society for almost a decade. Immediately after the coup, political activists were cracked down on and persecuted, publishers were shut down, and the military and intelligence apparatus took over the political realm. Despair and a sense of defeat dampened philosophical discussion. The deafening silence was captured in a poem by Mehdi Akhavan-Sales, in his *Akhar-e shahnameh* (The End of the Book of Kings), published three years after the 1953 coup: "In this cemetery-like and pulse-less city, one cannot hear even the sound of an owl."

This torpor was shattered in June 1963, when a series of political riots – referred to as "15 Khordad" (5–6 June) – protesting the arrest of Ayatollah Ruhollah Khomeini, shook the country and announced the conspicuous re-entry of religion into politics and against the monarchy. The state's violent oppression pushed the younger political activists away from civil disobedience and towards organized guerrilla warfare – a strategy of political activism that had considerable global popularity at the time and was led largely by Marxists, so that guerrilla fighters seemed to feel compelled to also adopt that ideology. This association complicated life for Islamist activists, many of whom were becoming guerrillas: they had to either negotiate their Islamist ideology with the heavily Marxist guerrilla organizations or abandon one in favour of the other.

In this dialogue in the 1960s and 1970s, three main Islamist players emerged. On a spectrum ranging from Marxist collaborationists to staunch anti-communists, the list would probably appear this way: the guerrilla MKO; the Sorbonne-educated historian of religion Dr Ali Shariati (1933–1977) and his followers; and the high-ranking religious authority Ayatollah Khomeini and his followers. In the Islam–Marxism dialogue, these three camps had different views on religion and spirituality in the struggle for social justice and on socialism in a school of thought informed by religion. Khomeini's position was the most straightforward: as a religious authority, he opposed Marxist philosophy and any collaboration with Marxist activists, but his ideal of social justice and his promotion of the interests of the lower classes resembled socialist ideals. The MKO, in contrast, had the most positive view towards Marxism; not only did it accept socialism as its economic model, it also considered Marxism "the science of political warfare." Shariati's stance was perhaps the most complex of the three; and the term "Christian communist tradition" used of Weitling's ideas finds its closest equivalent in him. Both Shariati and the MKO's projects helped secularize Iranian religious thought during the 1970s. Both drew many young Iranians to religion but in the process, and as an unintended consequence, also facilitated their secularization.

Shariati's Revolutionary Shi'ism

Ali Shariati's dialogue with Marxism was much more sophisticated and more elaborate than the MKO's. His political socialization had begun back in the 1940s, through his work with the Movement of God-Worshipping Socialists (MGWS), as the title of his first book makes clear: *Abuzar: The God-Worshipping Socialist*. The MGWS ideology was based on socialism, as the foundation of its ideal economic system, and on monotheism, as the ground of its philosophical perspective. Its founders criticized Marxist activists for their deep theoretical contradiction – "being materialist in their thoughts and idealist in their ethics" – and proposed that "a natural and organic relation existed between faith in God and the struggle for socialism and social justice" (Rahnema 2000, 26). This argument remained fundamental and enduring for Islamist activists till about a decade after the 1979 revolution.

Shariati's thoughts on the link between Islam and socialism find their most elaborate shape in his *Islamology* (*Islam-shenasi*), which outlined a comprehensive, militant, radical, action-oriented, and ideologically based interpretation of Islam. His theoretical model consisted of four elements: a monotheistic worldview that provides a grand reading of the universe, resembling Kant's notion of *is*; an ideology derived from that worldview, rather like the Kantian *ought*; a resultant image of the ideal/utopian society, built on the three principles Book (religious instruction), Scale (social justice), and Iron (militancy); and the ideal human being as the successor of God on earth and as the final destination. In addition, the worldview manifests itself in the ideology through three perspectives: an "anthropological position" (a philosophical definition of human); a "sociological perspective" (on the forces shaping societies); and a "philosophy of history" (how history has evolved). These last two components express Shariati's dialogue with Marxism most powerfully (Rahnema 2000, 26).

Shariati's philosophy of history, as well as his sociological perspective, creatively reproduce Marx's historical materialism (something that caused the Iranian secret police to refer to him and his perspective as 'Muslim communist' and 'Islamic socialism'; for an elaborate discussion, see Shayegan 2014; and see Alijani 2003, 66 and 82). History, he says, starts with a conflict mentioned in the holy books of the three Abrahamic religions – between Abel and Cain – as representatives of two types of societies, a *classless* pastoral community and a *class-based* agricultural society, respectively. Cain's murder of Abel signals the noisy arrival of classes and the brutal erosion of the initial classless community, marking the beginning of history. Looking past the highly religious symbolism of his language, one cannot help but remembering the first sentence of the *Communist Manifesto*: "The history of all hitherto existing society is the history of class struggles." But the similarity does not end there. In Shariati's perspective, this history ends through a global revolution, which will eradicate all classes, establish a classless society, and turn the oppressed masses into the new rulers of the world; and this is an inevitability dictated by historical necessity. Again, the *Communist Manifesto* (last paragraph): "The Communists ... openly declare that their ends can be attained only by the forcible overthrow of all existing social conditions. Let the ruling classes tremble at a Communistic revolution. The proletarians have nothing to lose but their chains. They have a world to win."

What is the essence of Shariati's project, and what are its implications for religion in Iran? The time of his writing – the 1960s and 1970s – was one of anti-colonial struggles in the developing world and political radicalism in the developed, both heavily influenced by revolutionary Marxist ideas. In interpreting Islam in a way compatible with historical materialism, Shariati was indeed subsuming Islam in the 1970s' zeitgeist. But this had a notable secularizing effect; as Shayegan (2014, 246) observes: "He was not aware that, through sociologizing the sacred nature of Islam, he was indeed secularizing it and making it erode in the unstoppable process of historical evolution." This turned Islam from a goal in itself into a means to establish a just society. This utilitarian approach to religion replaced its sacredness with its usefulness, which was decided by goals defined outside it. This dynamic effectively secularized religion.

The MKO's Ideological Shift

The MKO's secularizing effect was related to its ideological shift from Islam to Marxism in 1975, which I mentioned in chapter 3. As the largest anti-shah guerrilla organization of the 1970s, it enjoyed the support of many politically active religious leaders and the religiously inclined traditional merchant class, as well as recognition by some major regional players such as Fatah, the largest faction of the Palestine Liberation Organization. For politically active religious Iranians, the MKO seemed like a dream child, consisting mostly of university-educated young professionals, with a strong belief in Islamic principles, knowledge of the modern world, and a mastery of guerrilla warfare.

Although it moved to Marxism in 1975, the MKO's initial Islamism had Marxist elements. Indeed, at some point, the shah's secret service and state-run media started calling its adherents "Islamic Marxists." While the government was using this label to discredit it among religious Iranians, the moniker had some validity. As we saw above, the MKO's founders had declared Islam the foundation for their beliefs and Marxism the basis for their "science of political warfare." The former gave them a philosophical worldview, in which God, prophets, and holy scripture were present; the latter provided a philosophy of history based on class conflict, a deep analysis of capitalism, the proletariat, the violent revolution, and, finally, a socialist utopia. In other words, they adopted Marxism's historical materialism, but replaced its dialectical materialism with an Islamic philosophy. But their increasing engagement in guerrilla warfare generated serious doubts about this theoretical innovation.

Initially, the members found individualistic responses to their questions. Some quietly abandoned Islam in favour of Marxism; others chose to leave the MKO altogether, out of respect for its declared Islamist ideology. Over time, however, it became clear that the problem was beyond individual solutions, and the organization needed to respond. The Marxist elements first found like-minded comrades and formed a Marxist faction. In 1975, almost ten years after the MKO's founding, the openly Marxist members, now the majority of rank-and-file members, published a manifesto abandoning Islamism and adopting Marxism as the MKO's official ideology. Three years later, under heavy criticism by various political organizations, the Marxist members left the MKO and formed the Organization for the Fight for the Emancipation of the Proletariat (*Saziman-e paykar dar rah-e azadi-ye tabaghe-ye kargar*). This ended ideological evolution within the organization, but had enormous, twofold implications for the state of religion in Iran.

Up to 1975, the MKO was regarded as a happy compromise between two old foes – religious Muslim activists and atheist Marxist fighters –

but this middle ground virtually disappeared with its 1975 sea change and left a deeply polarized landscape behind: a much more heavily and traditionally religious camp and an emboldened Marxist camp.

The reactions of the former are visible in the positions of Morteza Motahhari, one of the influential and most theoretically sophisticated activist clerics. According to Sahabi (2013, 33), before the MKO's 1975 conversion, Motahhari had gone so far in defending mojahedin that he had ended up disagreeing with the mainstream clergy and even his own spiritual leader, Khomeini, by saying that "today, it is their [mojahedins'] turn; they interpret the Quran much better than we do." After 1975, however, he invented the pejorative label "*menhayioon*" (minus-ists) for mojahedin (= Muslims minus the clergy) and advised younger religious activists to "accept the leadership of the clergy" to avoid repeating the mojahedins' experience.

In the Marxist camp, confidence began to emerge, reflected in a response by Taghi Shahram, a leader of the MKO's Marxist faction, to criticism from the communist Fadaian-e Khalgh about the MKO's Marxists' keeping the original name MKO after the ideological shift. Shahram defended this decision, emphasizing that this would show the conversion as an organic and natural progression according to the laws of historical materialism. His rationale was that the move showed that, with the deepening of the class conflict and under the pressure of historical forces, mojahedins' initial Islamic, petit-bourgeois ideology *had to* transform into proletarian Marxism (Mojahedin-e Khalgh Organization 1975b).

As for its implications for secularizing in Iran, the MKO's initial ideological schizophrenia – the syncretism of Islamism and Marxism – came under severe strain as it dealt with the harsh realities of guerrilla warfare. This pressure revealed the inconsistencies and the weak points in its ideology, which did not survive the test of time. Despite some minor differences, this is roughly what the Islamic Republic's ideology went through a decade later, when the Islamists took over the state and had to run a country. In both cases, reality launched powerful secularizing forces. In other words, causes – engagement with reality – imposed themselves on reasons – ideological beliefs.

A similar dynamic acted again after the revolution, this time within the religious camp itself. Its new debates contended not with socialism or materialism, but with democracy, freedom, human rights, and, most important to it, the place of religion in society and in history.

The contents of these debates revealed a new fault line, across which a shadow of Martin Heidegger faced a shadow of Karl Popper.

1980s–90s: KARL POPPER VERSUS MARTIN HEIDEGGER

The migration of a large number of shia clerics from seminaries and theological schools to government offices after the revolution shook up philosophy. Their engagement in day-to-day administrative tasks took them away from pressing theoretical debates, while the defeat of their Marxist rivals made them feel that their mission was accomplished, and no more creative thinking was needed. With the mainstream shia establishment absent from the philosophical debates, other people stepped in and took on the heavy lifting. The most influential were two philosophers: Ahmad Fardid and Abdulkarim Soroush. Besides dealing with Islam's intellectual and ideological rivals, these two thinkers had also to wrestle with the faith itself; and both activities rendered Islam marginal in their theoretical systems. In other words, their engagement with Islam reduced its role in their philosophical theorizing – something we may refer to as "philosophical secularization."

Fardid was the linchpin of a group of Iranian intellectuals who met regularly during the 1960s–70s to discuss philosophical issues of interest. Many of those conversations revolved around themes of European philosophy and particularly the ideas of the German philosopher Martin Heidegger. Since these regular gatherings were held in Fardid's home in Tehran, this group came to be known as the "Fardidian circle" (*fardidiyeh*). Some of the regulars became influential thinkers – for example, Dariush Ashoori, Reza Davari-Ardekani, Dariush Shayegan, and Javad Tabatabayee. Eventually most of them either distanced themselves from Fardid or turned completely against him, personally and/or intellectually – except for Davari-Ardekani, a professor of philosophy at the University of Tehran, who has remained faithful to the main line of Fardid's thought (see Davari-Ardekani 2011, 311).

Abdulkarim Soroush, in contrast, emerged only after the revolution. A pharmacist by training, he had left Iran for Britain about 1970 to continue his graduate studies in both chemistry and analytical philosophy. His strong anti-Marxist positions, his scientific and philosophical training, and his command of Persian poetry made him an ideal philosophical spokesperson for the new Islamic Republic in its dealings with its Marxist rivals after 1979. In the mid-1980s, with the almost-complete disappearance of the Marxist groups, Soroush started promoting the ideas of the analytical philosopher Karl Popper. But Popper's liberal values and relativistic epistemology could not sit well with the anti-liberal values and absolutist orientation of the ruling clergy, which frowned also on Soroush's promotion of a mystical Islam, as embodied in the works of the 12th-century sunni jurist-turned-mystic Jalaluddin Rumi.

The first systematic critique of his position, however, came not from the clergy, but from Ahmad Fardid and Reza Davari-Ardekani. Philosophical warfare ensued, and the ruling clergy eventually joined in on Fardid's side. In a few short years, Soroush was pushed into the opposition ranks, was deprived of all his government and academic positions, was denied the right to give public lectures, and, eventually, was forced into self-exile in the United States.

Over the past two decades, these two camps – the "Fardidians" and the "Soroushians" – have been criticizing each other's ideas in an undeclared yet fierce philosophical warfare. While the Heidegger-Popper divide is still at its heart, the conversation has gone in entirely new directions. The Fardidians have dealt with modernity, intellectualism, Orientalism, the West, the arts, and literature. The Soroushians have explored democracy, modernity, human rights, secularism, hermeneutics, and, most recently, the nature and mechanism of God's revelation, the traits of the Prophet Muhammad, and the authenticity of the Quran. The following pages introduce the main ideas of these two thinkers and their implications for what I call "philosophical secularization" in Iran.

Abdulkarim Soroush

During the 1980s, Abdulkarim Soroush engaged in two distinct lines of intellectual activities. One involved a critique of the philosophical foundations of Marxism, the other promoted the philosophy of science; and in both, he drew on Karl Popper's ideas in works such as *The Open Society and Its Enemies* (1945) and *The Logic of Scientific Discovery* (1959). But with the eventual elimination of the Marxist opposition groups in Iran and the decline and fall of global Communism, Marxism lost its place as principal rival ideology for the Islamic Republic. As a consequence, the philosophical fault line moved inside the religious camp. As the Islamic Republic and the ruling clergy gradually developed more authoritarian tendencies, Soroush became the champion of a more liberal and democratically oriented interpretation of Islam within the religious camp. In this new battle, he dropped the anti-Marxist element in Karl Popper's philosophy and picked up its anti-fascism. The Popper-Marx struggle had now given way to a Popper-Heidegger conflict, represented by Soroush and Fardid, respectively.

Soroush secularized gradually through a fascinating intellectual journey (for an excellent review of the early part of this journey, see Ghamari-Tabrizi 2008). Right after the revolution, when he was one of the main philosophical spokespersons of the new state, he also believed in the possibility of government-led Islamization. He was therefore involved in the project to Islamize the universities, as one of the six members of the Cultural Revolution Board appointed by Khomeini to oversee the project. One of its main goals was to "cleanse" the campuses of dissident students and instructors, most of them Marxists or opposition sympathizers. After the government eliminated the Marxists, Soroush's focus shifted towards philosophy of science, mystical poetry, and a philosophical reading of *Nahj-ul-balagha*, one of the main *shia* Muslim references attributed to the first Imam, Ali. During 1988–90, and with the appearance of a series of articles entitled "The Theoretical Contraction and Expansion of Sharia" (TTCES) (later published as a book, Soroush 1992), he started exploring the notion of the secular, first implicitly, and later explicitly (for a thorough discussion of his ideas in these articles, more in relation to democracy than secularism, see Jahanbakhsh 2001).

In TTCES, Soroush explored non-religious influences on religious thinking and, particularly, on jurisprudence and *sharia*. His key argument was threefold: religion is nothing but the history of religion, or the different readings of religion produced throughout its history; one's reading of religion is influenced by one's other, non-religious thoughts, beliefs, and assumptions; and, as an implication of the first two points, we can legitimately reread religion, as a result of a change in our basic assumptions. Soroush formulated this as a descriptive account of religious knowledge and the way it evolves, rather than offering a prescriptive statement about how it should change (the latter being what seems to be implied by Jahanbakhsh 2001). However, this view of religious teachings diminished their sacredness and direct descent from God and gave them a more human quality, which paved the way for Soroush's later, more secular interpretations of religion.

Soroush's first step in a secular interpretation of Islam was his promotion of secularism as separation of mosque and state. Soroush (2000a) structured his argument as follows: unlike traditional peoples, who take the world as granted, "modern humankind has assumed the role of an aggressive and active agent in the world" by using scientific knowledge (55); then, "a revolution analogous to the one in natural sciences has overtaken the social sciences, and secularism in this sense is nothing but the 'scientification' and rationalization of social and political thought and deliberation" (57). Soroush then offers his definition of secularism:

> We may define secularism as a regime in whose polity no values and rules are beyond human appraisal and above public scrutiny. Everything is open to critique, from the head of state to the manner of government and the direction of policy determination. This is the meaning of secularism. Naturally, when politics is desacralized (that is, when it becomes rational and scientific) while religion remains sacred, the two are separated. This is the meaning of and the reason for the separation of religion and state in secular societies. (60)

Crucial here: secularism – defined as the separation of religion and state – can coexist with individual religious commitments. For Soroush, "scientific treatment of political and economic affairs does in no sense preclude a well-defined role for God and religion in political, social, and natural affairs"; even further, such commitments can in turn render the polity religious, without violating the notion of secularism: "If a society is religious, its government too will take a religious hue" (61). Thus belief in the sacred can coexist with a commitment to a secular polity (this aspect of Soroush's ideas have been discussed at length, under the notions of "scaral defence of secularism" and "religious secularity," in M. Sadri 2001; Ghobadzadeh 2015).

But more recent works by Soroush show his unease with the above proposition. Belief in the sacred would inevitably imply a hierarchical authority structure, in which the prophets remain at the top and lay-people at the bottom, so the sacred may always spill over into secular politics. Besides, the clerics, as self-declared guardians of sacred teachings and knowledge, will always remain in a superior position. Soroush therefore tries to reduce the distance between lay believers and prophets, first by elevating laypeople's ability to have prophetic experiences, then by highlighting the earthly nature of the prophets' experience. The first goal he addressed in *The Expansion of the Prophetic Experience* (2006); the second in *Prophetic Dreams* (2016).

The first title was an extension of his earlier work, *The Theoretical Contraction and Expansion of Sharia* (1992). While the latter "demonstrated the humanized, historic, and earthly nature of one's understanding of religion," the new book showed "the humanized and historic nature of the religious experience and religion itself" (Soroush 2006, i). The author introduces a series of ideas that together shrink "the sacred canopy" (Peter Berger's term) covering the prophetic experience. He challenges fundamental elements of the dominant, mostly clergy-driven narrative of the prophetic experience, including: the belief that the Prophet Muhammad's experience of the divine was unique to him and that it was the last experience of this nature; that the verses of the Quran are the exact words of God delivered to Muhammad by the Archangel Gabriel (Jibril); that the Quran was sent to the Prophet in its entirety all at once; that every single element in its verses is an essential element placed there by God's design; and that those verses contain everything that humankind needs in order to live on the right path.

In contrast to these beliefs, Soroush draws an alternative picture with at least five unconventional arguments: God has given Muhammad his key messages and has then entrusted him to deliver it in his own words; many Quran verses are not essential but rather coincidental, revealed in reference to historical events or queries directed at the Prophet; Quranic teachings provide Muslims with the minimum that is necessary, not the maximum that is possible, for them to run their lives, so believers must generate additional instructions in line with the spirit of the verses provided; Muhammad's prophetic experiences evolved over time, entering new dimensions and higher capacities; and, finally, as a result of all these, followers can continue having experiences similar to the Prophet's. Soroush's conclusion: "Today, the prophetic mission has come to an end, but the door is wide open for expanding the prophetic experience" (Soroush 2006, 27).

The secularizing implications of Soroush's propositions are undeniable, partly confirmed through the vehement reaction from the established mainstream clergy. These propositions, if implemented and acted on, would reduce the height of the hierarchy that separates the Prophet from ordinary Muslims and, by doing so, give more agency to believers to navigate through the mass of religious teachings, without any need for the clergy to mediate between them and the divine messages.

The liberation of individual Muslims from the controlling gaze of the clergy allows them to exercise their personal preferences and to arrive at conclusions more consistent with their other beliefs and opinions and more compatible with their personal way of life. For instance, by designating some Quranic teachings as historical and coincidental, as opposed to essential, Soroush's proposition reduces the scope of life that has to be informed by religious teachings and leaves more to secular calculations. Similarly, by proposing that the religious teachings are only the necessary minimum needful for a meaningful life, he legitimizes the incorporation of other – even non-religious – ideas into people's lives and gives those ideas the same credibility as the purely religious ones. Finally, by suggesting that an ordinary Muslim can have prophetic experiences, he generates a space for the sort of unique and very individualistic religious experiences that may not be in line with mainstream beliefs. All these changes point to a transformation similar to what Durkheim ([1897] 2013) calls "religious individualism" in his description of the shift in Christianity from Catholicism to Protestantism.

Such a transformation received further reinforcement from Soroush's two later propositions: that the wordings of the Quran are those not of God but of the Prophet Muhammad and that such wordings were the product of Muhammad's prophetic dreams. The seed of the first idea was already present in *The Expansion of Prophetic Experience*: "Let me only hint that the best way to solve the problems associated with the notion of God's talking is to consider the latter as Prophet's talking" (Soroush 2006, 14). What Soroush proposed gave the Prophet more agency vis-à-vis God, in opposition to the dominant Muslim position that Muhammad was merely a Messenger who delivered God's messages to humanity, without any creativity of his own with regard to content or style. In an interview, Soroush points to the contrast: "According to the traditional account, the Prophet was only an instrument; he merely conveyed a message passed to him by Jibril. In my view, however, the Prophet played a pivotal role in the production of the Koran" (Hoebink 2009, 272). The deviation of these views from mainstream shia theology created a maelstrom inside Iran and triggered rebuttals by high-ranking clerics (for some of those reactions, see the English translation of some of Soroush's articles on this topic, edited by Forough Jahanbakhsh, in Soroush 2009).

Soroush further humanized prophetic experience in *Prophetic Dreams* (2016a, 2019), where he addresses the mechanism through which God's messages reached the Prophet. The conventional Muslim position is that those messages were delivered by the angel Jibril. Dissatisfied with that answer, Soroush argues that the rich imagery of the Quranic verses suggests delivery through images in the Prophet's dreams, which he then put into words and passed on to his followers. This hypothesis explains the mechanism of revelation, rendering unnecessary the fixation on the detailed wording of the Quran as the exact words of God – as the traditionalists put it.

As corollaries to his theory of prophetic dreams, Soroush points to two of its implications. First, one can interpret the Quran's contents the same way as any other dream. Second, traditional seminary training will not provide that method; instead, this task should be given to the secular sciences such as anthropology, history, psychology, and sociology. This exercise in the phenomenology of revelation would further expand the individual's agency vis-à-vis revelation and God and allow more room for secular knowledge and values to determine the contents of one's religion.

Let's recapitulate how Soroush's propositions so far point in a secular direction. First, he considers secularism – the separation of religion and state – a fruit of the rationalization and scientification of socio-political life. This would automatically restrict the institutional power of the religious establishment, as it treats religiosity as an individual property, instead of an institutional force. Second, once religion is moved to the individual domain, according to Soroush, religious knowledge should be separated from religion itself and subject to earthly, historical, and human influences. Third, religion itself is historical and therefore human. Fourth, the prophetic experience is accessible to ordinary Muslims. Fifth, the text of the Quran is the words of the Prophet, not those of God. Sixth, dreams are the mechanism for the transfer of revelation, eliminating divine mechanisms such as delivery by Jibril that are out of reach of the layperson. While Soroush's propositions are those of a pious Muslim offered to Muslims, they provide for a more secular religious orientation. In that sense, secularity could be considered an unintended consequence of Soroush's philosophical-theological system.

Ahmad Fardid

During the 1990s, when Soroush and his followers began facing mistreatment by the Islamic Republic, Ahmad Fardid's followers were moving into senior government jobs. During the 2000s, these opposing trends reached their apex, with Fardid's disciples being offered cultural positions, and Soroush and many of his followers forced into self-exile. It looked as if, in the Islamic Republic's philosophical battleground, Heidegger had triumphed over Popper.[2]

It is particularly difficult to write about Fardid, due largely to his peculiar style of thinking and reasoning that earned him the labels "oral philosopher," "confused mind," and "word piercer" – labels sometimes used even by his admirers. There are three reasons for these labels: he usually lectured and had published only three articles during more than fifty years of active intellectual and academic life; his lectures were stream-of-consciousness, with no clear starting and ending points and no articulate thought process; and his etymology was peculiar, finding common roots or elements for some key words in different languages and then building some elaborate philosophical arguments on those commonalities – some well-justified, some intriguing, and others outrageous and unwarranted. Due to this lack of written works, the references to most of his thoughts and ideas cite other people's recollections of his speeches and their conversations with him, students' notes taken during his lectures, his letters, and his own sporadic notes.

None the less his intellectual project was identifiable and quite innovative: combining the ideas of Marx, the German philosopher Martin Heidegger, and the Andalusian Muslim mystic Muhyiddin Ibn Arabi into a grand anti-modernist philosophical system, both to explain humanity's past and to predict its future. The influence of Marx was visible in his philosophy of history. Like Marx, Fardid viewed the history of humankind as consisting of five main phases, which he creatively called: the day before yesterday, yesterday, today, tomorrow, and the day after tomorrow. Again like Marx, he considered the two most desirable of these five phases to be the first and the last – the day before yesterday, and the day after tomorrow – which corresponded in many respects to Marx's primitive and final communism. Heidegger's influence is visible in his idea that the bulk of the history of humankind – that is, the three middle phases – is the story of great negligence and the search for a lost paradise. Identifying these three middle phases with their intellectual and philosophical foundations, Fardid viewed them as corresponding to the Classic (Greek) era, the Modern era, and the Post-modern era. After drawing on Heidegger to conceptualize the great negligence that occurred in those three in-between eras, Fardid subscribes to Muhyiddin Ibn Arabi to explain how things were in the first desired phase and how they will be, and should be, in the last.

Fardid viewed the five phases of human history as driven and defined not by the Marxian notions of socio-economics and the class system but by their "historical destinies" – i.e., Heidegger's concept of Geschick – assigned to them by God. In defining these destinies, Fardid borrowed heavily from Islamic mystic traditions, particularly the ideas of Ibn Arabi. The starting and ending phases of human history, for him, are marked by classless and undifferentiated communities, attentiveness to God as the absolute existence, a shift away from the instrumentalist rationality of mind towards the poetic mysticism of heart to acquire knowledge, and access to "immediate insight" (*elm-e hozoori*) as opposed to "acquired knowledge" (*elm-e hosooli*).

In a secondary yet somewhat curious classification, Fardid labels the first and the last phases as "east" and the other three as "west." Human history, in this perspective, began with the "east," decayed into the "west," and will eventually return to a resurrected "east." These two terms, however, refer not to any geographical entities but rather to two philosophical perspectives and modes of viewing the world and thinking about it. According to Abdolkarimi (2015, 145-6), Fardid's notion of "westoxication" – i.e., the corrupting dominance of "west" – is the equivalent to Heidegger's "becoming metaphysicalized," a process that for him started when metaphysical reasoning took over the mystical approach in Greece about five centuries BCE and brought with it the great "negligence of Being." Fardid's innovation was that he took this notion – for Heidegger, a conceptual tool to explain the intellectual history of the West – and extended it to the history of the whole of humanity, including both west and east. In that sense, during the first and the last of Fardid's five historical phases, it is the whole world/humanity that is "easternized"; similarly, in the middle three phases, it is the whole world/humanity that is "westoxicated."

It was this anti-western element that provided the necessary link between Fardid's philosophy and the Islamic Republic's discourse. Fardid's ideas seemed to offer a philosophical critique of the intellectual foundations of modernity, as historically manifested in the West; and the Islamic Republic's discourse was a political rebellion against the world order created and protected by the West. As a result, it found a philosophical justification for its political cause in Fardid; and Fardid saw in it the beginning of a resurrected "east" and confirmation of his otherwise poorly recognized and extremely incoherent ideas. That he sees a strong connection between the Islamic Revolution and Heidegger's theory is obvious: "I use Islam to interpret Heidegger; he is the only contemporary thinker whose ideas are lined up with those of the Islamic Republic," and "Heidegger, the great teacher of contemporary thought, and Imam Khomeini are like-minded" (quoted in M.M. Hashemi 2004, 84).

For the reader familiar with Heidegger's anti-theology position, it might seem curious that Fardid could find a connection between his ideas and those of the leader of a revolution in the name of religion led by a shia Muslim cleric set on establishing a theocracy. Certainly the place of the sacred in Heidegger's philosophical system has long been a subject of controversy, with most interpreters leaning towards its absence. However, the French Orientalist Henri Curban, who introduced the German philosopher to the French, later introduced him to Iranian intellectual circles through a more religious prism.

According to Abdolkarimi (2015, 96), Curban categorically denied the possibility of a secular and non-spiritual interpretation of Heidegger and even criticized some of his young followers for ignoring the obvious connection between theology and Heidegger's key concept of hermeneutics. While both Heidegger and Curban were critical of classical Greek metaphysics and the instrumental rationality of the modern West, the former sought the solution in pre-Socratic thought, and the latter in Eastern mysticism, particularly in the ideas of the Persian mystic Sheikh Shahab-al-din-e Suhrawardy. In other words, through Curban, Iranian intellectuals learned about a Heidegger who was both more religious and more connected to Persians than Heidegger actually was (Abdolkarimi 2015). Fardid initially picked up Curban's version of Heidegger, but later replaced the mysticism of the Persian Suhrawardy with that of the Andalusian Muhyiddin Ibn Arabi.

This innovative combination of ideas made Fardid's views attractive to "an important segment of the community of Iranian intellectuals eager to reassert their own identity during a time of change both in the East and in the West" (Boroujerdi 1996, 65). Initially, these followers were not particularly religious, and were longing only for a "nativist" philosophical position that would set Iran apart from the modern Western world. But, with the Islamic Revolution and Fardid's frequent expressions of loyalty towards the Islamic Republic, the non-religious figures gradually left the crowd and the religious ones moved closer to him. For this new audience, the appeal of Fardid's ideas was no longer limited to its broad critique of the philosophical foundations of modernity, but lay in his direct attacks on its pillars and manifestations, such as modern science, modern technology, and humanism. These critiques could now help the Islamic Republic's state-supported intellectuals to give themselves a global and historic place, but also to suppress its local opposition as a bunch of westoxicated individuals.

In Fardid's post-revolution remarks, one can find many positive references to Islam, *shi'ism*, the Islamic Republic, and even the concept of jurist-ruler:

> It is through the Mohammadan truth and with the intervention of the 12th Imam that humanity will be saved ... The source of wisdom is the Quran ... The righteous are those who are under the prophetic leadership and the leadership of Imam Ali and the 12th Imam ... The truth that will emerge through Muhammad is different from what had emerged through Moses and Jesus ... The Shia principles are much less contaminated by philosophy ... The great advantage of us Iranians is that we have the Quran and we believe in Muhammad as the last prophet ... The world today needs a revolutionary Messianic mission, and a clear example of that could be found in the Islamic Republic and ... the concept of the leadership/rulership of the *faqih*. (quoted in Abdolkarimi 2015, 299–303)

Fardid went so far as to justify the new state not as theocracy, with its negative connotations, but as an "Allah-cracy" (quoted in Abdolkarimi 2015, 43). An alliance between Fardid and the Islamic Republic was gradually emerging.

It may appear that Fardid's ideas could promote the government's cause of Islamization by providing it with a relatively coherent philosophical foundation. In reality, however, while Fardid's framework offered the state a philosophical framework for anti-Western rhetoric, it did not sit well with Islam (or Christianity, for that matter). Both faiths had emerged in Fardid's *yesterday* phase of human history – the

Classical era and the Middle Ages – which he saw as a deviation from the initial, desirable phase. He considered the dominant mode of thinking in Islamic civilization a mere reflection of Greek philosophy. The only exception for him was the mysticism, and that only of Ibn Arabi. Fardid seemed to be fully aware of this contradiction in his philosophical system, as, according to Hashemi (2004, 137), he chose to remain silent "on the general issue of religiosity, and the particular issue of the historical Islam … [and indeed] on any issue directly related to religion [Islam]."

Furthermore, Fardid's admiration for Islam and the Islamic Revolution comes into an unresolvable conflict with Heidegger's anti-theology. Fardid himself couldn't miss it; hence his statement that "Heidegger and I think similarly but we do not say the same thing, because I am an Iranian Shia Muslim and he is a German Christian philosopher" (quoted in Abdolkarimi 2015, 300). None the less Fardid did not offer any theoretical resolution, so his pro-Islamic position remained an ad-hoc addition that was never integrated into his philosophical system. As a result, his critics have considered his positive assessment of Islam either politically opportunistic or due to the prevalence of romanticism in the early years after the revolution.

SUMMARY

This chapter offered not a detailed account of philosophical currents in Iran, but a sketch of the main philosophical debates during the twentieth century and the place of religion in them. My reading of those intellectual trends is that greater engagement with realities on the ground transformed each, leading to increasing secularism in one form or another. This was evident during the 1920s–30s in the strongly anti-clerical reading of Voltaire; during the 1960s–70s, in the MKO's ideological shift from Islam to Marxism; and during the 1980s–90s, in the increasing incorporation of secular elements in the ideas of Soroush and in Fardid's muted treatment of Islam.

In many respects, these currents mirrored those in the state's political philosophy, which we examined in chapter 5. There, too, increased engagement with day-to-day realities constantly challenged the initial ideas and forced a more pragmatic and secular stand. While the language in both realms remains rich in religious symbolism, the essence of the arguments becomes increasingly secular. An accurate reading of post-revolution religious trends requires a careful separation of these two layers, external and internal, form and essence, language and thinking. Such a separation would then allow for a more accurate understanding of sacred and secular, which treats them not as mutually exclusive, but rather as heavily intertwined.

10

Everyday Theology

Revealing Episodes since 1979

Chapters 4 to 8 covered the main transformations in religion in Iran in the four decades since the Islamic Revolution of 1979. The central theme throughout was that, beneath a religious façade, an intense secularization has been under way, which has manifested itself in many areas of life, from the political philosophy of state to the religious beliefs and practices of ordinary people, and from institutional domains to individual lives. Our analyses of these changes have revealed the kinds of processes that transform a society at a broad structural or deep foundational level, somewhat similar to what Fernand Braudel would call the *longue durée*; but we should supplement them with a look at the short-range alterations similar to what Paul Lacombe calls "episodic history" (for a discussion of these, see Braudel and Wallerstein 2009). We need to combine the long-term and short-term happenings because the former are not always perfectly linear; rather, they go through ebbs and flows, which can be captured in episodic history.

In this chapter, I discuss some of these episodic and short-term changes, which can give us a picture of where the country stands at the moment. Specifically, I discuss six of these and their influences on religious trends in Iran: the Iran–Iraq War of 1980–88; the rise of ceremonial/ritualistic religiosity and shia–sunni identity politics; the new wave of "spiritism" and "spiritualism"; the deepening of the religious-secular divide in urban space; women's-rights movements; and intensifying out-migration from Iran.

THE IRAN-IRAQ WAR (1980–88)

The eight years of war between Iran and Iraq changed the fabric and content of religiosity in post-revolution Iran, initially having a sacralizing effect and later a secularizing one. The fact that the war started only twenty months after the revolution, and that it was initiated by Iraq, allowed for the revolutionary discourse to stretch its relevance for several more years. In that discourse, which was greatly influenced by religious symbolism associated with the historical minority status of shia Muslims, injustice was viewed as the prime evil, and the struggle for justice as the greatest virtue. Volunteer participation in the war was therefore viewed by many people, especially the young, as an opportunity to fulfil this religious duty.

Against this background, the post-revolution state effectively used its arsenal of religious symbolism – particularly that associated with the events of Ashura/Karbala commemorating the martyrdom in 680 of the third Imam, Hossein – to mobilize human and material resources in support of the war effort. In this state-initiated discourse, participation in the conflict was portrayed as an act of joining in with a great shia Muslim imam in his fight against injustice, even if 1,400 years later. In this struggle, there was no possibility of defeat, as one either wins the fight – victory in the war – or wins the battle, if he is killed and reaches the honourable status of a martyr. This simple message with its dual elements – the responsibility to participate and the irrelevance of the outcome – was promoted through the works of two figures: Sadegh Ahangaran, a religious mourning singer, whose encouraging lyrics and innocently simple musical structure became a prerequisite fixture for any major military operation; and Abdolhossein Dastgheib, a high-ranking ayatollah whose books on Islamic morality and spirituality were widely read by the volunteer fighters, and whose main message was a special kind of fatalism: the irrelevance of individuals' desires and purposes vis-à-vis God's will and plans. This campaign intertwined the war and religious sentiment.

But the conflict's end in 1988 ushered in a new phase, with great consequences for religion, but in an opposite direction. For one thing, the war ended with no obvious victory for Iran. Even though Iran had contained the Iraqi invasion, this was not its goal. Energized by their own great success in pushing Iraqi forces back to the border by the end of the conflict's second year, Iranian political leaders and the Revolutionary Guard commanders had aimed not only to liberate the remainder of their territory but also to free Palestine from Israeli occupation and end injustice in the world. The famous slogan of the war's last few years – "*Jang, jang, ta raf'e fitne dar alam*" (War, war, till the erasure of injustice in the world) – clearly reflected that aim. The no-victory/no-defeat outcome was a far cry from this ambitious goal and hence brought significant political and religious ramifications.

Politically, Ayatollah Khomeini likened his decision to end the war without a clear victory to "drinking the cup of poison"; admitting such a lethal political mistake – supporting, for eight years, a struggle that could not be won – robbed him of his once-larger-than-life image and triggered a process of what Weber would call the "routinization of charisma." In religion, massive doubts followed, given the parallelism evoked between the war's events and the history of shia Islam and the heavy use of religious symbolism to justify continuing the conflict.

For those who remained faithful, the post-war environment and the beginning of "reconstruction" called for a different type of religiosity. First, the revolutionary forces were moved from the military realm into the economic. The pragmatist political leaders – led by the new president, Akbar Hashemi Rafsanjani – wanted to deflect the extreme frustration of the Revolutionary Guards, who had invested heavily in the war and harshly criticized the politicians' decision to end it. Some of them were eager to create other conflicts in order to prove themselves (for an excellent discussion of the role of the factional politics in the continuation of the war, and the religious consequences of Iran's lack of victory in the war, see Ayatollahi-Tabaar 2018, chapter six). Second, the Islamic Republic, now desperately in need of foreign investment, entered a process of détente with its former regional and global enemies and started behaving as a reliable player in the new world order. Third, economic liberalization started creating business opportunities for some citizens and worsening conditions for others. In this new liberal vision, people were seen no longer as potential revolutionary soldiers, but as businesspeople, customers, and consumers. The new president called for his fellow Muslims to behave according to this new framework through a "show of excessive consumption" (*manovr-e tajammol*). Together, these changes rendered the previous revolutionary religious discourses irrelevant and anachronistic.

Religion now had to play a different role or, more precisely, various roles, depending on the audience and the clientele. Ritualistic religiosity arose, linked to *shia–sunni* identity politics, and a host of new spiritual practices emerged.

THE RISE OF CEREMONIAL/RITUALISTIC RELIGIOSITY, LINKED TO SHIA-SUNNI IDENTITY POLITICS

With the declining legitimacy of the state-sanctioned religious discourse, those people who were more religious realized, according to Rahmani (2014, 149), that they needed a new way of practising their religion that was different from both the pro-government type of religiosity (promoted by the state) and traditional Islam (promoted by the seminary-centred clergy). The outcome was the emergence of a "popular/communal religion" (for a detailed historical review of the changes in the mission, function, and structure of religious confraternities in Iran, see Mazaheri 2011). The new practice had two defining features: shia identity (instead of the previous, now-failed sunni–shia unification campaign) and rituals (at the expense of beliefs). The new shia-centred policy was followed at home and abroad, leading to formation of what Vali Nasr has called a "shia crescent" in the Middle East. Domestically, it led to a vast campaign to augment shia rituals and ceremonies, as well as expand shia religious sites (e.g., Jamkaran, Arba'een in Iraq, restoration of many shrines). There was also a corresponding shift away from religious knowledge to religious sentiment; hence the larger roles for religious singers and preachers compared to religious scholars (for an elaborate discussion, see Mazaheri 2019). All these traits feature heavily during Ramazan, with activities around fasting, and even more during Muharram, the month of mourning for the martyrdom of shia's third Imam, Hossein ibn Ali.

The Muharram observances have even crossed over into shia-majority Iraq. During the past few years, an annual 80-kilometre procession has been held in Iraq, between Najaf and Karbala, to commemorate the fortieth day of Hossein's martyrdom. In this Arba'een Procession (*Rahpaymayee-ye arba'een*), more than 2 million Iranians join their Iraqi fellow shia Muslims, making it comparable in scale to the *hajj*, to Mecca and Medina. The ceremonies, in both countries, reveal a great deal about the new religious atmosphere in Iran.

On the domestic side, Rahmani (2014) sees, in post-revolution Iran, a new type of religiosity among the urban lower classes, because of their dissatisfaction with the traditional clergy and as a response to the state-affiliated clergy. This movement centres around the Muharram mourning rituals; he calls it the "Karbala discourse" for the city of Hossein's martyrdom. Its defining elements are symbolism associated with the martyrdom, an exaggerated sense of inferiority towards the main figures of that tragic story, participants' inflicting pain and suffering upon themselves during the mourning rituals, which centre around a group of religious pop singers, and over-representation of young people as well as the disadvantaged urban lower classes. Rahmani notes this movement's distance from almost all other major religious groups in Iran.

Focusing on the Arba'een Procession in Iraq, Mazaheri (2018a, 230) points to its fluidity as empowering for participants, because it gives them a say in its format and contents – an antidote to the influences of both state and religious establishments. This may also help explain the expansion of ceremonial expressions of religiosity, as reflected in the many tents and temporary *hosseiniehs* set up during Muharram.

Despite all the religious elements in this new movement, it is not all that religious. After all, under a theocratic state enforcing powerful religious symbolism, even the most secular activities will have to find a religious appearance in order to survive. Shekarchi (2018) shows some of these non-religious elements, in an empirical study of the reactions by the Iraqi hosts of the Arba'een ceremony to the Iranian visitors. Their positive comments revolve around religious devotion, discipline and order, good hygienic practices, and so on; their complaints relate to decidedly unreligious behaviour, such as not observing women's Islamic dress code, carrying knives, buying and selling street drugs, and incest and sodomy.

Besides, Iran, like any other society, has an embedded "structure of opportunities," which makes certain types of activities more accessible and affordable than others and, through that, encourages people to take advantage of those opportunities. The contributors to Mazaheri's (2018b) *The Arba'een Procession: Some Sociological Reflections* (*Piyade-ravi-ye Arba'een: ta'amolat-e jame'e-shenakhti*) have shown the many such secular forces at work during these religious ceremonies. These include socialization for younger people, particularly for young single women, otherwise restricted in mobility; inexpensive foreign travel, especially attractive to people with limited resources; social prestige and distinction upon return, as evident in extravagant ceremonies held by returning travellers' families; and suspension of everyday routines in favour of an extraordinary socio-psychological experience (for an excellent dicussion of this, see Razavi-zadeh 2018).

NEW "SPIRITUALITIES"

The era after the Iran–Iraq War witnessed the rise of new spiritual perspectives and exercises in Iran, all cultivating practitioners' individual and inner selves. This has taken at least three distinct forms: secular, informed by the ideas of Carlos Castaneda, Paulo Coelho, Gibran Khalil Gibran, and Krishnamurti, as well as Mohammad-Ali Taheri's "cosmic mysticism"; government-promoted, captured in the notion of the "Friends of God" (*awliya' allah*), seeking to purify the soul and cut off worldly attachments; and oppositional, with roots in post-revolution religious reformism and informed by Mostafa Malekian's "rationality and spirituality" project (for an excellent discussion of these trends, see Doostdar 2018).

The first trend revolves around spiritism – i.e., communication with the spirits of deceased people and with *jinn* – and is more popular among urban professionals and the upper middle class. Often, small groups gather in one member's home and, under the supervision of a master, engage in spiritual exercises that range from simple practices like meditation and yoga to more complex and taxing ones like encounters with occulted entities such as spirits and *jinn*, sometimes informed by abstract concepts such as "cosmic mysticism." Based on rich anthropological fieldwork, Doostdar (2018) has shown that, while the practices sometimes resemble those of traditional religion, participants often try to reconcile these experiences with rational and scientific thinking.

The second trend – centered on the Friends of God – is heavily promoted by government initiatives, perhaps to appease religious segments of the population left behind in the post-war boom and to create an alternative to secular spiritual practices. This campaign promotes non-interest in economics and disengagement from politics – both instrumental for a totalitarian state trying to control its populace and prevent it from making any claims on the limited pool of existing socio-economic opportunities.

The third trend – "spirituality and rationality" – was introduced by Mostafa Malekian (Malekian 2001), a philosopher with prior ties to a philosophical-political movement known as "religious intellectualism" (*roshanfekri-ye dini*). Politically, this trend is located somewhere between the other two: it differentiates itself from state-sanctioned spirituality by emphasizing rationality, and from the secular one by drawing on religious language and symbolism and allowing religious experience to take centre stage. It is also non-ritualistic. According to Malekian (2008; 2015, 277–8; 2016), a spiritual life contains three elements: a set of moral virtues such as honesty, humility, fairness, kindness, love, and caring; a set of psychological traits such as life satisfaction, happiness, and peacefulness; and a life that is meaningful and worthwhile. Such a spiritual life, Malekian argues, is perfectly compatible with rationality, as long as the latter is "thorough and deep" and acknowledges emotive and conative dimensions alongside cognitive capacity, does not deny the reality of something that it cannot explain scientifically, and maintains a connection between facts and values.

THE DEEPENING OF THE RELIGIOUS-SECULAR DIVIDE IN CITIES

Paradoxically in an Islamic Republic, religious groups sense that they are fast becoming a minority both numerically and in terms of power. Mazaheri (2019) attributes this increasing sense of insecurity to the fact that the non-religious view them as benefitting from the state's preferential policies and opportunities and justifying the state's malpractices and abusive treatment of its citizens. This sense of mutual suspicion has increasingly segregated the two segments of the population in urban areas, particularly in the larger cities, creating visibly religious neighbourhoods and a host of restaurants, clubs, and other gathering places reserved for religiously observant customers. The non-religious, too, particularly in Tehran, have found the northern cities around the Caspian Sea as their place of escape and refuge. Northern Iran, once the site of resistance to the advancing Muslim army in the seventh century, now seems to offer a place for cultural resistance to the Islamic Republic.

This segregation will profoundly affect religion in Iran. Limiting social interaction between religious and non-religious would diminish intellectual and social exchanges, severely polarizing society. Any major event – natural disaster, political crises, war – that requires collaboration and sacrifice would aggravate the cleavages and intensify competition over vital resources. In extreme conditions, this could result in a partitioned country or even civil war. In religion, such a polarized and segregated society would further solidify both the religious and the secular perspectives, with little chance of change.

THE WOMEN'S-RIGHTS MOVEMENT

As we saw in chapter 8, women's participation in the revolution of 1979 and their demands pushed the Islamic Republic away from orthodox Islam in order to accommodate them. This dynamic, however, seems to have morphed since 2009, a year of massive protests over a contested presidential election in which young Iranian women had a visible presence (for a discussion of the discursive implications of those protests, see Ayatollahi-Tabaar 2018). Ever since, in addition to their heightened political engagement, women have also escalated their oppositional activities over the compulsory dress code (*hijab*), domestic abuse, and sexual harassment. This visible shift in many women's political leanings, from pro-government to opposition, seems to have convinced the state that it can no longer count on their support, so it has stopped making concessions, even taking back some older ones, in order to appease its more traditionally religious supporters.

As a result, the government has adopted a much more conservative approach to women's rights. Since this new discourse is much closer in tone to traditional Islamic teachings, it may suggest that the state has abandoned its secular philosophy and switched to a more religious mode of operation. However, the underlying rationale has been purely political and pragmatic. A government's political decision to use a tap-on/tap-off approach in religious discourse does not make it more religious; it uses religion only for secular purposes.

INTENSIFICATION OF EMIGRATION

A more recent, yet powerful force affecting many aspects of social life in Iran, including religion, is greater migration from the country. While there has been a global increase in migration, current data suggest how unusual is Iran's experience. Figure 10.1 (based on Gallup 2017) compares it to several other Middle East countries. Its negative values show the higher number of people who, if given an opportunity, would like to leave Iran permanently, compared to those who want to remain. How can such a trend affect religion inside the country?

We need to put this information beside Iranian emigrants' level of religiosity. In a study of immigrants in Canada, Moghissi et al. (2009) have shown that Iranian emigrants are among the most secular compared to emigrants from other countries. This is hardly surprising, given Iran's highly religious political environment, which is oppressive for many

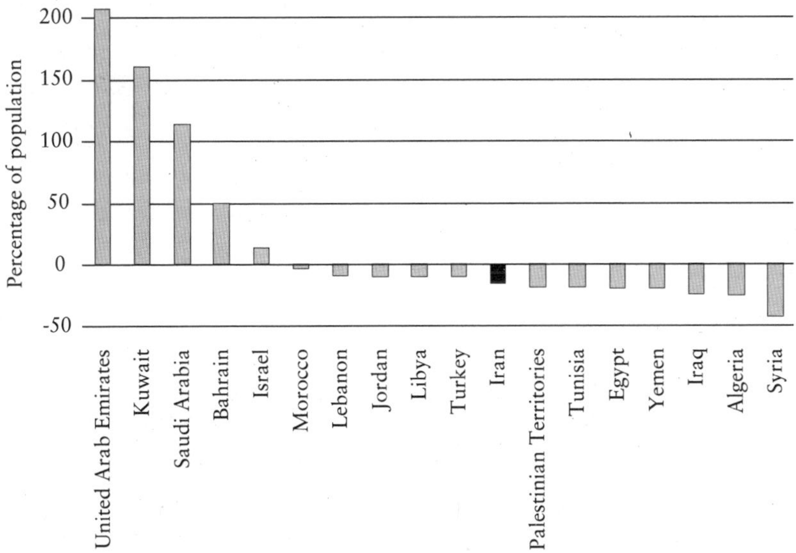

Figure 10.1 Potential net migration index (in- minus out-migration), 2013–16. *Source*: Gallup 2017.

middle- and upper-class educated people, who also constitute the majority of emigrants. Given these two realities – more out-migrants and their more secular tendencies – the recent exodus has removed a sizable chunk of the secular population, leaving behind more religious, less educated, and lower-class people. This may explain the recent increase in the visibility of religion in certain segments of the Iranian population.

SUMMARY

Chapters 4 to 9 explored long-term trends of religiosity in Iran. This chapter analysed some short-term factors that have affected the nature and level of religiosity in the country. The Iran-Iraq War initially increased religiosity, but the way it ended created an effect in the opposite direction. Likewise, women's involvement in the revolution jolted the dominant state ideology away from religious orthodoxy; but their moves to the opposition created a strong, negative reaction among state and religious authorities. The 1990s saw a popular movement towards spirituality in various forms, and the state's failure in sunni-shia unification led to a shia-centred campaign both regionally and domestically. Finally, substantial out-migration deepened an already polarized situation vis-à-vis religion, where the religious and the secular segments of the population lived increasingly distant from each other.

In the next, final chapter, I reflect on all the long- and short-term trends we have discussed and offer an overview of the religious landscape in Iran and where it may be heading.

CONCLUSION

Putting It Together a New Way?

This study lies at the intersection of three major debates and lines of scholarship: the history of religion in Iran, the historiography of the country's 1979 revolution, and the place of religion vis-à-vis secularism and secularizing trends in the world. In each of these three areas, the findings of this study offer a counter-argument to at least three powerful existing narratives: first, Iran's history as being inherently religious – for some, even before the advent of Islam (see, for instance, Dustdar 2004; Nasr 2010); second, the simplified and largely post-facto analysis that presents religion and the clergy as the masterminds behind the 1979 revolution and sees the current state of affairs as a straightforward materialization of their initial plans (see Afary and Anderson 2005); and, third, the widespread belief in "Muslim exceptionalism" (as examples, see Shoja'i-Zand 2002a, 2002b), in regard to secularization and secularism in the Muslim world in general, and in Iran in particular.

Three aspects separate this study from many existing works in this field. First: theoretically, it uses a structural and relational approach and focuses on the unintended consequences of actions. In doing so, it avoids three common errors: relying heavily on scriptural contents in explaining Muslims' behaviour, viewing outcomes as fixed, and assuming that the "intended" consequences of action shape social outcomes. Second: as for method, it relies on a vast amount of empirical data, rather than drawing conclusions based only on theory. Together, these two features allow for a much more dynamic and nuanced picture of reality. Third: substantively, the book's central argument is that, as a result of the Islamic Revolution and the establishment of the Islamic Republic with a heavy Islamization mandate,

Iranian society has undergone deep and widespread secularization. As well, even the Islamizing state itself has experienced a unique type of secularism.

Where would Iran go from here, in terms of the place of religion in the country? In many respects, post-revolution religious events resemble other, largely similar happenings at the start of the Sassanids' rule (224–651) in Persia, that is, more than three centuries prior to Islam's arrival. According to Zarrinkoob (2006, 177–98), King Ardashir, the founder of the dynasty, facing the almost complete disintegration of his country and lack of unity among the population, merged kingdom and religion and used religion to unify the populace. "The unity of kingdom and faith" became the basic principle of the state's structure and policies. This sat well with the spirit of the time, as the country was recovering from eighty years of rule by the Seleucids, whom Persians viewed as appointees of the invader Alexander (the Great) and carriers of his Hellenistic culture.

This unity of religion and state gave a special place to Zoroastrian religious institutions and authorities. The strategy bore fruit, as the Zoroastrian clerics convinced the centrifugal regional movements to adhere to the centre and remain loyal to the state. However, these clerics gained unprecedented sway in every aspect of governmental affairs, influencing even the appointment of officials and kings.

Disturbed by this vast power, later Sassanid kings tried to balance it by supporting Christian minorities and normalizing diplomatic relations with the arch-rival Christian Byzantine empire. The monarchs then faced a dual internal opposition: the clergy would not accept the restriction of its power, and army commanders saw normalization of ties with the Byzantines as undermining their roles as military leaders. The merger of religion and state had also pushed ordinary people away from the established religion and towards some minority religious movements led by Mani and Mazdak. The brutal oppression of both of these groups alienated the masses, paving the way for Muslim invaders to defeat the Sassanids and put an end to their reign.

The merger of religion and state by the Sassanids undid a policy of religious tolerance and neutrality adopted by Cyrus the Great (reigned 559–530 BCE), founder of the Achaemenids. Zarrinkoob (2006) describes this policy in detail: after conquering new lands, Cyrus, rather than forcibly converting them to the official faith, allowed his new subjects to maintain their religion, as he respected their religious traditions, practices, institutions, and places of worship. Some of his successors continued this approach, but more as a useful policy than as a matter of conviction. Cyrus's approach resembles contemporary policies of secularism, freedom of religion, and multiculturalism.

Toleration by some Achaemenid kings affected the lives of their religious minorities. Those minorities remained devoted to their religions but also showed strong attachment to the state, especially the Jewish communities, which have given Cyrus particularly favourable treatment in their histories. The effect of such a policy on Zoroastrians' religious commitments, however, is less clear. However, because Sassanid oppression disenchanted people with Zoroastrianism and made them welcome Muslim invaders, one may speculate that Cyrus's secularism and multiculturalism had kept ordinary people more strongly attached to their religion.

The situation in Iran today strongly resembles the Sassanids'. In both cases, widespread disillusionment with the government's policy on religion seems to have created a movement away from the state-sanctioned religion. While in the distant historical past – or, using Auguste Comte's terms, in the "metaphysical" age of humanity – such alienation might result in people's converting to other religions, today they might adopt an atheistic outlook and a secular way of life. It can also trigger a massive exodus from the land of imposed religiosity to more religiously free countries, which seems to be also happening among Iranians.

An area that demands great attention in future scholarship on religion in Iran concerns possible changes in the nature and content of Iranian religiosity. Because of the country's theocratic/autocratic state and highly politicized religion in an increasingly globalized and interconnected world, the content and fabric of its religion will undoubtedly change further, and more empirical social-scientific research is needed to capture those unique transformations.

APPENDIX A

Report on *Sunni* Militant Organizations' Conversion to *Shi'ism*

مؤسسه تحقیقاتی انتشاراتی:
نهضت جهانی اسلام

جمهوری اسلامی ایران

شماره: ....
تاریخ: ....
پیوست: ۴

بسمه تعالی

یکی از برادران جهاد اسلامی بنام محمود احمد الصاوی که از دوستان نزدیک خالد اسلامبولی بوده و اکنون در ایران بسر میبرد چنین گفت:

در مصر ما در مجموع محاسبات خویش در انقلاب مصر به یک کمبود اساسی برخورده‌ایم و آن اینکه مردم مصر آن تعبد و اطاعت شرعی که مردم شیعه نسبت به مراجع تقلید خود دارند، نداشته و خود را ملزم به اطاعت از علمای ما نمیدانند!!

افکار این برادران به اندازه‌ای به تشیع نزدیک است که گفت:

در مصر ما در مجلس شورای خود این فکر را طرح کرده‌ایم که هر چند پنهانی و از روی تقیه تشیع را بپذیریم تا زمینه این اندیشه در کل سازمان آماده شده و انشاءالله اگر حضرت امام نماینده‌ای تعیین فرمودند با ایشان بیعت کرده و همان معادله‌ای که انقلاب را در ایران پیروز کرد، در مصر برقرار سازیم.

همین آقای محمود احمد الصاوی در چند روزی که در منزل ما بود مرتب تحریر الوسیله حضرت امام را مطالعه میکرد و حتی در مسایل نماز و طهارت طبق فقه شیعه عمل میکرد.

کمکهای ما به این برادران مقداری پول و انتقال تجارب مبارزات ایران در زمان شاه بوده و مخصوصاً نسبت به برقراری رابطه مبارزات در مصر با علمای مصر و مقام رهبری در ایران، کمکهای فکری شایانی به آنان نموده‌ایم.

۳- عراق. در اینجا به دلیل اطلاعاتی که از موقعیت گروه‌های عراقی داشتیم، پس از پیروزی انقلاب در ایران با همکاری و همفکری برادر شهید حجة الاسلام محمد منتظری بر آن شدیم تا از راه دیگر به تشکل نیروها بپردازیم و لذا چند طرح زیر مورد توجه قرار گرفت:

مؤسسه تحقیقاتی انتشاراتی :
نهضت جهانی اسلام

جمهوری اسلامی ایران

شماره : ....
تاریخ : ....
پیوست : ....

۷

بسمه تعالی

اشتغال دارند. یا عده دیگر از ائمه جماعت مراکشی است که فعالیت های تدریس علوم اسلامی در مساجد مسلمانان مغربی در بلژیک اشتغال دارند.

جمعیت های اسلامی مانند جند الاسلام نیز که از گروه های شناسا شدین و نزدیک با انقلاب اسلامی است از کمک های فکری و تبلیغاتی ما بهره مند شده اند. در میان علمای بزرگ مراکش که در خارج از کشور زندگی می کنند و تاکنون چند بار به ایران آمده و به زیارت عتبات نیز نایل گشته اند، جو تشیع و نزدیکی به مکتب اهل بیت زیاد است تا آنجا که برای اولین بار از سوی ایشان فکر بیعت دسته جمعی علمای اهل سنت مراکش با حضرت امام پیشنهاد شده که بنظر نگرانی که در کار بود انجام نگرفت.

یکی از همین علما اظهار داشته است «من در مجموعه بررسی های عمیق خود به این نتیجه رسیده ام که در میان مذاهب اسلامی، تشیع تنها مذهبی است که می تواند در مقابل طواغیت به عنوان یک مکتب فکری انسان ها را تغذیه و رهبری نماید»

همین شخص آنچنان شیفته اهل بیت بود که در مراسم برگزاری یکی از شهدای عملیات برادر عمو رضائیان در اصفهان در هیئت ها چنان می گریست که برای حضار صحنه شگفت انگیز بود. همین عالم سنی در اثر آشنا شدن با مبانی انقلاب اسلامی در ایران و تجاربی که با او منتقل گشته بود بالاخره با تردید سئوال نمود من آماده ام تشیع خویش را اعلام کنم هرچند جو متعصبین اهل سنت اقتضای آن را ندارد. که من به ایشان سفارش کردم تقیه کند. نام این شخص آقای شیخ العینین است.

APPENDIX B

Aspects of Religiosity and the 1974/2000 Survey Questions Used to Measure Them

Aspect of religious beliefs, sentiments, and behaviour	*Survey question (NSVA 2000)*	*Survey question (Asadi 1974, published 1977)*	*Remarks*
Individual – practice	Some people believe that "faith/religion is one of the best ways to overcome life's difficulties." How strongly do you agree/disagree with such a belief? (Strongly disagree/disagree/neutral/agree/strongly agree) (q. 51).		The question gauges the personal feelings of the respondent regarding how central religion is in their life. It is also obvious that, in answering the question, the respondent considers the degree to which religion helps them overcome their practical difficulties in their life, as opposed to measuring such aspects as abstract feelings towards heaven, etc.
Individual – belief	How strongly do you agree/disagree with the idea that "all of our good/bad deeds in this world will be awarded/punished in the other world"? (Strongly disagree/disagree/neutral/agree/strongly agree) (q. 52).		The question highlights the existence or absence of a belief in life after death.
Collective (political) – belief	Some believe that "the religious beliefs of an individual is a personal and private matter, and there is nothing wrong in socializing with those who are not religious." How strongly do you agree/disagree with this idea? (Strongly disagree/disagree/neutral/agree/strongly agree) (q. 53).		The question singles out those who are of the opinion that religious beliefs are not just a private matter, but are in the public sphere and therefore a legitimate arena for government interference.

Aspect of religious beliefs, sentiments, and behaviour	*Survey question (NSVA 2000)*	*Survey question (Asadi 1974, published 1977)*	*Remarks*
Collective (political) – belief	Some believe that "the books whose contents are in conflict with religious beliefs should NOT be allowed to be published." How strongly do you agree/disagree with this idea? (Strongly disagree/disagree/neutral/agree/strongly agree) (q. 54).		The question highlights a view about which civil rights should accrue to an individual depending on their beliefs about religion.
Collective (political) – belief	Some believe that "the speakers who do not believe in religion should NOT be allowed to have public lectures." How strongly do you agree/disagree with this idea? (Strongly disagree/disagree/neutral/agree/strongly agree) (q. 55).		The question highlights the view based on which the civil rights should be accrued to individual depending on their beliefs about religions.
Individual – belief	How often do you ask God for help? (Never/seldom/sometimes/often/always) (q. 56).		
Individual – practice	How often do you think you have got closer to God? (Never/seldom/sometimes/often/always) (q. 57).		The question looks more at the experiential aspect of religion.
Collective (political) – belief	Some believe that "a religious person is one who is decent in heart, even if s/he does practise religious rituals (such as praying, fasting)." How strongly do you agree/disagree with this idea? (Strongly disagree/disagree/neutral/agree/strongly agree) (q. 58).		The question puts more emphasis on those aspects of religiosity that are 'visible', so the outsiders can judge whether or not a person is religious. This variable loads heavily alongside the items which emphasize that 'privileges' [rights] should be accrued to individuals based on whether or not they are religious.

Collective (political) – belief	Some believe that "religion will remain purer if it stays away from politics." How strongly do you agree/disagree with this idea? (Strongly disagree/disagree/neutral/agree/strongly agree) (q. 59).		
Collective (political) – belief	Some believe that "whoever is of the opinion that religion should stay away from politics should NOT be allowed to hold a governmental job." How strongly do you agree/disagree with this idea? (Strongly disagree/disagree/neutral/agree/strongly agree) (q. 60).		The question clearly distinguishes among those believe in the separation of church-state, and those who do not.
	Do you think that, five years from now, people in our society will be more religious, less religious, the same? (q. 61).	In your opinion, in the future, will there be more, less, or the same level of attention to religion? (More/less/the same).	
Individual – practice	Do you observe the required religious practices (daily prayers, fasting, etc.) (Never/seldom/sometimes/often/always) (q. 63).	If you are a Muslim, which one of the required religious duties (prayers, fasting …) do you observe, and how often? (Always/sometimes/never).	The examples included in the brackets all emphasize the individual aspect of religious practices.

Aspect of religious beliefs, sentiments, and behaviour	*Survey question (NSVA 2000)*	*Survey question (Asadi 1974, published 1977)*	*Remarks*
Collective – practice	How often do you participate in collective prayers? (Never/seldom/sometimes/often/always) (q. 64).	Do you go to mosque for prayers? How often? (Everyday/2–3 times a week/once a week/2–3 times a month).	Collective prayers are held in mosques three times a day, in the morning, at noon, and in the evenings. Normally, the morning ones are the quietest ones, and the evening ones the most crowded. The daily prayers that are often done individually and at home, can also be done collectively and in a public place like local mosque. Since the revolution, the prayers leaders (Imams) are increasingly appointed through governmental bodies. The large number of people to see during this function, mostly those from the same neighbourhood, is an attraction.
Collective – practice	How often do you participate in Friday congregations (prayers)? (Never/seldom/sometimes/often/always) (q. 65).		Friday Congregation (prayers) are held once a week, at Friday noon. There is one large congregation in each city, and the prayers leader (Imam) is directly appointed through a governmental body. The large number of people to see during the function is an attraction by itself.
Individual – practice	To what extent do you consider yourself religious? (Not at all/very little/little/average/very much/very very much/perfectly) (q. 66).		The question does not specify what aspect of religion it is looking at as a sign of religiosity. But, the fact that most people in Iran identify religiosity with individual practices such as daily prayers and fasting qualifies it as a variable related to the individual practice aspect of religiosity.

Notes

PREFACE

Chapter 6 is a modified and expanded version of A. Kazemipur and Ali Rezaei, "Religious Life under Theocracy: The Case of Iran," *Journal for the Scientific Study of Religion* 42, no. 3 (2003): 347–2, used with the journal's permission. Chapter 7 is a modified and expanded version of A. Kazemipur and M. Goodarzi, "The Iranian Youth and Religion: An Empirical Study," *Critical Middle Eastern Studies* 18, no. 2 (Summer 2009): 161–76, used with the journal's permission.

1 The term "Islamic Revolution" is widely used, especially among non-Iranian observers, in discussions about contemporary Iran. Iranians themselves differ widely about its meaning and appropriateness. Some, out of concern about what they consider "true Islam," question the accuracy of the adjective "Islamic" for the 1979 revolution, given the actions and policies of governments since then; others use it to denounce the whole revolutionary movement; and yet a third group emphasizes it to justify the Islamization measures taken by the Islamic Republic. My use of the term does not mean I'm taking sides; rather, I use it interchangeably with "1979 revolution." So, the reader may consider all uses of the term in this book as being placed between quotation marks.

CHAPTER ONE

1 "*Homo Islamicus*" is suggested by various scholars, some Muslims, others not, to underscore Muslims' distinctiveness in beliefs, attitudes, and behaviour. Farooq (2011), for instance, uses it in contrast to "homo

economicus," highlighting the latter's self-interestedness and the former's altruism. Nasr (2000) contrasts it with "modern man," who has forgotten about the essence of humanity and the spiritual dimension of this world. The concept is somewhat similar to "homo sovieticus," which was suggested as a description of the distinct cultural and personality features developed in the Soviet Union (Krzystof 2009; Zinoviev 1986).

2 According to Berger et al. (2008, 131), Islam "has from its beginnings been not only a faith, but a system of political and social organization."

CHAPTER TWO

1 Shahab Ahmed, *What Is Islam?: The Importance of Being Islamic* (Princeton, NJ: Princeton University Press, 2016), 3.

2 Will Durant, *The Story of Philosophy* (New York: Pocket Books, 1991), 247.

3 See Spellberg (2013), for an excellent study of how the US founders imported both the European anti-Muslim dominant view on religion and state, as well as a more Muslim-friendly minority view – particularly as they pertained to the rights of potential Muslim citizens – but adopted the minority view as their official position.

4 For the limitations of this perspective, see Magee (2001, 17–18).

5 In assessing some of the following works, I rely on the excellent annotated bibliography in (Shariati 2017).

CHAPTER THREE

1 Bernard Lewis, *The Middle East: 2000 Years of History from the Rise of Christianity to the Present Day* (London: Weidenfield & Nicolson, 1995), 60.

2 The many studies of this period, initiated by various seminary-affiliated institutes, more or less follow the official historiography (see, for instance, Babayee 2010). This sort of reasoning reduces the whole of Reza Shah's reign to a confrontation with the political opposition, which it shrinks to the dissident clergy. In doing so, it ignores the other opposition voices (such as communists and nationalists) and the lack of unanimity among the clerics, not to mention the significant advances the shah made in physical infrastructure and in modernizing public institutions. For an example of this type of reasoning, see Amini (2003), for an excellent review and critique, see Razavi (2017), and for a less biased and richer analysis, see Basiratmanesh (1997).

3 As for the academic discipline in which Shariati received his doctorate, he and others have suggested variously comparative literature, history, and sociology. Jalal Matini – dean of the Faculty of Humanities at the University of Mashhad when Shariati was hired as an assistant professor – mentioned hagiography, as a sub-field of comparative literature. Shariati himself, however, spoke frequently of history of religion and sociology of religion as his specialty. He had registered in a research-based comparative-literature program that had no course requirements, but he then took some elective courses in sociology and history of religion, later using them to define his own disciplinary background (for more information on this, see Markaz-e Asnad-e Enghelab-e Islami 2018; Matini 2014).

CHAPTER FOUR

1 There has recently been a surge of scholarly interest in Iran's seminaries (see, for instance, Forati 2011; Hosseini-zadeh 2010; Shirkhani and Zare'e 2005).

2 For an example, see Soleimanieh's article (2016) on the post-revolution men labelled "Dr Ayatollah" – graduates of seminaries who have also obtained degrees at universities to be eligible for posts at either or both – as opposed to the traditional "*Alem* [Academic]," who had studied at both to learn and to synthesize traditional and secular knowledge.

3 For more details, see the rise and fall of Montazeri below in this chapter.

4 This was not unique to the Islamic Republic. The tension between the multiplicity of religious decrees and the state's need for only one was also one reason why the Roman Empire eventually adopted monotheistic Christianity, to do away with all the Greek gods. According to Drake (2014, 406), "The first Christian emperor [Constantine] ... defended his choice of monotheism by pointing to the lack of a clear chain of command in polytheism ... [asking] How could I cultivate one without dishonouring the others? ... From which one should I expect to learn the cause of a crisis and how to resolve it? ... complete and utter confusion."

CHAPTER FIVE

1 An example would be the state's policy and behaviour towards pop music, changing from total denunciation of it as "westoxicating" to allowing it and then adopting it in the state media (for an elaborate discussion of those developments, see Siamdoost 2017); for another example on women-only urban spaces, see Shahrokni (2019).

CHAPTER EIGHT

1 Ahmad Mahmoud, *The Burnt Land*, 50.
2 "If you fear that you cannot act justly towards the orphans, then marry such women as seem good to you; two, three, four of them. But if you fear that you cannot do justice, then one only, or, those you possess. It is likelier then that you will not be partial" (Quran, chapter *nisa*, verse 3).

CHAPTER NINE

1 The shia clergy's very few works attacking Marxism, even in the 1940s and 1950s, responded not to any Tudeh publication but to Communist Party works of the 1930s, especially those of its main theoretician, Dr Taghi Arani, who died in Reza Shah's prison in 1936. A prominent attack on Arani's ideas was Allameh Mohammad-Hossein Tabatabayee's five-volume *Principles of Philosophy and the School of Realism* ([1954] 1980) – a critique of Marx's dialectical materialism. In his Introduction to the *Principles*, Morteza Motahhari ([1954] 1980) gives this rationale for going after Arani's works: "Despite the fact that Dr. Arani died about fifteen years ago, nobody from among the believers in dialectical materialism has been able to write better than he did … Dr Arani presented dialectical materialism in a fashion that was even superior to the way Marx and Engels and Lenin had done it" (22).
2 Interest in Fardid has risen recently (see, among others, Abdolkarimi 2015; M.M. Hashemi 2004; Ma'aref 2011; Madadpoor 2014; Mirsepassi 2017), including two recent documentaries (Mirsepassi and Yousefi 2015; Motahhar 2019).

References

Abdi, Abbas, and Mohsen Goodarzi. 2017. *Sedayee ke shenide nashod.* [The Voice That Did Not Get Heard.] Tehran: Nashre-Nay.

Abdolkarimi, Bijan. 2015. *Heidegger dar Iran: Negahi be zendegi, asar, va andishe-haye seyed Ahmad Fardid.* [Heidegger in Iran: A Glimpse into the Life, Works, and Ideas of Seyed Ahmad Fardid.] Tehran: Amir Kabir.

Abrahamian, Ervand. 1982. *Iran between Two Revolutions*. Princeton, NJ: Princeton University Press.

– 1989. *The Iranian Mojahedin*. New Haven, CT: Yale University Press.

Afary, Janet, and Kevin B. Anderson 2005. *Foucault and the Iranian Revolution: Gender and the Seductions of Islamism*. Chicago: University of Chicago Press.

Ahmadi-Amooyee, Bahman, ed. 2003. *Eghtesad-e siasi-ye jomhouri-ye eslami.* [The Political Economy of the Islamic Republic.] Tehran: Gam-e-no.

Alavian, Morteza. 2003. *Roohaniat va jame'e-paziri-ye siasi.* [Clergy and Political Socialization.] Qom: Mo'aseseye Amoozeshi-Pazhooheshiye Imam Khomeini.

Alijani, Reza. 2003. *Shariati va SAVAK: moroori tahlili bar se jeld asnad-e SAVAK darbare-ye doctor Shariati.* [Shariati and SAVAK: An Analytical Review of the Three Volumes of SAVAK's documents about Dr Shariati.] Tehran: Nashr-e Kavir.

Amanat, Abbas. 2017. *Iran: A Modern History*. New Haven, CT: Yale University Press.

Amini, Davood. 2003. *Chalesh-ha-ye roohaniat ba Reza Shah.* [The Clergy's Challenges vis-à-vis Reza Shah.] Tehran: Nashr-e Sepas.

Amuzegar, Jahangir. 1991. *Dynamics of the Iranian Revolution: The Pahlavis' Triumph and Tragedy*. New York: State University of New York Publisher.

Arjomand, Said Amir. 2016. *Sociology of Shi'ite Islam: Collected Essays*. Leiden and Boston: Brill.

Asad, Talal. 2003. *Formations of the Secular*. Stanford, CA: Stanford University Press.

Asadi, Ali. 1977. *Gerayesh-ha-ye farhangi va negaresh-ha-ye ejtema'ee dar Iran: gozaresh-e yek nazar-khahi-ye melli, 1353*. [Cultural Trends and Social Attitudes in Iran: Report of a National Opinion Poll in 1975.] Survey conducted in 1974. Tehran: Pajooheshkadeh Oloom Ertebati va Tousse'eh Iran.

Ashraf, Ahmad. 1990. "Theocracy and Charisma: New Men of Power in Iran." *International Journal of Politics, Culture, and Society* 4, no. 1: 113–52.

Aslan, Reza. 2011. *No god but God: The Origins, Evolution, and Future of Islam*. New York: Random House Trade Paperbacks.

Ausmus, H.J. 1982. *The Polite Escape: On The Myth of Secularization*. Athens: Ohio University Press.

Ayatollahi-Tabaar, Mohammad. 2018. *Religious Statecraft: The Politics of Islam in Iran*. New York: Columbia University Press.

Babayee, Omid. 2010. *Sazeman-e roohaniat-e shi'e dar asr-e Reza Shah Pahlavi*. [The Organizational Structure of Shia Clergy in Reza Shah Pahlavi's Era.] Qom: Shi'ite-Studies Institute.

Bangali, Shashank, and Ramin Mostaghimi. 2016. "More Women in Iran Are Forgoing Marriage. One Reason? The Men Aren't Good Enough." *Los Angeles Times*, 11 November. https://www.latimes.com/world/la-fg-iran-unmarried-snap-story.html.

Barzegar, Jamshid. 2014. "Hagh-e ra'aye zanan: Az fahsha ta hefz-e Islam." [Women's Right to Vote: From Corrupter to Islam's Safeguard.] BBC Persian, 15 July. https://www.bbc.com/persian/iran/2014/07/140715_l10_jb_women_vote.

Basiratmanesh, Hamid. 1997. *Ulama va regim-e Reza shah*. [Ulema and Reza Shah's Regime.] Tehran: Nashre Orooj.

Berger, Peter, Grace Davie, and Effie Fokas. 2008. *Religious America, Secular Europe? A Theme and Variations*. Burlington: Ashgate.

Berger, Peter L. 1967. *The Sacred Canopy: Elements of a Sociological Theory of Religion*. Garden City, NY: Doubleday.

– ed. 1999. *The De-secularization of the World*. Washington, DC: Ethics and Public Policy Centre.

Bhargava, Rajeev, ed. 1998. *Secularism and Its Critics*. New Delhi: Oxford University Press.

Bibby, Reginald W. 2001. *Canada's Teens: Today, Yesterday and Tomorrow*. Toronto: Stoddart.

Bolick, Kate. 2011. "All the Single Ladies." *Atlantic*, November, 116–36.

Boroujerdi, Mehrzad. 1996. *Iranian Intellectuals and the West: The Tormented Trimph of Nativism*. Syracuse, NY: Syracuse University Press.

Boroujerdi, Mehrzad, and Kourosh Rahimkhani. 2018. *Postrevolutionary Iran: A Political Handbook*. Syracuse, NY: Syracuse University Press.

Braudel, Fernand, and Immanuel Wallerstein. 2009. "History and the Social Sciences: The Longue Durée." *Review* 32, no. 2: 171–203.

Buss, Allan R. 1978. "Causes and Reasons in Attribution Theory: A Conceptual Critique." *Journal of Personality and Social Psychology* 36: 1311–21.

– 1979. "On the Relationship between Causes and Reasons." *Journal of Personality and Social Psychology* 37: 1458–61.

Buss, Andreas. 1999. "The Concept of Adequate Causation and Max Weber's Comparative Sociology of Religion." *British Journal of Sociology* 50, no. 2 (June): 317–29.

Campbell, Anne. 2004. "Female Competition: Causes, Constraints, Content, and Contexts." *Journal of Sex Research* 41, no. 1 (February): 16–26.

Capoccia, Giovanni, and R. Daniel Kelemen. 2007. "The Study of Critical Junctures: Theory, Narrative, and Counterfactuals in Historical Institutionalism." *World Politics* 59, no. 3 (April): 341–69.

Casanova, José. 1994. *Public Religions in the Modern World*. Chicago: University of Chicago Press.

CIA. 2021. *The World Factbook: Iran*.

Clayton, Richard R., and James W. Gladden. 1974. "The Five Dimensions of Religiosity: Toward Demythologizing a Sacred Artifact." *Journal for the Scientific Study of Religion* 13, no. 2: 135–43.

Cliteur, Paul. 2010. *The Secular Outlook: In Defense of Moral and Political Secularism*. Chichester, West Sussex: Wiley-Blackwell.

Cole, Juan R.I., and Nikki R. Keddie, eds. 1986. *Shi'ism and Social Protest*. New Haven, CT: Yale University Press.

Corbin, Henry. 1971. *En Islam iranien: Aspects spirituels et philosophiques, tome I*. Paris: Gillmard.

Courtwright, David T. 2008. "Gender Imbalances in History: Causes, Consequences and Social Adjustment." *Ethics, Bioscience and Life* 3, no. 1 (March): 32–40.

Dabashi, Hamid. 2011. *Shi'ism: A Religion of Protest*. Cambridge, MA: Belknap Press.

Dabbagh, Soroush. 2014. *Deen, akhlagh, va secularism.* [Religion, Ethics, and Secularism.] University of Calgary. https://castbox.fm/episode/سخنرانی-سروش-دباغ-با-عنوان-دین،-اخلاق-و-سکولاریسم-id1569317-id105785862?country=ca.

Davari-Ardekani, Reza. 2011. *Falsafe-ye mo'aser-e Iran.* [Contemporary Iranian Philosophy.] Tehran: Sokhan.

Davie, Grace. 2002. *Europe: The Exceptional Case: Parameters of Faith in the Modern World*. London: Darton, Longman and Todd.

– 2006. "Is Europe an Exceptional Case?" *Hedgehog Review* 8, nos. 1–2: 23–35.

Derakhsheh, Jalal. 2005. *Gofteman siasi-ye shia dar Iran-e mo'aser.* [Shia Political Discourse in Contemporary Iran.] Tehran: Entesharat-e Daneshghah-e Imam Sadegh.

Doostdar, Alireza. 2018. *The Iranian Metaphysicals: Explorations in Science, Islam, and the Uncanny*. Princeton, NJ: Princeton University Press.

Drake, H.A. 2014. "The Church, Society and Political Power." In *The Cambridge History of Christianity*. Volume 2. *Constantine to c. 600*, ed. Augustine Casiday and Frederick W. Norris, 403–28. New York: Cambridge University Press.

Durant, Will. 1933. *The Story of Philosophy*. New York: Garden City Publishing Co.

Durant, Will, and Ariel Durant. 1965. *The Story of Civilization*. Vol. 9. *The Age of Voltaire*. New York: Simon and Schuster.

Durkheim, Émile. (1893) 1984. *The Division of Labor in Society.* New York: Free Press.

– (1897) 2013. *Suicide: A Study in Sociology*. New York: Free Press.

– (1912) 2008. *The Elementary Forms of Religious Life*. New York: Oxford University Press.

Dustdar, Aramech 2004. *Emtena'a-e tafakkor dar farhang-e dini.* [The Impossibility of Free Thinking in a Religious Culture.] Paris: Khavaran.

Dyson, Tim. 2012. "Causes and Consequences of Skewed Sex Ratios." *Annual Review of Sociology* 38: 443–61.

Emami, Saeed. 2006. "Lecture in Abou-Ali University of Hamadan." Published 14 March 2019. http://written-blood.blogspot.com/2010/04/blog-post_05.html.

Eshghi, Leila. 2000. *Romani gheyr-e roman-ha.* [A Novel Unlike All the Others.] Trans. Ahmad Naghibzadeh. Tehran: Mo'assesse-ye farhang va honar va ertebatat.

Esmaeeli, Hamid-Reza. 2007. *Din va siasat dar andishe-ye siasi-ye mo'aser.* [Religion and Politics in Contemporary Political Thought.] Tehran: Pazhoohesh-kade-ye motale'at-e farhangi va ejtema'ee-ye vezaret-e oloom.

Faghfoory, Mohammad Hassan. 1993. "The Impact of Modernization on the Ulema in Iran: 1925–41." *Iranian Studies* 26, nos. 3–4: 277–312.

Farhani-Monfared, Mahdi. 1996. *Mohajerat-e olama-ye shie az jabal amel be Iran dar asr-e safavi.* [The Migration of Shia Ulema from Jabal-Amel to Iran during the Safavids.] Tehran: Amir-Kabir.

Farooq, Mohammad Omar. 2011. "Self-interest, Homo Islamicus and Some Behavioral Assumptions in Islamic Economics and Finance." *International Journal of Excellence in Islamic Banking and Finance* 1, no. 1: 52–79.

Fenn, Richard K. 1978. *Toward a Theory of Secularization.* Ellington, CT: Society for the Scientific Study of Religion.

Financial Tribune. 2017. "Iran Median Age Rises to 31.1 Years." 3 April. https://financialtribune.com/node/61716.

Fischer, Michael M.J. (1980) 2003. *Iran: From Religious Dispute to Revolution.* Madison: University of Wisconsin Press.

Fish, M. Steven 2011. *Are Muslims Distinctive? A Look at Evidence.* Oxford: Oxford University Press.

Foot, David K., and Daniel Stoffman. 1996. *Boom, Bust and Echo: How to Profit from the Coming Demographic Shift.* Toronto: Macfarlane Walter & Ross.

Forati, Abdolvahhab. 2011. *Roohaniat va siasat: masa'el va peyamad-ha.* [Clergy and Politics: The Problems and the Consequences.] Tehran: Pajoohesh-gah-e farhang va andishe-ye Islami.

Foucault, Michel. 1988. "Iran: The Spirit of a World without Spirit." In *Michel Foucault: Politics, Philosophy, Culture*, ed. Lawrence D. Kritzman, 211–26. New York: Routledge.

Freedman, Jane. 2004. "Secularism as a Barrier to Integration? The French Dilemma." *International Migration* 42, no. 3 (August): 5–27. https://doi.org/10.1111/j.0020-7985.2004.00287.x

Gellner, Ernest. 1993. "Marxism and Islam: Failure and Success." In *Power-Sharing Islam?*, ed. Azzam Tamimi. London: Liberty for Muslim World Publications.

Ghaffari-far, Hassan. 2011. *Tahlili bar chegoonegi-ye shekl-giri-ye shi'a dar sadr-e Islam, ba rooykard-e jame'e-shenasi.* [A Sociological Account of the Formation of Shiism in Early Islam.] Qom: Boostan-e Ketab.

Ghamari-Tabrizi, Behrooz. 2008. *Islam and Dissent in Postrevolutionary Iran: Abdolkarim Soroush, Religious Politics and Democratic Reform*. New York: I.B. Tauris.

– 2014. "The Divine, the People, and the Faqih: On Khomeini's Theory of Sovereignty." In *A Critical Introduction to Khomeini*, ed. Arshin Adib-Moghaddam, 239–55. New York: Cambridge University Press.

– 2016. *Foucault in Iran*. Minneapolis: University of Minnesota Press.

Ghobadzadeh, Naser. 2015. *Religious Secularity: A Theological Challenge to the Islamic State*. New York: Oxford.

Gilsinan, Kathy. 2015. "Could ISIS Exist without Islam? Why 'Is the Islamic State Muslim?' Is a Trick Question." *Atlantic*, July 3. https://www.theatlantic.com/international/archive/2015/07/isis-islam/397661.

Glasner, Peter E. 1977. *The Sociology of Secularization: A Critique of a Concept*. London: Routledge and Kegan Paul.

Glock, Charles Y., and Rodney Stark. 1965. *Religion and Society in Tension*. Chicago: Rand McNally & Company.

Gobineau, comte de. 2009. *Comte de Gobineau and Orientalism: Selected Eastern Writings*. Trans. Danie O'Donoghue. Culture and Civilization in the Middle East series. New York and London: Routledge.

Goethe, Johann Wolfgang. (1809) 2008. *Elective Affinities*. London: Penguin Books.

Guttentag, Marcia, and Paul F. Secord. 1983. *Too Many Women?: The Sex Ratio Question*. Newbury Park and Beverly Hills, CA: SAGE Publications.

Hajjarian, Saeed. 2000. *Jomhooriyat: Afsoon-zodayee az ghodrat*. [Republicanism: Dymystificatoin of Power.] Tehran: Tarh-e No.

– 2001. *Az shahed-e ghodsi ta shahed-e bazari: Orfi shodan-e din dar sepehr-e siasat*. [From the Sacred Witness to the Profane Witness: Secularization of Religion in the Sphere of Politics.] Tehran: Tarh-e No.

Halliday, Fred. 1978. *Iran: Dictatorship and Development*. London: Penguin Books Ltd.

Hashemi, Mohammad Mansour. 2004. *Hoviat-andishan va miras-e fekriye Ahmad Fardid*. [Identity Thinkers and the Intellectual Legacy of Ahmad Fardid.] Tehran: Kavir.

Hashemi, Nader. 2018. "Charles Taylor's *A Secular Age and Secularization from Below in Iran*." In *A Secular Age beyond the West: Religion, Law and the State in Asia, the Middle East and North Africa*, ed. Mirjam Kunkler, John Madeley, and Shylashri Shankar, 185–212. Cambridge: Cambridge University Press.

Hashemi Rafsanjani, Akbar. 1998. *Oboor az bohran, 1360, jeld-e 1 & 2.* [Passing through the Crisis: Memoirs of 1981. Vols. 1–2.] Tehran: Nashre Ma'aref Eslami.

– 2007a. *Aramesh va chalesh: 1362.* [Calmness and Challenge: Memoirs of 1983.] Ed. Mehadi Hashemi. Tehran: Ma'aref-e Enghelab.

– 2007b. *Be sooye sarnevesht: 1363.* [Towards Destiny: Memoirs of 1984.] Ed. Mohsen Hashemi. Tehran: Ma'aref-e Enghelab.

– 2007c. *Pas az bohran: 1361.* [After the Crisis: Memoirs of 1982.] Ed. Fatemeh Hashemi. Tehran: Ma'aref-e Enghelab.

– 2008. *Omid va delvapasi: 1364.* [Hope and Anxiety: Memoirs of 1985.] Tehran: Daftar-e Nashr-e Ma'aref-e Enghelab.

– 2011. *Payan-e defa'e, aghaz-e bazsazi: 1367.* [The End of the Defence, the Beginning of Reconstruction: Memoirs of 1988.] Tehran: Daftar-e Nashr-e Ma'aref-e Enghelab.

Hashemian-far, Seyed-Hossein. 2011. *Goone-shenasi-ye raftar-e siasi-ye maraje'e taghlid-e shi'e.* [*A Typology of the Political Behaviours of the Shia Sources of Emulation.*] Tehran: Imam Sadegh University.

Hinkle, Steve, and Daniel F. Schmidt. 1984. "The Buss Cause/Reason Hypotheses: An Empirical Investigation." *Social Psychology Quarterly* 47, no. 4 (December): 358–64.

Hoebink, Michel. 2009. "The Word of Mohammad: An Interview with Abdulkarim Soroush (by Michel Hoebink)." In *The Expansion of Prophetic Experience: Essays on Historicity, Contingency and Plurality in Religion*, ed. Abdolkarim Soroush, 271–5. Leiden: Brill Academic Publishers.

Honig, Bonnie. 2008. "What Foucault Saw at the Revolution: On the Use and Abuse of Theology for Politics." *Political Theory* 36, no. 2: 301–12.

Hoodfar, Homa. 2009. "Activism under the Radar: Volunteer Women Health Workers in Iran." *Middle East Report* no. 250 (Spring): 56–60.

Hooglund, Eric. 2009. "Thirty Years of Islamic Revolution in Rural Iran." *Middle East Report* no. 250 (Spring): 34–6.

Hosseini-zadeh, Seyed-Mohammad-Ali. 2010. *Shekl-giri va tahavvol-e howze-ha-ye shie.* [The Formation and Evolution of Shia Seminaries.] Qom: Boshra Cultural Institute.

Howe, Neil, and William Strauss. 2000. *Millennials Rising.* New York: Vintage Books.

Howe, Richard H. 1978. "Max Weber's Elective Affinities: Sociology within the Bounds of Pure Reason." *American Journal of Sociology* 84, no. 2 (September): 366–85.

Huntington, Samuel P. 1996. *The Clash of Civilizations and the Remaking of World Order*. New York: Simon & Schuster.

Inglehart, R., C. Haerpfer, A. Moreno, C. Welzel, K. Kizilova, J. Diez-Medrano, M. Lagos, P. Norris, E. Ponarin, B. Puranen, et al., eds. 2018. "World Values Survey: Round Four – Country-Pooled Datafile = WVS Wave 4 (2000–2004)." Madrid, Spain, and Vienna, Austria: JD Systems Institute and WVSA Secretariat. Accessed 1 July 2020. https://doi.org/10.14281/18241.6.

Inglehart, Ronald, and Pippa Norris. 2003. *Rising Tide: Gender Equality and Cultural Change around the World*. Cambridge: Cambridge University Press.

Islami, Reza. 2015. *Madkhal-e elm-e fiqh: Advar, manabe, mafahim, ketabha, va rejal-e fiqh-e mazaheb-e Islami*. [An Introduction to Islamic Jurisprudence.] Qom: Research Deputy of Howzah Elmiyyah – Centre for Educational Planning and Textbook Compliation – Qom Seminary.

Jafarian, Rasul. 2004. *Jarian-ha va sazeman-ha-ye mazhabi-siasi-ye Iran: Salhaye 1320–1357*. [Religio-political Currents and Organizations in Iran: 1941–79.] Tehran: Centre for Islamic Revolution Documents.

Jahanbakhsh, Forough. 2001. *Islam, Democracy, and Religious Modernism in Iran (1953–2000): From Bazargan to Soroush*. Leiden: Brill.

Joppke, Christian. 2015. *Secular State under Siege: Religion and Politics in Europe and America*. Cambridge: Polity Press.

Judaki, Mahbubeh. 2009. *Hosseiniye ershad be revayat-e asnad*. [Hosseiniye-ye ershad, According to Documents.] Tehran: Markaz-e asnad-e enghelab-e eslami.

Kadivar, Jamileh. 1999. *Tahavvol-e gofteman-e siasi-ye shi'e dar Iran*. [The Evolution of Shia Political Discourse in Iran.] Tehran: Tarh-e No.

Kadivar, Mohsen. 2001. *Nazariye-haye dolat dar fiqh-e shie*. [Theories of State in the Shi'ite *Fiqh*.] 5th ed. Political Thought in Islam series, vol. 1. Tehran: Nashr-e Ney.

Kamyab, Parviz. 2008. *Secularism dar Islam va masihiyyat*. [Secularism in Islam and Christianity.] BBC Persian, 18 January. http://www.bbc.com/persian/arts/story/2008/01/080117_wmt-secular-soroush1.shtml.

Karimi-Zanjani-Asl, Mohammad. 2006. *Dar-ul-elm-ha-ye shi'i va no-zayee-ye farhangi dar jahan-e Islam*. [Shia Academic Institutions and the Cultural Renaissance in the Muslim World.] Tehran: Ettela'at Publishing House.

Kazemipur, Abdolmohammad. 2014. *The Muslim Question in Canada: A Story of Segmented Integration*. Vancouver: University of British Columbia Press.

Kazemipur, Abdolmohammad, and Ali Rezaei. 2003. "Religious Life under Theocracy: The Case of Iran." *Journal for the Scientific Study of Religion* 42, no. 3: 347–61.

Keddie, Nikki R. 2003. *Modern Iran: Roots and Results of Revolution.* New Haven, CT, and London: Yale University Press.

– 2007. "Iranian Women's Status and Struggles since 1979." *Journal of International Affairs* 60, no. 2: 17–33.

– 2008. "Introduction: Innovative Women: Unsung Pioneers of Social Change." *Journal of Middle East Women's Studies* 4, no. 3: 1–11.

Kelly, John, and Bruce Etling. 2008. *Mapping Iran's Online Public: Politics and Culture in the Persian Blogosphere.* Harvard Law School. https://cyber.harvard.edu/sites/cyber.harvard.edu/files/Kelly&Etling_Mapping_Irans_Online_Public_2008.pdf.

Khalaji, Mehdi. 2010. *Nazm-e nowin-e rohaniat dar Iran.* [The New Order of the Clerical Establishment in Iran.] Bochum, Germany: Aida Verlag.

Khomeini, Ruhollah. 1986. *Sahifeh-ye noor: rahnemood-ha-ye imam khomeini.* [An Anthology of Imam Khomeinis Speeches, Messages, Interviews, Decrees, Religious Permissions, and Letters.] Vol. 18. Tehran: Entesharat-e Sazeman-e Madarek-e Farhangi-ye Enghelab-e Eslami.

– 1990a. *Sahifeh-ye noor: Rahnemood-ha-ye imam khomeini.* [An Anthology of Imam Khomeini's Speeches, Messages, Interviews, Decrees, Religious Permissions, and Letters.] Vol. 20. Tehran: Entesharat-e Sazeman-e Madarek-e Farhangi-ye Enghelab-e Eslami.

– 1990b. *Sahifeh-ye noor: Rahnemood-ha-ye imam khomeini.* [An Anthology of Imam Khomeinis Speeches, Messages, Interviews, Decrees, Religious Permissions, and Letters.] Vol. 21. Tehran: Entesharat-e Sazeman-e Madarek-e Farhangi-ye Enghelab-e Eslami.

– (1944) 1999. *Kashf-ul-asrar.* [Secrets Revealed.] Isfahan: Ghaemiyeh.

– (1970) 1999. *Velayat-e faqih.* [The Rulership of the Jurist.] Isfahan: Ghaemiyeh.

Kołakowski, Leszek. 1978. *Main Currents of Marxism: The Founders, The Golden Age, The Breakdown.* 3 volumes. New York: W.W. Norton & Company.

Kruger, Daniel J., and Erin Schlemmer. 2009. "Male Scarcity Is Differentially Related to Male Marital Likelihood across the Life Course." *Evolutionary Psychology* 7, no. 2: 280–7.

Krzystof, Tyszka. 2009. "'Homo Sovieticus': Two Decades Later." *Polish Sociological Review* 4, no. 168: 507–22.

Kunkler, Mirjam, John Madeley, and Shylashri Shankar, eds. 2018. *A Secular Age beyond the West: Religion, Law and the State in Asia, the Middle East and North Africa*. Cambridge: Cambridge University Press.

Kuru, Ahmet T. 2009. *Secularism and State Policies toward Religion: The United States, France, and Turkey*. Cambridge: Cambridge University Press.

Lewis, Bernard. 1987. *Islam: From the Prophet Muhammad to the Capture of Constantinople*. Volume 1. *Politics and War*. New York: Oxford University Press.

– 1991. *The Political Language of Islam*. Chicago: University of Chicago Press.

– 1995. *The Middle East: 2000 Years of History from the Rise of Christianity to the Present Day*. London: Phoenix.

– 2002. *What Went Wrong? Western Impact and the Middle Eastern Response*. New York: Oxford University Press.

Lloyd, Kim M., and Scott J. South. 1996. "Contextual Influences on Young Men's Transition to First Marriage." *Social Forces* 74, no. 3: 1097–119.

Ma'aref, Seyed Abbas. 2011. *Negahi dobare be mabadi-ye hekmat-e onsi.* [Revisiting the Principles of Mystical Philosphy.] Abadan: Nashr-e porsesh.

Macklin, Ruth. 1972. "Reasons vs. Causes in Explanation of Action." *Philosophy and Phenomenological Research* 33, no. 1: 78–89.

Madadpoor, Mohammad. 2014. *Didar-e farrehi va fotoohat-e akhar-ul-zaman*. [The Grandiose Meeting and the Victories of the End-of-time.] Tehran: Mo'assesse-ye farhangi-ye chap va nashr-e nazar.

Magee, Bryan. 2001. *The Great Philosophers: An Introduction to Western Philosophy*. New York: Oxford University Press.

Mahmood, Saba. 2015. *Religious Difference in a Secular Age: A Minority Report*. Princeton, NJ: Princeton University Press.

Mahoney, James, and Kathleen Thelen. 2010. "A Theory of Gradual Institutional Change." In *Explaining Institutional Change: Ambiguity, Agency, and Power*, ed. James Mahoney and Kathleen Thelen, 1–37. Cambridge: Cambridge University Press.

Malekian, Mostafa. 2001. *Rahi be rahayee: Jostarhayee dar aghlaniat va ma'naviat*. [A Way to Liberation: Essays on Rationality and Spirituality.] Tehran: Negah-e Mo'aser.

– 2008. *Moshtaghi va mahjoori: Goft-o-gooyee dar bab-e farhang va sisasat*. [Eagerness and Separation: A Conversation about Culture and Politics.] Tehran: Negah-e Mo'aser.

– 2015. *Hadise arezoomandi: Jostarhayee dar aghlaniat va ma'naviat.* [The Story of Dreamfulness: Essays on Rationality and Spirituality.] Tehran: Negah-e Mo'aser.

– 2016. *Mehr-e mandegar: Maghalati dar akhlagh-shenasi.* [Enduring Kindness: Essays on Morality.] Tehran: Negah-e Mo'aser.

Markaz-e Amar-e Iran (Statistical Centre of Iran). 1999. *Namagar-ha-ye jam'ee-yati-ye Iran: 1335–1375.* [Iran's Demographic Indicators: 1956–96.] Tehran: Statistical Centre of Iran Press.

– 2012. "Population Estimation – Country's Population, Urban and Rural Areas." Accessed 8 November 2012. http://www.amar.org.ir/LinkClick.aspx?fileticket=gjGZoFMVMDY%3d&tabid=32.

Markaz-e Asnad-e Enghelab-e Islami. 2018. *Shariati dar asnad-e SAVAK – 3 jeld.* [Shariati in SAVAK's Documents. 3 volumes.] Tehran: Markaz-e asnad-e enghelab-e Islami.

Markaz-e tahghighat-e shora-ye negahban. [Guardian Council Research Centre.] 2006a. *Majmoo-e-ye nazarat-e shora-ye negahban dar mored-e mosavvabat-e majles-e shora-ye eslami, dore-ye 3: Khordad 1367–khordad 1371.* [Collection of Guardian Council Views on Parliament's Deliberations, Cycle 3: June 1988–June 1992.] Tehran: Nashr-e Dadgostar.

– 2006b. *Majmoo-e-ye nazarat-e shora-yenegahban dar mored-e mosavvabat-e majles-e shora-ye eslami, dore-ye 4: Khordad 1371–khordad 1375.* [Collection of Guardian Council Views on Parliament's Deliberations, Cycle 4: June 1992–June 1996.] Tehran: Nashr-e Dadgostar.

– 2006c. *Majmoo-e-ye nazarat-e shora-yenegahban dar morede mosavvabat-e majles-e shora-ye eslami, dore-ye 5: Khordad 1375–khordad 1379.* [Collection of Guardian Council Views on Parliament's Deliberations, Cycle 5: June 1996–June 2000.] Tehran: Nashr-e Dadgostar.

– 2007. *Mashrooh-e mozakerat-e shora-ye negahban, dore-ye 1: Sal-e 1359.* [Detailed Debates of Guardian Council, Cycle 1: June 1980.] Tehran: Nashr-e Dadgostar.

– 2009. *Majmoo-ye nazarat-e shora-ye negahban dar mored-e mosavvabat-e majles-e shora-ye eslami, dore-ye 1: Khordad 1359–khordad 1363.* [Collection of Guardian Council Views on Parliament's Deliberations, Cycle 1: June 1980–June 1984.] Tehran: Mo'aventat-e hoghooghi-ye riasat-e jomhoori.

– 2010a. *Majmoo-e-ye nazarat-e shora-ye negahban dar mored-e mosavvabat-e majles-e shora-ye eslami, dore-ye 1: 1359.* [Collection of Guardian

Council Views on Parliament's Deliberations, Cycle 1: 1980.] Tehran: Mo'avenat-e hoghooghi-ye riasat-e jomhoori.

– 2010b. *Majmoo-e-ye nazarat-e shora-ye negahban dar mored-e mosavvabat-e majles-e shora-ye eslami, dore-ye 2: Khordad 1363–khordad 1367*. [Collection of Guardian Council Views on Parliament's Deliberations, Cycle 3: June 1984–June 1988.] Tehran: Mo'avenat-e hoghooghi-ye riasat-e jomhoori.

– 2010c. *Majmoo-e-ye nazarat-e shora-ye negahban dar mored-e mosavvabat-e majles-e shora-ye eslami, dore-ye 7: Khordad 1383–khordad 1387*. [Collection of Guardian Council Views on Parliament's Deliberations, Cycle 7: June 2004–June 2008.] Tehran: Mo'avenat-e hoghooghi-ye riasat-e jomhoori.

– 2012. *Majmoo-e-ye nazarat-e shora-ye negahban dar mored-e mosavvabat-e majles-e shora-ye eslami, dore-ye 6: Khordad 1379–khordad 1383*. [Collection of Guardian Council Views on Parliament's Deliberations, Cycle 6: June 2000–June 2004.] Tehran: Mo'avenat-e hoghooghi-ye riasat-e jomhoori.

Martin, David. 1978. *A General Theory of Secularization*. Oxford: Basil Blackwell.

Marx, Anthony W. 2003. *Faith in Nation: Exclusionary Origins of Nationalism*. New York: Oxford University Press.

Matin-Asgari, Afshin. 2018. *Both Eastern and Western: An Intellectual History of Iranian Modernity*. New York: Cambridge University Press.

Matini, Jalal. 2014. *Khaterat-e Jalal Matini: Doctor Ali Shariati dar daneshgah-e Mashhad (Ferdowsi)*. [Memories of Jalal Matini about Dr Ali Shariati in Ferdowsi University.] Los Angeles: Sherkat-e ketab.

Mazaheri, Mohsen Hesam. 2011. *Resane-ye shi'e: Jame'e-shenasi-ye ayeen-ha-ye soogvari va hei'at-ha-ye mazhabi dar Iran*. [Shia Media: A Sociology of Mourning Ceremonies and Religious Confraternities in Iran.] Tehran: International Publishing Co.

– 2018a. "Arba'een-e Irani." [The Iranian Arba'een.] In *Piyade-ravi-ye Arba'een: Ta'amolat-e jame'e-shenakhti* [The Arba'een Procession: Some Sociological Reflections], ed. Mohsen Hesam Mazaheri, 199–238. Isfahan: Arma.

– ed. 2018b. *Piyade-ravi-ye Arba'een: Ta'amolat-e jame'e-shenakhti*. [The Arba'een Procession: Some Sociological Reflections.] Isfahan: Arma.

– 2019. *Saken-e khiaban-e Iran: Masa'el va chalesh-ha-ye dindari dar jomhouri-ye Islami*. [The Resident of the Iran Street: The Problems and Challenges of Being Religious in the Islamic Republic.] Isfahan: Arma.

McKinnon, Andrew M. 2010. "Elective Affinities of the Protestant Ethic: Weber and the Chemistry of Capitalism." *Sociological Theory* 28, no. 1 (March): 108–26.

Meisami, Lotfollah. 2008a. *Khaterat-e lotfollah meisami, vol. 1 (az nehzat-e azadi ta mojahedin).* [Memoirs. Vol. 1.] Tehran: Samadiye.

– 2008b. *Khaterat-e lotfollah meisami, vol. 2 (anha ke raftand).* [Memoirs. Vol. 2.] Tehran: Samadiye.

Memarian, Omid, and Tara Nesvaderani. 2015. *The Youth.* August. https://iranprimer.usip.org/resource/youth.

Merton, Robert K. 1968. *Social Theory and Social Structure.* New York: Free Press.

Miller, R. Robin, and Sandra Lee Browning. 2000. "Sharing a Man: Insights from Research." *Journal of Comparative Family Studies* 31, no. 3: 339–46.

Mir-moosavi, Seyed-Ali. 2005. *Sonnat, dowlat-e modern: No-sazi va tahavvol dar andishe-ye siasi shi'e.* [Islam, Tradition, Modern State: Modernization and Evolution of Shia Political Thought.] Tehran: Nashr-e Ney.

Mirsepassi, Ali. 2017. *Transnationalism in Iranian Political Thought: The Life and Times of Ahmad Fardid.* Cambridge: Cambridge University Press.

Mirsepassi, Ali, and Hamed Yousefi. 2015. *The Fabulous Life and Thought of Ahmad Fardid.* Documentary. Accessed 22 November 2020. https://vimeo.com/143555867.

Mirzayee, Hossein. 2014. "Lenin-e nakam: Moroori bar zendegi va zamane-ye taghi-ye shahram." [The Failed Lenin: A Review of the Life and Times of Taghi Shahram.] *Mehr* 5, no. 38: 74–8.

Mitchell, Leslie G. 1999. "Introduction." In *Edmund Burke's (1790) Reflections on the Revolution in France*, vii–xix. New York: Oxford University Press.

Modarresi, Hossein. 1993. *Crisis and Consolidation in the Formative Period of Shi'ite Islam: Abu Ja'Far Ibn Qiba Al-Razi and His Contribution to Imamite Shi'ite Thought.* Princeton, NJ: Darwin Press.

Moghissi, Haideh, Saeed Rahnema, and Mark J. Goodman. 2009. *Diaspora by Design: Muslim Immigrants in Canada and Beyond.* Toronto: University of Toronto Press.

Mohammadi-Gorgani, Mohammad. 2017. *Khaterat va ta'amolat dar zendan-e shah.* [Memoirs and Reflections in the Shah's Prison.] Tehran: Nashr-e Ney.

Mohseni, Manouchehr. 2000. *Barresi-ye agahi-ha, negaresh-ha va faftar-ha dar Iran.* [An Examination of Knowledge, Attitudes, and Behaviours in Iran.] Survey conducted 1996. Tehran: Shoraye Farhange Omoomiye Keshvar.

Mojahedin-e Khalgh Organization. 1974. *Jozve-ye sabz.* [The Green Pamphlet.] Peykar Press. Accessed 21 February 2019. http://peykar.info/PeykarArchive/Mojahedin-ML/pdf/Jozveye-Sabz.pdf.

– 1975a. *Bayaniye-ye taghyeer-e mavaze'e ideologic.* [Manifesto of the Ideological Positions.] Peykar Press. Accessed 21 February 2019. http://peykar.info/PeykarArchive/Mojahedin-ML/pdf/Bayaniyeh-1354-1.pdf.

– 1975b. *Door-e aval-e mozakerat-e mojahedin (M.L.) va cherikha-ye Fadaii.* [Round One of the Unification Negotiations between Mojahedin-e Khalgh Organization and Cherik-ha-ye Fadayee-ye Khalgh.] Peykar Press. Accessed 21 February 2019. http://peykar.info/PeykarArchive/Mojahedin-ML/mojahed_fadaii.html.

– 1977a. *Door-e dovom-e mozakerat-e mojahedin (M.L.) va cherikha-ye fadaii.* [Round Two of the Unification Negotiations between Mojahedin-e Khalgh Organization and Cherik-ha-ye Fadayee-ye Khalgh.] Peykar Press. Accessed 21 February 2019. http://peykar.info/PeykarArchive/Mojahedin-ML/mojahed_fadaii-dore2.html.

– 1977b. *Goftegoo beyn-e sazeman mojahedin-e khalgh (M.L.) va gorooh-e monsha'eb az cherikhaye fadaii-ye khalgh.* [Unification Negotiations between Mojahedin-e Khalgh Organizaton and the Group Branched out of Cherik-ha-ye fadayee-e khalgh.] Peykar Press. Accessed 21 February 2019. http://peykar.info/PeykarArchive/Mojahedin-ML/mojahed_fadaii-2.html.

– 1977c. *Masa'el-e hadd-e jonbesh-e ma.* [The Most Urgent Problems of Our Movement.] Peykar Press. Accessed 21 February 2019. http://peykar.info/PeykarArchive/Mojahedin-ML/pdf/Masaele-Hadde-Jonbeshe-Ma.pdf.

– 1977d. *Masael-e hadd-e jonbesh-e ma – zamimeh.* [The Most Urgent Problems of Our Movement: The Attachment.] Peykar Press. Accessed 21 February 2019. http://peykar.info/PeykarArchive/Mojahedin-ML/pdf/Masaele-Had-Zamimeh.pdf.

– 1977e. *Tahlil-e amoozeshi-ye bayaniye-ye opportunist-ha-ye chap-nama.* [Instructional Analysis of the Manifesto of Ideolgocial Positions of the Ostensible Leftist Opportunists.] Peykar Press. Accessed 21 February 2019. https://www.iran-archive.com/sites/default/files/sanad/mojahedine_khalgh-tahlile_amoozeshi.pdf.

Montazeri, Hosseinali. 2000. *Khaterat-e ayatollah montazeri: Az 1301 ta 1378 hejri-shamsi.* [Memoirs: 1922–99.] Ettehadieye Nasheran-e Irani dar Oroopa. Accessed 29 September 2021. https://amontazeri.com/static/books/Khaterat-Scan-A4.pdf

Moomivand, Bijan. 2014. "Tarikh-e yek ertedad." [The History of an Apostasy.] *Mehr-Nameh* 5, no. 38: 72–3.

Motahhar, Mehdi. 2019. "Theorician-e khoshoonat: Andishe-ha va tafakkorat-e Ahmad Fardid." [The Theorist of Violence: Ideas and Thoughts of Ahmad Fardid.] Accessed 21 January 2021. https://www.youtube.com/watch?v=-Q_SFwaaGdk.

Motahhari, Morteza. (1973) 1978. *Elal-e gerayesh be maddigari.* [The Causes of the Adoption of the Materialist Philosophy.] Tehran: Bonyade- Elmi-Farhangi-ye Ostad-e Shahid Morteza Motahhari (motahari.ir).

– (1954) 1980. "Introduction." In *Tabatabayee, osool-e falsafe va ravesh-e realism, volumes 1–5.* [Tabatabayee: Principles of Philosophy and the School of Realism. Vols. 1–5.] Tehran: Daftar-e Entesharat-e Eslami.

– (1962) 2003. *Dah goftar.* [Ten Lectures.] Tehran: Sadra.

Mozaffari, Ayat. 2008. *Monasebat-e roohaniat va dowlat dar Iran-e mo'aser, ba rooykard-e jame'e-shenasi-ye siasi.* [Relations between Clergy and State in Contemporary Iran: A Political Sociological Approach.] Qom: Nashr-e Ma'aref.

Naghibzadeh, Ahmad, and Vahid Amani-Zawarem. 2003. *Naghsh-e roohaniat-e shie dar piroozi-ye enghelab-e Islami.* [The Role of the Shia Clergy in the Victory of the Islamic Revolution.] Tehran: Markaz-e Asnad-e Enghelab-e Islami.

Nasr, Seyyed Hossein. 2000. *Islam and the Plight of Modern Man.* Chicago: ABC International Groups.

– 2010. *In Search of the Sacred: A Conversation with Seyyed Hossein Nasr on His Life and Thought (by R. Jahanbegloo and T. Moore).* Santa Barbara, CA: Praeger.

– 2015. *Hekmat va siasat: Khaterat-e doctor seyed hossein nasr.* [Wisdom and Politics: The Memoirs of Seyed Hossein Nasr.] Ed. Hossein Dehbashi. Tehran: Sazeman-e asnad va ketabkhane-ye melli.

Nasr, Seyyed Hossein, Ramin Jahanbegloo, and Terry Moore. 2010. *In Search of the Sacred: A Conversation with Seyyed Hossein Nasr on His Life and Thought*. Santa Barbara, CA: Praeger.

Nategh, Homa. 1983. "Interview with Homa Nategh." Audio File. Harvard Oral History of Iran. Accessed 22 October 2020.

Nikfar, Mohammad Reza. 2007. *Eghtesad-e siasi-ye din.* [Political Economy of Religion.] Radio Zamaneh. Accessed 21 January 2021. http://seculariran.freetzi.com/Nikfar_Eghtesade_Siasie_Din.pdf.

– 2016. "Interview with Enayat Fani." *Be ebarat-e digar.* BBC Persian, February 16. https://www.youtube.com/watch?v=Ux9SzVmdhBA.

Norris, Pippa, and Ronald Inglehart. 2004. *Sacred and Secular: Religion and Politics Worldwide.* Cambridge: Cambridge University Press.

Norton, Anne. 2013. *On the Muslim Question.* Princeton, NJ: Princeton University Press.

NSVA. 2000. *Paymayeshe Melliye Arzesh-ha va negaresh-ha-ye Iranian: Natayej-e paymayesh dar 28 ostan.* [National Survey of Values and Attitudes of Iranians: Findings of Survey in 28 Provinces. 2 volumes.] Office of National Projects (Iran). Tehran: Iranian Ministry of Culture and Islamic Guidance.

– 2003. *Paymayeshe Melliye Arzesh-ha va Negaresh-ha.* [National Survey of Values and Attitudes.] Office of National Projects (Iran). Tehran: Iranian Ministry of Culture and Islamic Guidance.

Peters, Richard S. 1958. *The Concept of Motivation.* London: Routledge & Kegan Paul.

Petroshevsky, Ilia Pavlich [Karim Keshavarz]. 1971. *Islam dar Iran: Az hijrat to payan-e gharn-e nohom-e hejri.* [Islam in Iran: From Hijra to the End of the Sixteenth Century.] Tehran: Payam.

Petrushevsky, Ilya Pavlovich. 1985. *Islam in Iran.* New York: State University of New York Press.

Rahimpour-Azghadi, Hassan. 2018. "Rahimpour-Azghadi dar madrese-ye faizieh che goft?" [What Did Rahimpour-Azghadi Say at Faizieh School?] Accessed 21 January 2021. https://www.isna.ir/news/97053016111/ رحیم-پور-ازغدی-در-مدرسه-فیضیه-چه-گفت.

Rahmani, Jabbar. 2014. *Tagh'yeerat-e manasek-e azadari-ye moharram: Ensan-shenasiye manasek-e azadariye moharram.* [Changes in the Muharram Mourning Rituals: An Anthropology of Muharram Mourning Ritual.] Tehran: Tissa.

Rahnema, Ali. 2000. *An Islamic Utopian: A Political Biography of Ali Shari'ati.* London and New York: I.B. Tauris Publishers.

– 2005. *Nirooya-ye mazhavi bar baster-e harekat-e nehzat-e melli.* [The Religious Forces during the National Movement.] Tehran: Gam-e No.

– 2014. "Ayaotallh Khomeini's Rule of the Guardian Jurist: From Theory to Practice." In *A Critical Introduction to Khomeini*, ed. Arshin Adib-Moghaddam, 88–114. New York: Cambridge University Press.

– 2021. *Call to Arms: Iran's Marxist Revolutionaries, Formation and Evolution of the Fada'is, 1964–1976*. London: Oneworld Academic.

Ramezan-Nargesi, Reza. 2010. *Tabyeen-e jame'e-shenakhti-ye enghelab-e mashrooteh*. [A Sociological Account of the Constitutional Revolution.] Qom: Mo'aseseye Amoozeshi-Pazhooheshiye Imam Khomeini.

Ranjbar, Mohsen. 2010. *Jarian-shenasi-ye tarikhi-ye ghera'at-ha va rooykard-ha-ye ashoora az safaviyeh to mashrooteh (ba ta'akeed bar maghatel*. [Historical Classification of Ashoora Narratives, from the Safavids to the Constituionalist Revolution, with Special Focus on Maghatel.] Qom: Mo'asseseye Amoozeshi-Pajhouheshi-ye Imam Khomeini.

Rastgar, Karim. 2014. "Elteghati boodan-e sazeman goriz-napazeer bood (mosahebe ba Karim Rastegar)." [The Eclectic Ideology of the MKO Was Inevitable.] *Mehr-nameh* no. 38: 85–90.

Razavi, Kamal. 2017. "*Naghd-e ketab: Chalesh-ha-ye roohaniat ba Reza Shah*." In *Ketab-shenasi-ye enteghadi-ye jame'e-shenasi-ye tashayo*. [A Critical Annotated Bibliography of the Sociology of Shi'ism.] Ed. Sara Shariati, 330–41. Tehran: Nashr-e Negah-e Mo'aser.

– 2018. *Do-rahi-ye roohaniat: Jostarhayee darbare-ye marja'iat-e shie dar Iran-e mo'aser*. [Clergy at the Crossroads: Essays on Shia Marja'iat in Contemporary Iran.] Tehran: Nashre-arma.

Razavi-zadeh, Neda. 2018. "Da'avat shode-am be een ziarat-e ranj-alood." [I Have Been Invited to This Painful Ceremony.] In *Piyade-ravi-ye arba'een: Ta'amolat-e jame'e-shenakhti* [The Arba'een Procession: Some Sociological Reflections], ed. Mohsen Hesam Mazaheri, 145–98. Isfahan: Arma.

Reed, Jean-Pierre. 2020. "Elective Affinities between Sandinismo (as Socialist Idea) and Liberation Theology in the Nicaraguan Revolution." *Critical Research on Religion* 8, no. 2 (August): 153–77. https://doi.org/10.1177/2050303220924110.

Rezaei, Ali, and Abbas Abdi, eds. 1998. *Entekhab-e no*. [The New Choice.] Tehran: Tarh-e No.

Riedel, Bruce. 2008. "America and Iran: Flawed Analysis, Missed Opportunities, and Looming Dangers." *Brown Journal of World Affairs* 5, no. 1: 101–11.

Robinson, Francis. 1999. "Secularization, Weber, and Islam." In *Max Weber and Islam*, ed. Toby E. Huff and Wolfgong Schluchter, 231–46. London: Transaction Publishers.

Rosenfeld, Rachel A., and Kathryn B. Ward. 1991. "The Contemporary U.S. Women's Movement: An Empirical Example of Competition Theory." *Sociological Forum* 6, no. 3: 471–500.

Roy, Olivier. 2015. "Le djihadisme est une revolte generationnelle et nihiliste." [Jihadism Is a Generational and Nihilistic Rebellion.] *Le Monde*, 24 November. http://www.lemonde.fr/idees/article/2015/11/24/le-djihadisme-une-revolte-generationnelle-et-nihil-iste_4815992_3232.html.

Runciman, Walter G. 2005. "Not Elective but Selective Affinities." *Journal of Classical Sociology* 5, no. 2: 175–87.

Russell, Bertrand. (1946) 2005. *History of Western Philosophy*. London and New York: Routledge.

Sadri, Ahmad. 2006. "Foucault and the Iranian Revolution: Gender and the Seductions of Islamism (Book Review)." *Contemporary Sociology* 35, no. 5: 496–7.

Sadri, Mahmoud. 2001. "Sacral Defense of Secularism: The Political Theologies of Soroush, Shabestari, and Kadivar." *International Journal of Politics, Culture and Society* 15, no. 2: 257–70.

Sadri-Nia, Seyed Mohammad Ali. 2017. "Mostanad-e ghaem-magham." [Vice-leader: A Documentary.] Published 28 July 2018. https://www.youtube.com/watch?v=Yd7_NlxMPN4.

Sahabi, Ezatollah. 2013. *Nim gharn khatereh va tajrobe: Jelde dovom: Khaterat-e mohandes ezzatollah sahabi, jeld 2: Salhaye 1357–1379*. [A Half-century of Memories and Experiences, Memoirs of Ezzatollah Sahabi. Vol. 2. 1979–2001.] Paris: Khavaran.

Saleh, Seyed Mohsen. 2007a. *Jame'e-ye modarresin-e howze-ye elmiye-ye Qom, jeld-e 2: 1357–1384 (fa'aliyat-ha)*. [Qom Seminary Scholars' Community. Vol. 2. 1979–2005 (Activities).] Tehran: Centre for Islamic Revolution Documents.

– 2007b. *Jame'e-ye modarresin-e howze-ye elmiye-ye Qom, jeld-e 3: 1341–1384 (zendegi-name-ye a'aza)*. [Qom Seminary Scholars' Community. Vol. 3. 1962–2005 (Members' Biographies).] Tehran: Centre for Islamic Revolution Documents.

– 2007c. *Jame'e-ye modarresin-e howze-ye elmiye-ye Qom, jeld-e 4: 1341–1357 (bayaniye-ha)*. [Qom Seminary Scholars' Community. Vol. 4. 1962–79 (Communiqués).] Tehran: Centre for Islamic Revolution Documents.

– 2007d. *Jame'e-ye modarresin-e howze-ye elmiye-ye Qom, jeld-e 5: 1358–1361 (bayaniye-ha)*. [Qom Seminary Scholars' Community, Vol. 5: 1980–1983 (Communiqués).] Tehran: Centre for Islamic Revolution Documents.

– 2007e. *Jame'e-ye modarresin-e howze-ye elmiye-ye Qom, jeld-e 6: 1362–1368 (bayaniye-ha).* [Qom Seminary Scholars' Community. Vol. 6. 1983–99 (Communiqués).] Tehran: Centre for Islamic Revolution Documents.

– 2007f. *Jame'e-ye modarresin-e howze-ye elmiye-ye Qom, jeld-e 7: 1369–1376 (bayaniye-ha).* [Qom Seminary Scholars' Community. Vol. 7. 1990–2007 (Communiqués).] Tehran: Centre for Islamic Revolution Documents.

– 2007g. *Jame'e-ye modarresin-e howze-ye elmiye-ye Qom, jeld-e 8: 1377–1384 (bayaniye-ha).* [Qom Seminary Scholars' Community. Vol. 8. 1998–2005 (Communiqués).] Tehran: Centre for Islamic Revolution Documents.

Saleh, Seyed Mohsen, and Alireza Javadzadeh. 2007. *Jame'e-ye modarresin-e howze-ye elmiye-ye Qom, jeld-e 1: 1341–1357 (fa'aliyat-ha).* [Qom Seminary Scholars' Community. Vol. 1. 1962–79 (Activities).] Tehran: Centre for Islamic Revolution Documents.

Sefatgol, Mansour. 1982. *Sakhtar-e nahad va andishe-ye dini dar Iran-e asr-e Safavi: Tarikh-e tahavvolat-e dini-ye Iran dar sade-ha-ye dahom ta davazdahom-e hejri-ye ghamari.* [Religious Institutions and Thought in Safavid Iran: A History of Religious Developments in Iran during the Sixteenth to Eighteenth Centuries.] Tehran: Rasa.

Shahrokni, Nazanin. 2019. *Women in Place: The Politics of Gender Segregation in Iran.* Oakland: University of California Press.

Shahsavandi, Saeed. 2014. "Parchamdari ke na kashef bood va na forootan." [A Flag-bearer Who Was Neither an Original Thinker nor Humble.] *Mehr-nameh* no. 38: 79–84.

Shariati, Ali. 1977. *Majmoo'e-ye asar, jeld-e 1: Ba mokhatabha-ye ashena.* [Collection of Works. Vol. 1. With Familiar Audiences.] http://nimeharf.com/books/Ba-Mokhatabhaye-Ashna.pdf.

Shariati, Sara, ed. 2017. *Ketab-shenasi-ye enteghadi-ye jame'e-shenasi-ye tasha'yo.* [A Critical Annotated Bibliography of the Sociology of Shi'ism.] Tehran: Nashr-e Negah-e Mo'aser.

Shariati, Sara, and Kamal Razavi. 2018. "Marja'iat be masabe-he nahad-e ejtema'ee." [Marja'iat as a Social Institution.] In *Do-rahi-ye roohaniat: Jostarhayee darbare-ye marja'iat-e shie dar Iran-e mo'aser* [Clergy at the Crossroads: Essays on Shia Marja'iat in Contemporary Iran], ed. Kamal Razavi, 53–83. Tehran: Nashre-Arma.

Shayegan, Dariush. 2013. *Dar jost-o-jooye faza-ha-ye gom-shodeh.* [In Search of the Lost Spaces.] Tehran: Farzan.

– 2014. *Amizesh-e ofogh-ha.* [Merging the Horizons: Selected Works.] Ed. Mohmmad Mansour Hashemi. Tehran: Farzan.

Shekarchi, Ahmad. 2018. "Mizbanan-e arba'een." [The Hosts of Arba'een.] In *Piyade-ravi-ye Arba'een: Ta'amolat-e jame'e-shenakhti* [Arba'een Procession: Some Sociological Reflections], ed. Mohsen Hesam Mazaheri, 63–84. Isfahan: Nashr-e Arma.

Shirkhani, Ali, and Abbas Zare'e. 2005. *Tahavvolat-e howze-ye elmiye-ye Qom pas az piroozi-ye enghelab-e Islami.* [The Developments of the Qom Seminaries after the Islamic Revolution.] Tehran: Markaz-e Asnad-e Enghelab-e Islami.

Shoja'i-Zand, Ali-Reza. 2002a. *Deen, jame'e, va orfi shodan.* [Religion, Society and Secularization.] Tehran: Nashr-e Markaz Publishing Co.

– 2002b. *Orfi shodan dar tajrobe-ye masihi va eslami.* [Secularization in Christianity and Islamic Experience.] Tehran: Entesharat-e Baz.

Siamdoost, Nahid. 2017. *Soundtrack of the Revolution: The Politics of Music in Iran*. Stanford, CA: Stanford University Press.

Sick, Gary. 1985. *All Fall Down: America's Tragic Encounter with Iran.* New York: Random House.

Soleimanieh, Mahdi. 2016. "'Alem-daneshgahi' va 'doctor-hojjat-ul-islam.'" ["Alem-Academic" and "Doctor-Hojjat-ul-Islam."] *Deen Online.* Accessed 11 February 2021. https://www.dinonline.com/5940.

Soroush, Abdolkarim. 1988. "Ellat va dalil dar oloome ejtema'ee." [Cause and Reason in the Social Sciences.] *Nameye Oloom-e Ejtema'ee* no. 1: 53–72. http://ensani.ir/file/download/article/20110203101219-%C2%A0%20(2).pdf.

– 1992. *Ghabz va bast-e teoric shari'at – ya azariyeh-ye takāmol-e ma'refat-e dini.* [The Theoretical Contraction and Expansion of Sharia.] Tehran: Serat.

– 1998. *Modara va modiriyyat.* [Leniency and Governance.] Tehran: Serat Cultural Institute.

– 2000a. *Reason, Freedom, and Democracy in Islam (Essential Writings of Abdolkarim Soroush)*. Trans. Mahmoud Sadri and Ahmad Sadri. New York: Oxford University Press.

– 2000b. *Serat-ha-ye mostagheem.* [The Robust Paths.] Tehran: Serat.

– 2006. *Bast-e tajrobe-ye nabavi.* [The Expansion of Prophetic Experience.] Tehran: Serat.

– 2009. *The Expansion of Prophetic Experience: Essays on Historicity, Contingency and Plurality in Religion*. Trans. Nilou Mobasser. Ed. Forough Jahanbakhsh. Leiden: Brill Academic Publisher.

– 2014. "Secularization." 16 September. https://www.youtube.com/watch?v=5AemOkswfsA.

– 2016a. "Royayaye rasoolaneh: zehi kereshmeye khabi ke beh ze bidarist." [The Prophetic Dreams.] BBC Persian, 25 May–25 June. http://www.bbc.com/persian/blogs/2016/05/160525_l44_nazeran_sorush_bazargan.

– 2016b. "*Ta'abbod, ta'aghol, va ta'assob.*" [Religious Dedication, Rational Thinking, and Fanaticism.] 19 February. https://www.youtube.com/watch?v=Ly3GiLSqbn8.

– 2017. "*Az aten ta orshalim.*" [From Athens to Jerusalem.] 16 December. https://www.youtube.com/watch?v=dRKFR3qWAjo.

– 2019. *Kalam-e mohammad, royaye mohammad.* [Muhammad's Words, Muhammad's Dreams.] US: Soghrat.

Spellberg, Denise A. 2013. *Thomas Jefferson's Quran: Islam and the Founders*. New York: Vintage Books.

Stark, Rodney. 1999. "Secularization: RIP." *Sociology of Religion* 60, no. 3: 249–73.

– 2002. "Physiology and Faith: Addressing the 'Universal' Gender Differences in Religious Commitment." *Journal for the Scientific Study of Religion* 41, no. 3: 495–507.

Stark, Rodney, and William S. Bainbridge. 1987. *A Theory of Religion.* New York: Peter Lang Publishing.

Stark, Rodney, and Roger Finke. 2000. *Acts of Faith: Explaining the Human Side of Religion*. Berkeley: University of California Press.

Stone, Emily A., Todd K. Shackelford, and David M. Buss. 2007. "Sex Ratio and Mate Preference: A Cross-cultural Investigation." *European Journal of Social Psychology* 37: 288–96.

Tabatabayee, Mohammad Hossein. (1954) 1980. *Osool-e falsafe va ravesh-e realism (volumes 1–5).* [The Principles of Philosophy and the School of Realism.] Tehran: Daftar-e Entesharat-e Eslami.

Tabatabayee, Seyed Javad. 2017. "A Lecture at the Department of Political Science, Azad University of Meshad." 3 March. https://www.youtube.com/watch?v=6SLt7LYkBgE.

Tabatabayeefar, Seyed Mohsen. 2015. *Jarian-ha-ye fekri dar howze-ye mo'aser-e Qom.* [Intellectual Currents in Today's Qom Seminaries.] Tehran: Nashre Ney.

Taylor, Charles. 1998. "Modes of Secularism." In *Secularims and Its Critics*, ed. Rajeev Bhargava, 31–53. New Delhi: Oxford University Press.

– 2007. *A Secular Age*. Cambridge, MA: Belknap Press of Harvard University Press.

Thomas, J.J.R. 1985. "Ideology and Elective Affinity." *Sociology* 19, no. 1: 31–54.

Treiber, Hubert. 1985. "'Elective Affinities' between Weber's Sociology of Religion and Sociology of Law." *Theory and Society* 14, no. 6 (November): 809–61.

Turner, Bryan S. 1974. *Weber and Islam: A Critical Study*. London and Boston: Routledge & Kegan Paul.

Turner, Stansfield. 1985. *Secrecy and Democracy: The CIA in Transition*. Boston: Houghton Mifflin.

Ward, Kathryn B., and Fred C. Pampel. 1985a. "More on the Meaning of the Effect of the Sex Ratio on Female Labor Force Participation." *Social Science Quarterly* 66: 675–9.

– 1985b. "Structural Determinants of Female Labor Force Participation in Developed Nations, 1955–75." *Social Science Quarterly* 66: 654–67.

Warner, Michael, Jonathan Vanantwerpen, and Craig Calhoun, eds. 2010. *Varieties of Secularism in a Secular Age*. Cambridge, MA: Harvard University Press.

Weber, Max. (1920) 2010. *The Protestant Ethic and the Spirit of Capitalism*. Oxford: Oxford University Press.

Wilson, James Q. 2002. "Sex and the Marriage Market." *Commentary*, March. http://www.commentarymagazine.com/article/sex-and-the-marriage-market.

Wittke, Carl. 1950. *The Utopian Communist: A Biography of Wilhelm Weitling, Nineteenth-Century Reformer*. Baton Rouge: Louisiana State University Press.

Wood, Graeme. 2015. "What ISIS Really Wants." *Atlantic*, March. https://www.theatlantic.com/magazine/archive/2015/03/what-isis-really-wants/384980.

World Bank. 2021. *Iran's Fertility Rate*. Accessed 4 July 2021. https://data.worldbank.org/indicator/SP.DYN.TFRT.IN?locations=IR.

Yamane, David. 1997. "Secularization on Trial: In Defense of a Neosecularization Paradigm." *Journal for the Scientific Study of Religion* 36, no. 1 (March): 109–22.

Yong, William. 2010. "Iran's Divorce Rate Stirs Fears of Society in Crisis." *New York Times*, 6 December. http://www.nytimes.com/2010/12/07/world/middleeast/07divorce.html.

Zarei, Arman. 2015. "Post-secularism: Deen va hoze-ye omoomi dar andishe-ye Jurgen Habermas." [Post-secularism: Religion and the Public Sphere in Habermas's Thought.] *Pajoohesh-name-ye Oloom-e Siasi* 10, no. 2: 79–111.

– 2018. *Post-secularism: Deen, dolat, va hoze-ye omoomi dar gharb*. [Post-secularism: Religion, State, and the Public Sphere in the West.] Tehran: Nashre Ney.

Zargari-Nejhad, Gholamhossein. 2008. *Rasa'el-e mashrootiat*. [The Constitutional Letters.] Tehran: Human Sciences Research and Development Institute Press.

Zarrinkoob, Abdolhossein. 1999. *Roozegaran: Tarikh-e Iran az aghaz to payan-e saltanate pahlavi.* [The Past: The History of Iran, from the Start till the End of the Pahlavi Kingdom.] 6th ed. Tehran: Sokhan
– 2006. *Ashenayee ba tarikh-e Iran.* [An Introductory Look at Iran's History.] Tehran: Sokhan.
Ziadat, Adel. 1986. *Western Science in the Arab World: The Impact of Darwinism: 1860–1930.* New York: Macmillian Publishers.
Zibakalam, Sadegh. 2014. "To Rule or Not to Rule? An Alternative Look at the Political Life of Ayatollah Khomeini between 1960 and 1980." In *A Critical Introduction to Khomeini*, ed. Arshin Adib-Moghaddam, 256–74. New York: Cambridge University Press.
Zinoviev, Alexander. 1986. *Homo Sovieticus*. New York: Atlantic Monthly Press.

Index

Abrahamian, Ervand, 15, 51, 58–9
ahkam-e avvaliyyeh, 102
ahkam-e sanaviyyeh, 102
autocracy, 54, 62, 69, 77

Bazargan, Mehdi, 80, 97
Berger, Peter, 7, 9–10, 24–5, 29, 34, 148, 184
Boroujerdi, Ayatollah Hossein, 52–3, 55, 76–7, 87–8, 189

Casanova, José, 8, 14, 24–5, 27–9, 32–3
cause, 5, 19, 22, 34–42, 44–5, 48, 62, 65, 68, 78, 142–3, 150, 153, 166, 171, 179, 189–90
Christian communist, 174–5
clergy, 12–13, 15–16, 41–2, 46–7, 49–51, 55, 57–8, 60–7, 71–7, 79–80, 82, 85, 87–9, 95–8, 101, 108, 145, 147–8, 150–1, 165–6, 172–4, 179, 181, 184–5, 196, 203–4
cleric, 13, 48, 51–3, 55, 57, 60, 62–4, 66, 72–3, 77, 79–92, 94, 96–102, 105, 107–8, 110, 151, 173, 179–80, 183, 185, 189, 204. *See also* clergy; ulama
critical juncture, 19–20, 43–8, 50, 77, 171

Durant, Will, 3, 22, 34–5, 51
Durkheim, Emile, 23, 27–8, 34, 36, 45, 116, 151–2, 185

elective affinity, 42, 45

Fardid, Ahmad, 21, 126, 180–2, 187–91
fasting, 66–7, 115, 123, 141, 196
fatwa, 53, 61, 64, 87
fiqh: hokoomati, 91; *pooya*, 91; *sonati*, 91. See also *fiqhi*
fiqhi, 48, 65, 91–2, 104
Foucault, Michel, 4–5

GCC (Guardian Council of the Constitution), 100–3, 106–7, 109–10. *See also* Guardian Council
Ghamari-Tabrizi, Behrooz, 82, 99, 101, 110, 147, 182
Guardian Council, 96, 100–3, 106, 108, 149. *See also* GCC
guerrilla, 54–5, 57–61, 175, 177–9

Hashemi Rafsanjani, Akbar, 15, 51, 83–6, 96–101, 103, 148–50, 195
Heidegger, Martin, 172, 180, 182, 187–9, 191
historical institutionalism, 19, 43–4, 77
"*Homo Islamicus*," 6
Huntington, Samuel, 11, 34, 79

Iran-Iraq War, 21, 65, 89, 98, 102, 152, 193–4, 198, 201
Islamic Marxism, 178
Islamic Republic, 15–16, 20, 30, 38, 47, 62–6, 82–4, 86, 88–9, 91, 96, 99–104, 108, 111, 115–16, 123, 132, 135, 143, 145–6, 149, 165, 179–81, 187–90, 195, 199–200, 203
Islamization, 7, 14–15, 20–1, 32–3, 37–8, 45, 47, 62–4, 83, 115, 122, 128, 182, 190, 203

jurisprudence, 13, 65, 67, 89–94, 96, 98, 102–3, 112, 157, 166, 182. *See also* jurisprudential
jurisprudential, 48, 65, 67, 84, 87, 91, 95–8, 102, 110, 165
jurist-ruler, 41, 77, 79, 83–4, 89, 94, 110, 190. See also *velayat-e faqih*

Khamenei, Ali, 66, 77, 86–7, 90, 104, 111, 153
Khomeini, Ruhollah, 16, 52, 54, 57, 61–7, 72, 76–7, 79–94, 96–9, 101–6, 108, 110–11, 144–9, 175, 179, 182, 189, 195

laïcité, 24–5, 29, 32–3
Lewis, Bernard, 6, 11, 99

marja'a, 52, 64, 146
marriage squeeze, 146, 151, 153, 155, 157
Marx, Karl, 36, 49, 59, 172, 174, 176, 182, 187
Marxism, 5, 20, 41, 47, 57–61, 74–5, 126, 173, 175–9, 181, 191
maslahat, 20, 30, 48, 64, 66–7, 92, 95–6, 103–8, 110–11
maslahat-e nezam, 30, 103–7
Massachusetts circle, 62
merger of religion and state, 32–3, 204. *See also* laïcité; secularism
Mojahedin-e Khalgh-e Iran (MKO), 20, 47, 54–61, 81–2, 126, 175–9, 191
Montazeri, Hosseinali, 77, 82, 84–7, 92, 105, 111
Mossadegh, Mohammad, 56
Motahhari, Morteza, 39–41, 64, 72–3, 179
Muslim exceptionalism, 3, 5, 7, 9, 11, 13, 15, 17, 19, 203

Nasr, Seyed Hossein, 6, 11–12, 14, 16–17, 38, 62, 126, 196, 203
necessity, 20, 32–3, 65–6, 90–1, 94, 96, 98, 100–3, 106, 111, 177. See also *zarurat*
neosecularization, 27–8. *See also* secularization

Orientalism, 38, 181. *See also* Orientalist
Orientalist, 38, 189
Ottoman, 4, 131

Pahlavi, 15, 17, 20, 24–5, 47, 50–1, 53–4, 62, 72, 86, 144
path dependency, 19, 43, 44, 77

philosophy, 3–5, 13, 18, 20–1, 29–30, 34–6, 39, 45–6, 48, 80, 94, 100–1, 104, 106, 109, 111–12, 115, 169, 173, 175–6, 178, 180–2, 187–8, 190–1, 193, 200
Popper, Karl, 172, 180–2, 187
prayers: collective, 90, 102, 118–24, 128; Friday, 74–5, 102, 119–20

Rahnema, Ali, 51, 53, 55–6, 76, 82, 102, 176
reason, 12, 18–19, 22, 34–42, 44–5, 47–8, 51, 53, 61, 68, 92, 105, 109, 115, 130, 142–3, 154, 157, 171, 179, 183, 187
religiosity, 8–9, 24–9, 32–4, 38, 53–4, 67, 74–5, 115–16, 118–22, 127–35, 138–9, 143, 156, 186, 191, 193–7, 200–1, 205
revolution, 4–6, 9, 14–18, 20–1, 26, 30, 32–3, 36, 41–2, 46, 47, 50, 53–4, 58, 61–5, 67, 72–80, 82, 84–6, 88, 91, 95–7, 101, 103, 105–6, 115–19, 121–2, 126–7, 129, 131–3, 138–9, 142–3, 158, 160, 165, 167, 171–2, 174, 176–80, 182–3, 189–94, 196, 198, 200–1, 203–4

sacralization, 9, 31–3, 116. *See also* sacred
sacred, 4, 6, 8, 10, 12, 14, 16–20, 22–3, 26–34, 36, 38, 40, 42, 44–5, 48, 50, 52, 54, 56, 58, 60, 62, 64, 66, 68, 72, 76, 78, 80, 82, 84, 86, 88, 90, 92, 94, 96, 98, 100, 102, 104, 106, 108, 110, 112, 116, 118, 120, 122, 124, 126, 128, 130, 132, 134, 142, 146, 148, 150, 152, 154, 156, 158, 160, 162, 164, 166, 172, 174, 176–8, 180, 182–4, 186, 188–90, 192, 194, 196, 198, 200, 202, 204
Safavid, 20, 40–1, 47–51, 96
Sahabi, Ezzatollah, 73, 80, 82, 96–7, 142, 147, 179
Sassanid, 46, 204–5
SAVAK, 59, 61
secular, 4, 6–8, 10, 12–34, 36, 38, 40–2, 44–5, 48, 50, 52, 54–6, 58, 60, 62–6, 68, 72, 74–6, 78, 80, 82, 84, 86, 88, 90, 92–4, 96, 98, 100, 102, 104, 106–8, 110, 112, 115–16, 118, 120–2, 124–8, 130, 132, 134–5, 138–9, 142–4, 146, 148, 150–2, 154, 156, 158, 160, 162, 164, 166, 172, 174, 176, 178, 180, 182–6, 188–94, 196–202, 204–5. *See also* secularity
secularism, 6–7, 9–13, 15, 17–18, 20–1, 23–6, 29, 31–3, 44, 47, 51, 67, 71, 93, 110, 115, 119, 131, 181–3, 186, 191, 203–5. See also *laïcité*
secularity, 7, 10–11, 14–15, 18–19, 21–27, 29–35, 37, 39, 41, 43, 45, 74–5, 183, 186
secularization: from above, 8, 20, 24–6, 32–3, 47, 50, 54, 147; from below, 24–5, 27, 32–3
seminaries, 15, 46, 52, 57, 62–4, 67, 71–7, 79, 82, 84–95, 98, 103, 108, 126, 180
seminary, 45, 50, 52–3, 61, 63, 74–6, 83–5, 88–91, 93–4, 102, 186, 196
separation of church and state, 7, 9, 17, 24–5, 29, 32–3, 127, 172. *See also* merger of religion and state; secularism

sex ratio, 153–4, 157–8, 160, 167
Shah: Mohammad Reza, 50, 88; Reza, 20, 24–5, 50–4, 72, 88, 92, 172, 180–1
sharia, 65, 93, 150, 182, 184
Shariati, Ali, 4–5, 20, 47, 54–8, 61, 72–3, 175–7
Shariatmadari, Kazem, 83, 85–6, 88
shia, 6, 14–16, 40–2, 46–53, 61–7, 71–7, 79–80, 82–3, 86–9, 92–6, 98–9, 103, 105, 145, 148, 172, 180, 182, 185, 189–91, 193–6, 201. See also *shi'ism*
shia establishment, 47, 49–50, 53, 63, 71–2, 76, 86–8, 92–4, 145, 180. *See also* seminaries; seminary
*Shi'i*fication, 47, 49
Shi'ism, 6, 20, 46–51, 87, 94, 105, 176, 190
sociology, 19, 42, 74–5, 116, 151, 186
Soroush, Abdulkarim, 12, 21, 23, 34, 37–8, 72, 180–7, 191
Source of Emulation, 64, 73, 77, 79–80, 83–4, 86–7, 146. See also *marja'a*
Sources of Emulation, 42, 52, 73, 76, 83–4, 87, 89, 145
state exigencies, 30, 96, 111. See also *maslahat*; *maslahat-e nezam*
sunni, 16, 47–9, 61, 64, 72–3, 92–3, 95, 103, 105, 181, 193, 195–6, 201

Taylor, Charles, 9–10, 23, 26–7, 30–1, 34
theocracy, 69, 77, 189–90
theological, 3, 7–8, 14, 19, 34, 40, 49, 74–5, 90, 95–6, 105, 180
theology, 3, 8, 13, 16, 18, 23, 35, 185, 189, 191, 193, 195, 197, 199, 201

ulama, 16–17, 79, 144–5

velayat-e faqih, 41, 63, 76–7, 80–1, 93, 96. *See also* jurist-ruler
Voltaire, 34, 172–3, 191

Weber, Max, 8, 14, 28, 42, 195
Weitling, Wilhelm, 172, 174–5
women, 6, 15, 18, 21, 51, 56–7, 63, 65, 113, 117, 130, 143–67, 172, 193, 197, 200–1

Zarrinkoob, Abdulhussain, 48–9, 51, 204
zarurat, 48, 64–9, 91, 101, 103, 111. *See also* necessity